APOSTLE FOR OUR TIME
POPE PAUL VI

APOSTLE FOR OUR TIME

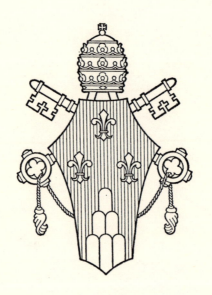

POPE PAUL VI

by
John G. Clancy

P. J. KENEDY & SONS
NEW YORK

Library of Congress Catalog Card Number: 63–21413
Manufactured in the United States of America

Nihil obstat: Rev. Charles K. Von Euw, S.T.L., S.E.O.D.
Censor Librorum

Imprimatur: ✠Richard Cardinal Cushing
Archbishop of Boston

Brighton, Massachusetts, September 13, 1963

The nihil obstat and imprimatur are official declarations that a book or pamphlet is free of doctrinal or moral error. No implication is contained therein that those who have granted the nihil obstat and imprimatur agree with the contents, opinions or statements expressed.

*To my Mother and Father
and in memory of Anne*

"We will love those who are near and those far from us. We will love our own country, and we will love that of others. We will love our friends, we will love our enemies. We will love Catholics, we will love the dissidents, the Protestants, the Anglicans, the indifferent, the Mohammedans, the pagans, the atheists. We will love all social classes, but especially those most in need of help, of assistance, of advancement. We will love children and we will love the old, the poor and the sick. We will love those who mock us, who scorn us, who oppose us, who persecute us. We will love those who merit and those who do not merit to be loved. We will love our opponents: we will want no man to be our enemy. We will love the time in which we live: our culture, our science, our art, our sport, our world. We will love, striving to understand, to have sympathy, to admire, to serve, and to suffer. We will love with the heart of Christ: Come to me, all of you . . ."

WORDS OF POPE PAUL VI

Foreword

In the long history of the Church no papal election has attracted the interest and attention of the whole world as did that which brought John Baptist Montini to the Chair of Peter. It seemed as if the entire world held its breath and waited and watched with the silent crowd keeping vigil in the square of St. Peter while the man who was to succeed good Pope John was chosen.

We cardinals, who by tradition and law have the solemn obligation of selecting the man who will be Peter in the Church of his day, were well aware as we entered the conclave not only of the grave responsibility that was ours but also that the eyes of the world were focused upon us. It was ours to choose the man capable of assuming the leadership of the Church of Christ here on earth—an awesome responsibility. But the one we would elect must be the man who could continue the monumental work begun by John XXIII; who must be what John was to the world. The Holy Spirit showed us the choice and directed our vote. We have a Pope; he has taken the name of Paul.

But if the Church sounded a shout of joy at this announcement; if the Christian world breathed a happy sigh of expectancy; if the whole globe approved of this election, there were still the questions on the lips of many. "What is he really like?" "What kind of a person is this Pope Paul?" If we know his past life and work, we can tell something of our future. Indeed, a knowledge of the life of John Baptist Montini—his youth, his priesthood, his service in the Church and his devotion to Christ —reveals that here truly God has raised up in His Church a great man, a holy and able man, a man whose whole life seems in the plan of Providence to have been a preparation for this critical task in an age of crisis.

One thing which strikes me about our new Pope is this: he is a man of the twentieth century, a priest of the modern world, a Pope for our time. His middle-class family background pre- sents almost a familiar scene to us Americans: his father a journalist and active in politics; his mother a quiet woman of firm faith. In the words of Monsignor Clancy, "there seems to have been a Christian rhythm to the lives of the Montinis which . . . in the example of his mother and father profoundly in- fluenced young Giovanni Battista."

And his early priesthood, so much of it dedicated to assisting idealistic and disillusioned youth of the university to discover the Christ-centeredness of the world, strikes a sympathetic note here in our society. The great pontiff of happy memory, Pope Pius XII, whom Monsignor Montini served so faithfully with Christlike self-effacement, said of his pro-Secretary of State: He possesses every priestly quality in the highest degree. His years of service in the Secretariat of State gave him valuable experience in administration and diplomacy, to be sure. But in the midst of those duties which can tend to be so routine, so impersonal, Monsignor Montini never lost sight of his priestly vocation and its divine purpose—*cura animarum,* the care of souls.

Two pictures stand out in my memory which for me charac- terize the man whom our Lord has chosen to be His Vicar and

our servant: the deep concern on Monsignor Montini's face
as he stood with Pius XII amid the wounded of Rome who
had been injured by an Allied bombing; the new Archbishop
kneeling and kissing the ground of his diocese as he entered
Milan. These reveal a man who is warm, who is compassion-
ate, who feels the anguish of our anguished world.

As Archbishop of Milan he electrified that city with a plan
and program of evangelization which revealed a man who knew
the twentieth century, who knew the problems of twentieth
century men. He soon became known with affection as "the
Archbishop of the workers." His personal charity, his quiet example, his tireless energy reflected the zeal and life of the apostle whose name he was to take as Bishop of Rome. The full
part which Cardinal Montini played in the preparations for
Pope John's Council of Renewal cannot yet be told. Suffice to
say that his was the first voice raised in praising the vision of
Pope John, in delineating the path of renewal we must follow.
"Reform," he said, "has been through the centuries the renewing ferment of Catholic tradition." His immediate decision
following his election to continue the Council without postponement gave joy and hope to the whole Christian world.

Speaking to his people of Milan about the then forthcoming
Council, Cardinal Montini proclaimed, "Something of the
prophetic is abroad in our times." These are words which
can be most aptly applied to the man who has taken the name
of Paul as he succeeds to the *cathedra* of Peter. In Pope Paul
VI we can indeed see with awe that something of the prophetic
is abroad in our times.

We have a Pope, whose name is Paul. And in him we have,
as Monsignor John Clancy has so appropriately entitled his
splendid biography, "an apostle for our time." Monsignor
Clancy has performed an admirable service in giving us this
excellent and timely life of John Baptist Montini. I commend
his work highly, not only for the valuable biographical matter

he has gathered but for the meaningful insights he discloses as he presents this apostolic life of our Holy Father. By knowing the past of Pope Paul we can predict with joyful enthusiasm, our future.

RICHARD CARDINAL CUSHING
Archbishop of Boston

Contents

Foreword by Richard Cardinal Cushing   vii

Author's Preface   xiii

1   The Home in Brescia   1

2   "Don Battista"   18

3   Vatican Beginnings   46

4   "Cloister of Ciphers and Secrets"   68

5   "And So I Came to Milan"   86

6   Mission to Milan   113

7   Portrait of a Cardinal   130

8   Sede Vacante   154

9   Successor to Peter—Successor to John   183

10   The Pauline Pontificate   204

     Appendix   233

     Index   235

Author's Preface

He has always been considered young—and yet he is sixty-six years old. He became a priest without ever having lived in a seminary, an archbishop without ever having been a parish priest. While still a priest he refused to be a cardinal, and in 1958, still not a cardinal, he was considered *papabile*. He was close to Pope Pius XII for long years marked by extraordinary devotion and intimacy, and yet in 1954, with the Pope aging and ill, he was named Archbishop of Milan and left the Vatican. He has been called a progressive—intemperately, by some, a revolutionary—and yet during Vatican Council II his was a muted voice, speaking only infrequently, and then words of calm moderation.

More often spoken of as a skilled diplomat than priest, and as lacking in human warmth and concern, his eight years as the loving and beloved archbishop of Milan far overshadowed the more spectacular thirty years of Vatican diplomacy. Called to the Vatican by the stern and conservative Pope Pius XI, formed by the great but exigent Pius XII, then raised to the cardinalate by the cheerful destroyer of no longer viable traditions, Pope John XXIII, John Baptist Montini, now reigning as Paul VI, possesses a vast and somewhat puzzling experience of the Church, her people, and of the world. It is an experience shaped and personalized by the extraordinary complex of qualities which distinguish him—brilliantly diffuse, and of dimensions which defy easy categorization.

There is, in this attempt to tell his life, a beginning to be made, an apology and explanation to accompany it. This is the life of Paul VI as it has been led until his accession to the papal throne, and an account of the first days of his pontificate. Most of the facts presently available are here, something of the nuance of his life, some hints, some shadow—a beginning.

Four months after his election we are still on the threshhold of his pontificate. To anticipate it is foolhardy. Yet there are signs and portents in Pope Paul's sixty-six years which the world may read and ponder as it offers him its hopes and its love in his first days on the throne of Peter. A Brescian by birth, a Roman by career, a Milanese by adoption, and now Pope to the world—to His Holiness, Paul VI, this book is offered in loving and devoted remembrance.

JOHN G. CLANCY

Rome
New York—Feast of Saint Augustine

APOSTLE FOR OUR TIME
POPE PAUL VI

1. The Home in Brescia

Half hidden by ancient plane trees, the stone of its façade bleached and weathered, the parish church of Concesio, dedicated to Saint Anthony, bears the scars of age and of successive remodeling with a dignity which befits a church of its antiquity. First built in the late 1600's, it is a church in the baroque style which replaces one that was new in the days when Alexander VI was Pope, when the discovery of the new Indies by Columbus was news at the court of Spain, and when the plains of Lombardy, in which the village of Concesio lies, were periodically ravaged by war and plundered by fierce *condottieri*, mercenaries under arms to warring states and nobles, living off the land and the people.

Concesio itself, at the entrance to the valley of Trompia in the foothills of the Italian Alps, has drowsed through the centuries, remaining a small center of the rich farming country which surrounds it, while seven miles away the city of Brescia has grown out to reach and almost engulf it. Today the village shares in the general prosperity of northern Italy, and under the impact of growing industrialization is losing much of the appearance and mood which characterized it at the beginning of the century. Then it still possessed the quiet

1

freshness and pace which drew well-to-do Brescians out of
the city from time to time to live in their country houses.
These homes still stand in the old quarter of Concesio, eighteenth-century in style, most of them two stories high and built
around a courtyard brilliant with flowers and showing a dis-
creet face to the street. The windows are shuttered, the huge
outer doors closed, the only touch of life the geraniums flow-
ering on the wrought-iron balconies over the entry ways.

A modest village Concesio, and yet with a certain pride of
place. It has given four bishops to the Church: Count Francesco Landrone, born in 1600; Count Sebastian Lodrone, in
1643; Giovanni Battista Bosio, former archbishop of Chieti,
in 1892; and in 1897, on September 26, Giovanni Battista
Montini. The last on this list, the second son born to Giorgio
and Giuditta Alghisi Montini, today sits in the seat of Peter
as Pope Paul VI, the 262nd successor of the Prince of the
Apostles.

The Montini family, while not of the *nobilità blasonata*,
that is, of the high nobility, with armorial bearings, was ancient and respected, members in those waning years of the
nineteenth century of the highly selective Brescian élite, professional, intellectual, profoundly Catholic. In their beginnings they had belonged to the lesser nobility which in the
fifteenth century, as the feudal and military castes began their
decline, slowly emerged into provincial prominence.

Giorgio Montini, born in 1860, was a ruggedly handsome
man of average height, the head high-domed and narrow, the
ears slightly prominent, the eyes steady and clear above the
aquiline nose and carefully trimmed mustache. He dressed
meticulously, even elegantly, and was distinguished as a
young man for his courtly and reserved manner. In his thirty-
seventh year, at the time of his son's birth, he was comfortably
established financially and free to pursue his passion for ideas,
for politics, and for journalism. Although he had studied law

at the University of Padua, he chose not to practice. He was an untiring initiator. He shared in the founding of the La Scuola Publishing Union, of the San Paolo Bank of Brescia, of the Morcelliana publishing house. Later in life he was to receive from Pope Benedict XV the leadership of the Catholic Electoral Union of Italy—one of the spearheads of Catholic Action in the country, and he was to be its last president.

Thus he stood at the very center of the cultural and economic life of the city of Brescia, called the most Catholic in Italy, and the Montini home was alive with the ferment of social and political and cultural ideas which possessed the Catholic Italian intellectuals at the beginning of the century. To it came some of the most significant figures of the time— Bazoli, Longinotti, Tovini, Murri. These are names which symbolized the struggle of fervent men to articulate on a political level their commitment to Christian principles in government, at a time in Italy of vast religious indifference and hostility to religion on the part of its political leaders, of anticlericalism, and all the other dreary baggage which accompanies assault on religion and its estrangement from public life.

With the fall of the Papal States in 1870, Pius IX's answer to the usurping House of Savoy was the *non expedit,* an advice to Catholics to abstain from presenting themselves as candidates for political office or from voting, acts which would imply a recognition of the occupation of Rome and of the infringement of papal rights. For nearly half a century, from 1870 to 1919, the *non expedit* would keep the men most capable of counteracting the atmosphere of secularism from taking part in the government of their country. The vacuum was filled, in part, by Catholic Action in the religious and social spheres, but there were those who felt that there should be men in government to give witness to Christian principles.

The great political challenge of the day for Catholics was

breaking through the isolation from national life which followed on the occupation of Rome, leaving them living marginal lives as Italians in order to protest an injustice as Catholics. Giorgio Montini succeeded in creating in his area an understanding with the moderate wing of the liberals of the day. He fought the famous Zanardelli and the Socialists with all his vigor, thus helping to create the basis for the Popular Party to whose formation he, together with Don Luigi Sturzo, made a notable contribution.

Sturzo, another giant of the period, was slight, ascetic, soft-spoken, but with a dynamism which bespoke his total conviction. He was born on November 26, 1871, in Caltagirone, a town of central Sicily. After his ordination as a priest, he pursued graduate studies at the Pontifical Gregorian University in Rome and returned to the Caltagirone seminary to teach philosophy and sociology. As deputy mayor and then mayor of Caltagirone, Don Sturzo gained experience in civic affairs and a knowledge of the needs of the people. His idea for a preponderantly Catholic political party did not win the support of many members of Italy's Catholic hierarchy, but he persisted stubbornly. Out of his brilliance and persistence was to come the Popular Party, formed in 1919, after the First World War, when Benedict XV withdrew the *non expedit*. As a member from Brescia, Giorgio Montini was to represent the Popular Party in three legislatures of the kingdom, from 1919 until 1926. When the Popular Party divided on the question of supporting Fascism, the clerical moderates went over to the side of Mussolini, but Giorgio Montini was not among them. He continued to support in Parliament the party's original principles, although he saw his friend Don Sturzo, stricken and ill, begin his lonely exile in England and then in the United States. In 1926 the Popular Party was suppressed by Mussolini, and Montini retired to Brescia, continuing to write and speak about freedom while he saw his country slip more deeply into Fascism.

In a long letter to a friend, written in 1940, he stated: "For a long period of years I was counselor of the commune and a member of other public administrations and Catholic projects; for twenty-five years provincial counselor; from 1913 to 1920, assessor of the commune of Brescia. In 1917, I could not refuse, because the offer came from the highest authority [the Pope], the presidency of the electoral union of Italian Catholics, one of the large components then constituting Catholic Action, but it was not a position suited to my talents, nor could I divide my time between Rome and Brescia where there were other obligations to fulfil; thus I resigned in 1918. In 1919 I was elected to the Chamber, and I remained there for three legislatures, without praise, but then, too, without blame."

With the defeat of Italy in the Second World War and its decision to become a republic, the Popular Party, seemingly so long dead, rose from the grave in 1944. In the general election of 1948 and under the leadership of Alcide De Gasperi, it was given a mandate, under its new name of Christian Democratic Party, to lead Italy into the brilliant recovery of its postwar years. Don Luigi Sturzo returned from exile and resided in Rome as the elder statesman, honored and consulted by Christian Democratic leaders until his death in 1959. But Giorgio Montini did not live to see this victory. He died in the war-troubled year of 1943, after a life of contribution to a future he would not witness.

Perhaps his greatest role was played as a journalist. For thirty-one years (1881-1912) he was publisher and editor of the Brescian daily *Il Cittadino*. He was only twenty-one when Giuseppe Tovini, a lawyer and a pioneer in Catholic Action in Brescia, called him from the University of Padua to this post.

Under Giorgio Montini's direction the daily was a paper both of information and formation, courageous and progressive in its defense of Catholic teachings during the many years of his association with it, long afterward to retain the impress he made upon it.[1] The Germans, during their occupation of Italy during the Second World War, were outraged at *Il Cittadino's* insistence on freedom and justice, and silenced it. But from one of its old issues, that of March 28, 1909, there comes alive the spirit of the man who was father to Paul VI.

Addressed by Giorgio Montini to Catholics who were wary of any alliance with the liberal ideas of the day, these words have a crackle and thrust which is almost startling: "You have the air of men who, having slept for thirty years, awaken suddenly and believe yourselves to be the ultimate expression of modernity. You fell asleep in 1880, in days when Catholics were without organization, without strength, distrustful of themselves, trampled by their adversaries. And since you have been asleep, you have not seen your fellows rise day by day from their abject situation, animated by a great faith, jealous of their rights . . . determined to recapture completely their civil identity, proud of their renewed energies and of the new social duties to which a great responsiblity and inspired voice calls them. Something else you have forgotten: Forty years ago you fell asleep with political formulas which could inspire a people with enthusiasm for their political potential . . . but now these people prefer the advance of a social program to sterile political ideas. . . . With Catholic social action we have been able to advance a complete system of ideas and of healing and progressive work. . . . You continue to sleep!"

Long years after these words were written, just one week after being raised to the Papacy, Giorgio Montini's son, Gio-

[1] Count Sforza once made the statement that the most deadly enemies of the Italians are nationalistic vanity and literary overemphasis. Giorgio Montini suffered from neither malady nor did his newspaper.

vanni Battista, was to speak of his father, the journalist, to the newspaper men and women of the world gathered in Rome to cover the conclave which had elected the new Pope: "Should We be required to say what consciousness of his profession animated him, We believe that, without being swayed by affection, We could outline the profile of a person who considered the press a splendid and courageous mission in the service of truth, of democracy, of progress; in a word, of public welfare. But We refer simply to this fact not to give praise to that most worthy man who was so very dear to Us, but to tell you gentlemen of the press how Our mind has an inclination to sympathy, esteem and confidence for what you are and what you do. We can almost say that Our family education makes Us one of you! That it makes you colleagues and friends!"

As the journalists broke into thunderous applause and the Pope smiled in acknowledgment, one could almost sense his nostalgia for those distant days when there had been a family together in a home, a home in which the father was a journalist, with that compulsion which all good journalists share of making people aware of their time and of their world. He wanted his sons to live in their century, to embrace reality. He taught them to be progressive; he gave them an interest in social questions.

He had a profound influence on young Giovanni Battista. The latter's gifts as an organizer, his involvement in social questions, his charity, his intense interest in art and philosophy, his love of writing, his commitment to all the aspects of modern life—these were to come to him from his father, as in his home he received the most modern of educations, free from the narrowness and provincial flavor which characterized so many homes in those years before the First World War. Above all, it was a home in which the faith was strongly lived. Three years before his death, Giorgio Montini was to write: "In my long life I have assisted at the sunset of men, of parties, of ideologies which appeared indestructible. But one thing with my eyes I have seen overcome the times and the tempests: this rock on which I stand—my faith—which I have always sustained. It consoles me indescribably, and in this vision I prepare for the inevitable sunset of my life. . . ." [2]

The wife of Giorgio Montini, Giuditta Alghisi, was a fragile, shy woman, born of an excellent family of the lesser nobility, in Verolovecchia and educated in Milan by the Suore Marcelline. At the time of her second son's birth (Ludovico had been born in 1896), she still had the clear, unlined complexion of a schoolgirl; pictures show her hair worn in the pompadour fashion of the day, a high-collared dress making her face appear somewhat plump, eyes heavy-browed, lips full and gently curved. She was a perfect counterpoint to her husband, restrained where he was impetuous, light and soothing where he tended to be heavy, calming him when he exploded with indignation over some pettiness or injustice. She shared his sense of commitment to the world in which they lived and was devoutly religious. A leader of the Catholic women of Brescia, she was not content as were so many in those days to keep to the house in a kind of elegant and christianized purdah. She is still remembered for her generosity to the poor.

Her interest in public affairs was as wide as her husband's and as her sons' was later to be. Ludovico would become a member of Parliament, and her third and last son, Francesco, a doctor and a leader in the resistance movement during the Second World War. The second son especially was to become a balanced blend of the qualities possessed by his two parents. He would be influenced, too, by what he saw and remembered of the life in their home in Brescia, filled, it always seemed, with the vital and intelligent leaders of the city and

[2] Letter to Dr. Comotti, March 13, 1940.

the province—someone always underfoot, ready to argue, and to laugh, at the house on the Via delle Grazie. It was no wonder that Giuditta Montini, in anticipation of the birth of her second son, determined to seek the peace of the country house in Concesio, so that her baby might be born away from the noise and excitement of the city.

The house in Concesio where Giovanni Battista was born still stands, at Via Vantini No. 14 (then No. 16) and it is largely unchanged. There is the same courtyard, green with plants and ivy, the shed for the farm equipment, the coachhouse. The section of the house once occupied by the family, the noble wing, passed by inheritance years ago to a cousin of the Pope, the engineer Vittorio, and he occupies it today, together with his family, during the summer months. The servants' wing and the section occupied by those who worked the Montini property is now rented by six families. The rooms of the house are large and austere, without frivolity, the furniture old and massive. The walls with their pictures of saints, the library filled with religious books, are an evidence of the atmosphere of the Montini home.

Four days after their baby was born, Giorgio and Giuditta Montini climbed into their carriage and rode to the parish church to have the infant baptized. It was the 30th of September, 1897. "It was on that day that I was really born," Giovanni Battista was to say later. He was the fiftieth child to be born that year in Concesio, and the pastor, Giovanni Fiorini, writing in his rural hand which made the r's appear like v's, entered the information in the baptismal records of the Church of San Antonio, on page 51, under date of September 30, 1897: "Giovanni Battista Enrico Antonio Maria Montini, son of Dr. Giorgio and Giuditta Alghisi, born on the 26th at 10 P.M., was today baptized by me, Giovanni Fiorini, Archpriest. The godfather, the Cavaliere Enrico de

Manzoni of Brescia." This name of Giovanni Battista the child would bear until, sixty-six years later, he himself as Pope would choose the name of Paul. After his election he would hear his own name no more, nor would he again be addressed by it until after his death, the Cardinal Dean would bend over the bed on which he lay and softly call "Giovanni Battista." There would be no answer—and truly the Pope would be dead. . . .

From the first days of the new baby's life the parents were concerned about him. He was small at birth, and he did not respond as expected to the care and love showered on him. The doctors decided, after the Italian fashion, that a change of air might do him good. Following the custom of the time among the upper classes, the infant was brought a few days after his baptism to a wet-nurse, Clorinda Peretti, who lived not far from Brescia in the town of Bovezzo, close enough for the child to be frequently visited. Signora Peretti was a strong, healthy woman with three children of her own—Margherita, Giovanni and Pietro—the serene type of woman who can always make room for one more by merely enlarging the scope of her care and love. The child made progress slowly, the young parents worried, and Giovanni Battista lived through the first year of his life.

Margherita Peretti, Clorinda's daughter, remembers that she and her brothers used to keep the baby company, and that he was still with her mother in his thirteenth month. Shortly afterward he was taken back to the house in Brescia, against the doctor's advice but on the insistence of his mother. Nevertheless, the next few years of his life found him still sickly, and his mother, seeking a formula to make him well, shuttled between Concesio, Bovezzo, and her own Verolovecchia, where she had inherited the seventeenth-century family home.

A photograph of Giovanni Battista taken at the age of

three reveals enormous eyes dominating a rather peaked face, solemn and innocent in this first encounter with a photographer. He was plagued with frailty in these early years, and this made his contacts with other children few and remote, and had an important influence on the character of the sensitive, delicate child. He was never to forget his second family, and as a cardinal he would visit Nina, as Clorinda was called, when her troubles became overwhelming and she remembered the *"piccolino,"* now a prince of the Church, who might help her as she had helped him when he was fighting for his life.

The early and adolescent years of Giovanni Battista were to be unusual ones because of his health. On the 6th of June, 1907, he made his first holy Communion at the chapel of the Sisters of Saint Mary the Child in Brescia; and on July 21 of that year he was confirmed by Bishop Giacomo Pellegrini in the chapel of the Jesuit Institute, Cesare Arici. This latter was the finest school in Brescia, located not far from the Montini home, on Via Trieste. Later to pass into the hands of the diocesan clergy, who maintain it today, it had at that time the high standards and demanding entrance requirements which the Jesuits traditionally exact. When he was confirmed there, young Montini, together with his brothers, was already enrolled at the Cesare Arici in what in Italy is called the elementary course, usually pursued from the age of six to ten, after which the young student would enter the *ginnasio* for the next period of his schooling, equivalent to our high school. Giovanni Battista followed the courses at the Institute until 1914.

The Institute Cesare Arici had been started in 1882, when Giuseppe Tovini, the father of ten children, began to despair of their obtaining in the State schools of the time an education which would enable them to live Christian lives and at the same time have access to the best of European culture.

He persuaded some other fathers of the city to join him in opening a school for the first five elementary classes. A building was rented and Jesuit priests agreed to staff it. Two years later, a large gift of money was offered to the school, and the handsome building in which little Giovanni Battista would attend classes was built. Each year another class was added, and the lawyer Tovini's intention was realized. "Our sons, if they have the faith, will never be poor, and without the faith they will never be rich," he said. After six years of operation, the Ministry of Public Instruction, at the petition of Brescian Masons under Giuseppe Zanardelli, refused further permission to the rector, Father Zanoni, to maintain the Institute. The battle was fought over the next four years, with victory for the school finally coming in 1892.

Young Giovanni Battista must have heard this story when he asked his father about the man whose picture was set into one of the windows of the school. He wore no Roman collar; he did not look so severe as the Jesuits whose portraits lined the halls. "Was he a priest?" young Giovanni asked. "No, son, he wasn't." "Was he a holy man?" A difficult question for the father. "That's hard to say, son. He loved his faith and he loved his sons, and he fought for both. He wouldn't care about being called holy. Let's settle for saying he was a good man."

During those years at the Jesuit Institute young Giambattista lived at home, and each morning during the short periods when his health permitted him to attend classes regularly, he walked the short distance between his home and the school. The register in which the achievements of the students enrolled for the year 1908-1909 are contained reveal that in this period of his formal schooling he achieved the following marks: Diligence, 10; written Italian, 8; oral Italian, 9; translation of Latin into Italian, 9; from Italian into Latin, 9; oral Latin, 9; arithmetic, 7; history and geography, 9;

general culture, 9; catechism, 10; conduct, 10. With our indulgent attitude toward what children should be asked to learn, we are somewhat surprised to realize that young Montini and his companions were at this time around eleven years old!

Throughout his years with the Jesuits, infrequently at school but studying at home and passing his examinations, his reports abound in 8's and 9's, rarely a 7. He was always first. The Jesuits were famous for their severity of discipline and marking, a severity of which young Montini was reminded whenever in the corridors of the Institute he looked up at the portraits of Jesuits of other times and remembered that their successors, proud of their traditions, were not at all undisposed to distribute 3's and 4's to scions of some of the most distinguished families of Brescia.

It could not be said that young Montini was indulged either because of his family or his health. Rather it would appear that under the goad of poor health (at this time it was determined that the cause of his almost chronic disability was a pulmonary weakness) he was obliged to become as precocious of will as he was of mind. His parents surrounded him with every care and indulged him more than they did the other two boys, but the greatest kindness they showed him was the strict disciplining of his time, the ordering of the day in such a way as to conserve his strength. This introduced a rhythm of work with a minimum of play which with the passing of each year became the structure of his life. Later in the Vatican Secretariat of State and in Milan he was to be the wonder and the despair of all who sought to keep pace with him as they wryly pondered his reputation for being frail.

Yet these must have been unhappy years for young Giambattista. He was a boy, and the most disturbing awareness a boy can have is to feel, to know, that he is different, and to experience at so early an age that isolation and loneliness which only maturity and grace make it possible for most men to support. He was not incapable of running and playing as did other boys, but he could do neither well. He spent much of his time reading, and thus began his consuming interest in books. Shut off from the quick, easy contacts with young people of his age, he grew somewhat aloof, and some of his school companions, unable in the thoughtlessness of youth to comprehend why he was different, and irritated that he was always first in class, called him a grind. He reacted, but he did not show it. His teachers would push him forward to join the others in play; he would obey, but it could be for only a short time.

How did he appear to others at this time? Domenico Pedersini, who lives in Concesio remembers that when he was a boy, five or six years older than Giambattista, he and some of the others in the local school would go each year to the Montini home for the final leave-taking of the school year. "Those invited would take their places on seats placed against the walls of the courtyard. The mayor would be there, the inspector, the lawyer Giorgio, his wife Giuditta and their sons. We would recite poetry . . . and as a reward we would be given fruit and biscuits. I can still see young Giambattista, always pale, and dressed in a suit of dark velvet."

Another resident of Concesio who remembers him is Luigi Bolognini, spry and alert at eighty-three. "He was a very serious little boy, with a mind and reasoning capacity far beyond his years. He was much attached to his mother and he would often run to her whenever he had some argument with his brothers. Giambattista never exploded into shouting or quarrels—you understand, of course, that even in noble families the brothers quarrel—but those few times in which they made him angry he would retire into himself, brooding over reprisals against his brothers which for the most part he never did anything about. He was very intelligent, but a little cold, very reserved, even as a boy. Only once did I ever see him really angry. Luisin, one of the sons of a farmer, had tied an old frying pan to the tail of a cat, and to tell the truth it was pretty funny at first to see how crazy scared that cat was when the pan banged along the ground. But we soon saw that the more the pan clanked, the more terrorized the cat was. It was then that Giovanni Battista, who couldn't have been more than seven or eight at the time, stepped forward. Mind you, he was a little fellow! He ordered Luisin to catch the cat and remove the pan. Luisin refused to do so and the two went at each other, their fists flying. Little Montini couldn't bear to see that poor cat suffer. Mind you, it was the only time I ever saw him really angry."

The parish priest of Farfengo, Don Luigi Benassi, in the area where the Montinis vacationed, remembers him. "He inherited from his mother her great wisdom and her profound faith. Once at Verolovecchia when he heard the bells ring at three in the afternoon to remind us of the death of our Savior, Battista at once stopped playing and started to pray . . . and without any human respect or self-consciousness he invited everyone, adults and children, to join with him in reciting the Angelus."

"I remember, too," says Don Luigi, "once, when we were together at my house, my grandmother, who was waiting on us at table, told him that I wanted to be a priest but that there was no money to send me to the seminary. There was a kind of silence and then Giambattista said, 'Nonna Margherita, there is always Providence.' Then, when he could get me alone, he whispered, 'Be ready, you'll be going to Brescia.' . . . Two days later I received a letter saying that I had been accepted for study at the seminary with all expenses paid. I found out then that the president of the fund was Giorgio Montini, the father of Giambattista."

One of his school companions in 1913-1914, the last pe-

riod of study he was to have under the Jesuits at the Cesare
Arici Institute, was Apollonio Zerla, now a dermatologist and
bachelor who lives with his sister in Brescia. "He was the best
of us all, and we stood in awe of him, even though he was as
thin as a toothpick. We weren't very close, you understand.
They were the Montinis, one of the first families of Brescia.
Those were other times. . . . What I remember most about
him was his vocabulary. He had a way of expressing himself,
even with us, so proper and precise, sticking to the point, a
style none of us shared. He wasn't with us for very long."

And the last words from an old professor, a Jesuit in the
Arici, Father Persico, now ninety-five but lucid in his memory
of the thin young man with the hollow eyes. He remembers
Giovanni Battista as the best student it was ever his pleasure
to teach. Young Montini was very close to Father Persico,
and it was to him that he first revealed his intention of becoming a priest, this when he was seventeen years old. "He
had marvelous talents as a writer," remembers Father Persico.
". . . I taught him only physics and philosophy, but I know
how well he wrote because he used to bring me articles to
read which he had written for the school paper. He would
have become a great journalist if he had taken the other road.
Of course, he had an excellent teacher in his father. I remember that he wrote articles for the student newspaper *La Fionda,* which expressed the thinking of young people about
Catholic democracy in those days."

Giovanni Battista was seventeen when he withdrew from
the Jesuit Institute and began the next phase of his studies as
an extern student of the Liceo Arnaldo da Brescia. In effect
it meant that he attended few if any classes, studying at home
for his examinations. His tutor was Professor Miglioni di
Viarigi, whose family still keeps the postcards of greeting
sent by the young student when from time to time he went off

on vacations to strengthen his health. He loved to go to the mountains with his brothers or friends, to hike in the clear air, and to come away refreshed and just the least bit less pale. The Easter vacation was spent in Concesio. He passed the summers with his family either at Concesio or Verolovecchia, but his favorite was Verolovecchia (once known as Verolo Alghisia, after his mother's family).

The whole family would go to Verolovecchia for a month, traveling on the little Brescia-Cremona train, and from the station by carriage to the villa where the whole town, it seemed, would be gathered to give welcome to "la Signora" and "il Signore" and "i signorini." Then the family would repair together to the parish church, and having prayed, greet the pastor.

There seems to have been a Christian rhythm to the lives of the Montinis, with that awareness of sacrament and mystery even in the things of earth which, in the example of his mother and father, profoundly influenced young Giovanni Battista. He was turning his thoughts, still secretly, in the direction of the priesthood, but he shared his hopes with only one person, Father Persico, and then only to question and examine his qualifications. When asked what he hoped to do with his life, he would smile and change the subject, as young men have done from time immemorial as they sought to know first their own hearts.

2.   "Don Battista"

In 1916, Giovanni Battista finished his examinations at the Liceo Arnaldo da Brescia, receiving his degree with highest honors. He was nineteen years old, his country was at war, and his class, that of 1897, had been called up. He was not accepted; again his health was the determining factor. A photograph taken in 1916 at the Cesare Arici Institute shows him with two friends, Castagna and Cognetto, who were just about to leave for the front. They wear the uniform of their country; he is dressed in a dark suit, white shirt and sober tie, an almost-too-large hat on his head, the eyes enormous, the lips firm. The three young men stare fixedly into the camera as if to assist it in capturing this moment, and it is their youth which lives so poignantly in this photograph now almost fifty years old.

For most of the young men in Europe of Giovanni Battista's age the decision as to what they would do with their lives was being made for them by their governments. They were going to war, hundreds of thousands of them to die. Seminarians as well as priests were being called up, and as young Montini came to the decision to become a priest, a young priest from Bergamo, a diocese not far from Brescia,

18

was being posted to one of the Italian fronts as a sergeant in the army. He was roly-poly, robustly healthy, cheerful; he grew a mustache to give himself an air of bravado; he made sly jokes and roared with laughter at the jokes of others; he was loved by all who met him—his name was Angelo Roncalli who, as John XXIII, was to be the predecessor of Montini on the throne of Peter.

Young Montini's desire to become a priest had been part of his life for some years, but with that prudence and caution which already marked him, he had remained silent about it, seeking only direction of a spiritual nature in its regard. Did he have a vocation? A good constitution was one of its requirements, and he had been plagued most of his life with delicate health. Did he have the temperament, the stamina, the zeal—was God's grace moving him to the first step leading to the priesthood?

His parents knew that he was wrestling with some inner problem; he grew more silent, more withdrawn, even while leaving them no doubt of his love. They suspected the nature of his struggle, but the wrong encouragement, the slightest pressure in any direction might have shattered his colloquy with God, might have introduced some too human factor. Any young man considering the priesthood sees his own unworthiness; he realizes the distance he must travel; he cannot believe that God is calling him when all around him are young men he thinks far better than he and who give this vocation no thought; he wonders if he is deceiving himself. A boy can only do what Giovanni Battista did: open his soul to a priest, receive from him an assurance that he has sufficient reason to believe he has a vocation, and then seek out the bishop of the diocese and reveal his desire to him. This Montini did. With his parents, delighted and relieved that he had come to a decision, he went to the bishop of Brescia, Giacinto Gaggia, an old friend of the family, and from him received permission to

begin his studies at the seminary of the diocese and to live at
home while doing so.

"The best seminary in the world is a good Christian home."
It is true that the Council of Trent, in its zeal for the reform of
the Church, had ordered the establishment of seminaries in
every diocese where, in isolation from the world, under the
surveillance of superiors, and following a strict regime of
work, study, recreation and prayer, young men might come to
know themselves and the Christ they sought to serve. However, the ultimate responsibility for the quality and training of
the young men in each diocese lay with the bishop himself,
and it was Bishop Gaggia's decision that no good purpose
would result from subjecting young Montini to rigors intended to produce qualities which he knew him already to
possess: strong discipline of self, absolute purity of life, intellectual capacity and a love of Christ.

If there was any doubt in the bishop's mind it centered not
in the character but in the personality of Montini. A diocesan
priest is not ordained to shut himself off from the world to
pursue his personal spiritual and intellectual perfection, but to
bring Christ to others, to win them to Him by every means,
human and divine. The diocesan priest must not live solely in
the world of ideas—his is the world of people, and they must
sense in him compassion for flawed humanity, his own and
theirs. They must be able to welcome as a man the one who
comes to them from Christ. The bishop may not have intended, even at that time, that Giovanni Battista should serve
in a parish of the provincial diocese of Brescia. Montini's
mind, for one thing, was too valuable not to be constantly
challenged, something which would not be possible in the
villages of the Brescian countryside. But the bishop had to
know, before in conscience he could ordain him, what he had
to know about all his candidates: that the priesthood which
would come to Giovanni Battista would be for others, not

merely for himself; that no matter how frail he was now and would remain, he would be willing to spend and to be spent. Was he too shy, too withdrawn, too introspective, too cold to give himself to others? These also were questions which the bishop asked himself before coming to his decision.

For the next three years young Giovanni Battista lived quietly at home, but attended classes with other students for the priesthood who lived in the seminary in Brescia under the rectorship of Father Mose Tovini, nephew of the founder of the Arici. The seminaries of the time were not distinguished for their emphasis on social and political questions, many of them narrow and provincial as opposed to catholic in their concern for life and men. But at home this son of the Montinis listened and shared in the conversation in the house on Via delle Grazie. While at the seminary he studied the usual courses in philosophy and theology and church history and scripture, at home he continued to grow in knowledge of the political and social forces shaping the world, a world which was to emerge so changed after the war that was convulsing Europe, a world of which he was very much aware.

There was always a balance in the forces that shaped Giovanni Battista intellectually. He lived in no ivory tower; his father, the practical journalist who was soon to enter the Italian Parliament, would not have tolerated it. Nor would Giorgio Montini's son ever become a priest fit only for sacristy musings, remote from the currents of his time. His condition of health, seemingly such a burden and impediment, was one of the contributory factors in the shaping of his life. It kept him at home, and it was in this home he learned to love freedom, to know that it had to be fought for over and over again. He learned the power of the written and spoken word, the necessity for a man not only to be good but to be committed, to be an apostle of the good, a communicator of truth.

A communicator of the truth was what his father had al-

ways sought to be, and in these years of testing his son sought
to be one too, but on a level and in a manner and with a success
geared to his youth and calling which enormously pleased
Bishop Gaggia. The young man spent much time teaching
catechism to children preparing for their first holy Communion at the Sanctuary delle Grazie, and also—although with
marginal success—to older children at the Oratory of Saint
Philip Neri, in the time assigned after school when they
longed to be out playing. The serious young man with the
gentle face and voice spoke to them about the things of God;
he did not seem to mind too much when they shuffled their
feet to remind him that the time was up. In the parish of San
Giovanni he organized a little Company of San Luigi, the
saint of purity; it lasted only so long as he with his enthusiasm
was around to sustain it.

He loved children and young people generally, and they
responded to him. Often he was found with the boys of the
student Association Alessandro Manzoni and with the staff of
the student newspaper *La Fionda,* which he and Andrea
Trebeschi, later to be a lawyer and to die at Dachau, founded
to speak of democracy and to combat on a student level the
anticlericalism and other antichurch attitudes of the time. Its
title, meaning "The Slingshot," bespeaks a youthfulness and
a brashness, a kind of independent noncomformity which it
is interesting to discover at this point in Montini's development.

The boys of the Association were poor for the most part,
with the problems and needs of poor boys everywhere. He
gave them affection and attention; he visited their families; he
interceded with their fathers—all with that unaffected manner
which bespoke his breeding but which lacked any note of
condescension. His boys loved him as young people were always to do, and his greatest joy as a priest would be to spend
his time among the young. Again his health played a role.

Having been denied many of the normal contacts with young people of his own age while he was growing up, now that he seemed to have somewhat outgrown his disability, he found that he had a natural facility in communicating with them, an instinctive understanding of them, and that they responded in kind. There was no longer any doubt in his bishop's mind that the priesthood of Giovanni Battista Montini would be for others.

On November 21, 1919, he received his ecclesiastical garb from Monsignor Defendente Salvetti, and became known, although still half a year away from ordination, as "Don Battista," Don being the affectionate, informal term of address for a priest in Italy. He seemed slimmer than ever in the black cassock, the white collar immaculate against his fair skin. The gravity which had always marked him seemed to deepen; these three years had given him insights into his vocation, its scope and its obligations which might have been terrifying to one less prepared than he. When, on May 29, 1920, he was ordained a priest by Bishop Gaggia, and kneeling before the prelate, his young hands clasped by those of the old man, he promised obedience and reverence to him and his successors, he rose no longer only a member of the Montini family but a priest to all men.

His first Mass was offered in the Sanctuary delle Grazie in Brescia in the presence of his family and friends, among whom were proudly numbered "his boys." He wore a chasuble made from the wedding-gown of his mother, and it was to her and to his father that he first brought Communion at that Mass, as it had been they who had been the first to kiss his anointed hands on the day of his ordination.

As a priest he was to spend little time in the diocese of Brescia. Already the bishop had formulated his plans for the young man, but for a while Don Battista was to exercise his ministry in Verolanuova, a suburb of Brescia. A story is still told with sly delight of the new priest who one day, while walking through the neighborhood, looking frail and wan in his cassock, his wide clerical hat sitting squarely on his head, was spotted by a good-hearted farmer who stood aghast at the slightness of his figure. Running into his chicken-house, he picked up a handful of eggs and brought them to the startled young passer-by. "Here, here, Don Battista," he said, "take these along; they'll do you a world of good!" How to carry the eggs was something of a problem, but to refuse would have embarrassed the man. So Don Battista carefully removed his hat, dropped the eggs into it, and with a hearty *"Grazie"* to the farmer strode off down the road. His father roared with laughter that night when he told him the story.

He celebrated his twenty-third birthday with his family, and on November 20 he left for Rome, sent by his bishop to live at the Lombard College in the Via del Corso and pursue his studies in philosophy at the Gregorian University maintained by the Jesuits, and simultaneously to take courses in the faculty of letters at the University of Rome. His capacity for work was being challenged; his future was being shaped. And he was in Rome!

It could not be said that Don Battista entered fully into the life of Rome in this first year of the 1920's. He lived the circumscribed life of the Lombard College—just reopened after the war under the rectorship of Monsignor Ettore Baranzini, the present archbishop of Syracuse—with its routine and restrictions, the first to which young Montini had been subjected outside of his home. His was the life apart of all young men who go to Rome for their seminary studies or to continue their education as priests, and he was as occupied as anyone must be who is pursuing degrees in two different universities, studying languages, and at the same time trying to exercise an apostolate to others through his priesthood. He was still being formed, but as much by the events of the day as by his studies. Italy, in 1920, dissatisfied with the scant fruits of victory after the First World War, was a country restless and convulsed as it took the first tentative, probing steps, which were soon to become giant ones, leading in 1922, to Fascism and Benito Mussolini.

The name of the Fascist dictator was to have personal as well as historical meaning to the Montini family. Don Battista's father had been elected to the Parliament in 1919, and was in Rome when his son arrived to take up residence at the Lombard College. As a member from Brescia of the Popular Party, Giorgio Montini was among the minority urging caution, for there were already signs that the Italian State was tending toward totalitarian government. The ideas and ideals of the Popular Party were the antithesis of totalitarianism. It proclaimed its Christian character, and was liberal in upholding civil and political liberties as the right of all, without party monopolies or prejudice against religion, race or classes. Such sanity, especially sanity clothed in Christian garments, was not to appeal to the Italian government at the time. Although the Popular Party had won 99 seats in Parliament out of 508 in the election of 1919, and was to do more than any other Italian organization to bar the way to Fascism, Mussolini continued to tighten his grip on the country.

The young student at the Lombard College could, of course, have taken no part in the battle being waged by Giorgio Montini and his colleagues, but he knew of the battle and of the principles it involved. From those days forward he was always to show an aversion for any form of dictatorship or curtailment of fundamental liberties.

On January 22, 1922, Pope Benedict XV died suddenly.[1]

[1] The fourth Pope since the Kingdom of Italy took possession of Rome, Benedict XV was the first at whose death the Italian government lowered the flags to half-mast in token of mourning.

A sad little man who has deserved better of history, he had spent his strength during the First World War in trying to bring about peace between the nations in conflict. Although he had been excluded from the Peace Conference, it was to be belatedly acknowledged that his peace proposals of 1917 were closely paralleled by Wilson's Fourteen Points of the next January. He was a man of enormous capacity and personal charm, without the qualities of genius but possessed of a vast prudence and patience. Small, frail and ugly, he had worked indefatigably to bring about recognition of the Church's moral influence in the world. His diplomatic skill had softened old bitternesses between Italy and the Papacy and a rapprochement now appeared possible. The war had convinced the Vatican that an Italy more than ever nationalist would never surrender Rome as its capital. On its side the Quirinal had come to recognize that however many governments come and go, the Papacy would not renounce its claim to independence of any temporal power. While Benedict XV did not fail to reiterate the protest of his predecessors against dependence upon the Kingdom, it now appeared that a solution would not be held incompatible with a nominal amount of territory, one sufficient to house the offices and staff of the Holy See, the palaces of the Vatican and of the Lateran, the summer residence of the Popes at Castelgandolfo, and certain other papal possessions such as churches and sanctuaries within the city of Rome and in other parts of Italy.

During the war Italy, watching the growing prestige of a Papacy stripped of secular sovereignty, had come to realize that there was a power other than that derived from the possession of Rome and of the old Papal States, and that this power was coming to be recognized more and more by other nations. At the beginning of Pope Benedict's pontificate only fourteen States had been represented at the Vatican; at his death the number had grown to twenty-six. After the conflict was over, his worldwide appeals had saved thousands from starvation in Central and Eastern Europe.

Benedict XV, the frail, sensitive nobleman was succeeded by the archbishop of Milan, Achille Ratti, former prefect of the Vatican Library and former nuncio to Warsaw, a rugged, forthright man as intransigent in his way as the mountains he loved to scale.[2] As his reign began, the Church was girding herself anew to deal with the forces being shaped in the world by the rise of Communism and Fascism; it was cautiously willing to cooperate in bringing order and harmony to Italy, but determined to maintain its allegiance to freedom and human dignity. During the reign of Pope Pius XI, Mussolini would lead his "march on Rome" and become the dictator of Italy; a dictator would seize power in Germany; Italy would invade Ethiopia; the civil war in Spain would explode, and the doughty Pontiff would leave the world just as it sought to commit suicide with the beginning of the war in 1939. In fearless encyclicals he denounced Fascism, Nazism and Communism; he sought to effect a transfusion of the spiritual and moral and intellectual forces of the Church into the arena of world affairs. Inheritor of the Roman Question, perhaps his greatest historical achievement was to bring about in 1929 the Lateran Treaty[3] in which the Italian government recognized the independence and sovereign power of the Papacy over its do-

[2] Sir Alec Randall, secretary, at this time, of the British Legation to the Holy See, in his book *Vatican Assignment* (London: William Heinemann, Ltd.) refers to his "strict discipline," his "uncompromising austerity"; describes him as "independent and unyielding." During his Milan years he was known as a "clerical liberal": a man closer to the ideas of Leo XIII and Rampolla than of Saint Pius X and Merry del Val.

[3] Of Pope Pius and the Lateran Treaty, Randall says (*op. cit.*, p. 58): "It needed someone of a dictatorial nature to clinch an agreement with a dictator." 1921 was the year in which Pope Pius made his famous remark about being willing to negotiate with the devil.

main of the Vatican State and its extraterritorial possessions, an independence and sovereignty which the Holy See had always contended that it possessed.

In the first year of Pius XI's pontificate, 1922, the serious twenty-five year old priest from Brescia, immersed in the task of gaining two doctorates, was called to the attention of Monsignor Giuseppe Pizzardo, the newly appointed Undersecretary of State at the Vatican. One of Pope Pius' first acts had been to confirm as his Secretary of State the Lord Cardinal Pietro Gasparri; and his assistant, Monsignor Pizzardo, small and birdlike, with his quick darting eyes and restless energy, was given, among more monumental tasks, that of recruiting additional personnel for the Secretariat. Father Montini had the intellectual capacities, the family background and priestly qualities which would have recommended him in any case, and it was now that the generosity of the bishop of Brescia and his personal interest in the young man culminated in Monsignor Pizzardo's invitation to Don Battista to prepare himself for the diplomatic service of the Church. To Father Montini's mild protest that he was already pursuing two doctorates, Monsignor Pizzardo gave him an airy wave of the hand and replied, "What difference does one doctorate more or less make?" He was to enter the Pontifical Academy of Noble Ecclesiastics, the training school for diplomat-priests, and to continue his studies in canon law at the Gregorian University. His studies for this degree were done at the Gregorian but the degree was to be issued, after an examination and defense of his thesis, by the Milan Pontifical Seminary.

Thus summoned in the first months of the new pontificate, Don Battista took the first recognizably significant step in the career which was to bring him to the papal throne forty-one years later. Entering the somewhat gloomy Academy in the Piazza Minerva, flanked on one side by the Pantheon, facing an early Gothic church built on the site of a temple to Minerva, he began his two-year course in languages, diplomatic style and history, while at the same time he continued to follow his courses at the Gregorian. More significantly, he was at the Academy to be observed and judged. The Vatican diplomatic service was wholly Italian in those days,[4] and the young men beginning their slow ascent in the Church through that service had to be thoroughly screened. They would hold positions of deep sensitivity in Rome and posts all over the world; many would be called from those posts to accept a cardinal's hat, and one of them might even, through the vote of his peers, ascend the throne of Peter.

Those who had begun as Father Montini was beginning looked down on him from the oil paintings that covered the walls of the Academy. There were Pacca and Consalvi, and even Merry del Val; Della Chiesa, too, who became Benedict XV. Pope Leo XIII had been there as a student, in the days when the diplomatic service was truly limited to the sons of nobles, and when the young priest noblemen brought their personal servants to care for their needs. But these were more democratic days, and the rooms of the servants, high on the fifth floor under the roof, were now occupied by students. They ate indifferent food, they celebrated Mass in the baroque chapel or in neighboring churches, attended classes in the library and at the Gregorian, took each other's measure and were in turn weighed, measured, and probed in all ways known to wise and cautious Rome.

Years later, on April 25, 1951, on the occasion of the celebration of the foundation of the Academy, the then Sostituto of the Secretariat of State, Monsignor Montini, setting forth the reasons for the continuation of Vatican diplomacy and its training school for diplomats, and emphasizing the sense of

[4] Cardinal Hinsley of Westminster made vigorous representation to Pius XI about the all-Italian character of the Curia, but the Pope was indifferent.

history it inculcates, had this to say: "When we were in the seminary we were taught to love souls, to love the parish, to love the diocese. Here we learned to love all peoples, to widen our hearts, to enlarge their scope with a magnanimity which is truly Roman, to open our souls to nations and to continents, to become aware of history in its most obscure aspects in order to deal with the most encompassing problems of human life. Here the school says to the students: you will be the servant of great causes and of high interests. A school, I repeat, of universal charity . . . the Academy . . . says to its students: the higher you rise, the greater must be your service; remember that to rise means to accept the weight of new responsibilities and realize what it means to be a representative: it is to serve as a symbol for another—that is to say, he must increase, I must decrease. And in the measure that you rise, your mission will make you tremble, and you will be obliged to sanctify yourself by prayer and in humility for the fulfilment of those duties that will be demanded of you."

In his address to the future diplomats of the Holy See Monsignor Montini defended papal diplomacy from charges that it was a survival of the past, "an almost ritualistic diplomacy, its personnel assuming traditional attitudes and recruited from closed social circles; a diplomacy swathed in forms and etiquette no longer in the spirit of our times." While he conceded that some of the "objections" had a certain foundation, he went on to say that they ignored the essential reality that "it is neither on such forms nor forces that the Church relies . . . she draws her vital forces from within." He defined the diplomacy of the Church as more than ever "a form of love for people," and added: "If civil diplomacy tends to reduce the antagonisms in the world by making reason prevail over force, and to contribute to the growth of the prosperity of individual States in the harmonious concert of an ever larger international organization, it finds in ecclesiastical diplomacy almost a model to which it can look; not so much because of any technical skill that the diplomacy of the Church might display or any successes it might obtain (for both the one and the other may be lacking), but rather because of the ideal from which it takes its departure and toward which it tends: the universal brotherhood of man."

"Does this Academy," Monsignor Montini went on to ask, "fulfill its mission to its students? Does it really prepare them?" He then chose two examples, the one, he said, illustrating the simplicity of spirit and the adaptability which animates the students of the Academy; the other an example of self-abnegation and of courage approaching the heroic.

"I remember," he said, "a very young colleague at the Academy, who after finishing his course was assigned to a distant country of South America. Before leaving he acquired as much information as he could regarding the country to which he was posted. Finally we asked him: 'What conclusions have you reached about the country and the appointment?' 'I have learned,' he said, 'that I will need a pair of leather pants in order to ride horseback.'" "And indeed he did," added Monsignor Montini, "because at a time when he was alone and chargé d'affaires, he traveled for fifteen days on horseback to reach a remote area in order to establish an apostolic vicariate."

His other example centered in the return from behind the Iron Curtain of certain of his colleagues from the Secretariat of State. "The countries in which they had been stationed had broken off relations with the Holy See, and they had been obliged to leave. We went to the railroad station to meet them on their return . . . and this is what our friends said to us, in simple but humanly moving words: 'What we regret is not being able to stay and to suffer with our brothers.'"

"This," said Monsignor Montini, "this is the Academy and these are the things which justify it." Then, addressing the

young students who sat where once he had sat, he added:
"May all of you be such representatives, may all of you have
the sense, the spirit, of this representation. Diplomacy is a
representation. We must have the sense of being representatives of Christ, of the Church. This is our purpose, and this
is our title of glory—to be able to say: 'I am Christ; I am the
Church.'"

In May of 1923 Don Battista was summoned by Monsignor
Pizzardo and informed that he had been made *addetto*, or
second secretary, to the nunciature in Warsaw, and that he
was to leave immediately. He knew no reason for the appointment, an unusual one since he had not completed his course
at the Academy; he was simply to go. There was a quick farewell to his parents, and armed with a diplomatic passport, he
left Italy for the first time.

His journey took him across Austria with its onion-domed
churches, into Germany and across the plains of Poland, to
Warsaw. The nuncio, Archbishop Lorenzo Lauro, who had
succeeded Achille Ratti in Poland and was later made a cardinal, received Don Battista as a father. The young man so
far from home, with his slight frame and exquisite manners,
generated sympathy and warmth wherever he went with the
nuncio during his few months in Poland. His manner was
totally self-effacing, he had a prodigious capacity for work,
and the *uditore* (auditor) of the nunciature, Monsignor Carlo
Chiarlo, later one of the cardinals of the conclave which elected
Paul VI, had no reason to regret the quiet and helpful presence of the young Brescian. Don Battista was recalled to
Rome the following November, since it had been thought best
not to subject him to the rigors of the Polish winter. Thus his
test in the field came to an end.

Father Montini returned to the Academy, his purposiveness
sharpened by those months of practical experience, and in
October 1924, he entered the Secretariat of State as *addetto*,

was named *minutante*[5] in April 1925, and there—ascending always to higher posts—he remained until he was named archbishop of Milan in 1954. Those thirty years would be years of refining, they would distill the man until only the fiber of his character would remain; they would drain him of any residue of self until his name would become at the Vatican the very emblem of the perfect servitor of the Pope. His strong personality was not destroyed but submerged, his mind and will not subverted but submitted, with his priesthood his first passion, enriched by his perfect obedience to what he was asked to do. The "diplomat priest" he would be called, the "patrician priest" also, but his first and greatest pleasure was in the title "the priest of the students." It came about this way.

Pius XI, among other of his distinctions, was to become known as the Pope of Catholic Action,[6] and in the first years of his pontificate he was encouraging in the Catholic world, and especially in Italy, the involvement of the laity in the work of the Church under the guidance of priests deputed by the hierarchy. In Italy it was an antidotal action to the lingering effects of the *non expedit*, to the long years of lethargy and indifference on the part of the country's Catholic laity who were content to leave the work of the Church to the priests, and to the equally long centuries of clerical control. There, as elsewhere in the world, a general awareness had not yet dawned that the Church's witness was in the marketplace, in the forum of men's activity and ideas, not a witness of worship only but one of social regeneration as well.

Pope Pius was by no means the first to formulate this concept; it was as old as Christianity itself and had been stressed by his immediate predecessors, but it was he who gave it new

[5] A *minutante* must read all reports on a given question, summarize them and integrate them into one trenchant précis.

[6] Pope Pius called Catholic Action ". . . the apple of Our eye," in a letter to Cardinal Bertram.

impetus. In Italy it would become at times for the Fascists an irritating counterpoise to their own ambitions for dechristianizing the country, an organized response by Catholic citizens on various levels of national life to attempts to deify the State, to restrict human rights, to subvert the young, and to dazzle university youth with talk of national glory divorced from moral principle and spiritual basis. At times it hesitated, at times it compromised, and even seemed at times to capitulate, but there were always those who came forth to give it fire and a new sense of purpose.

Monsignor Pizzardo had been appointed general chaplain for Catholic Action in Italy, and in 1924, at his suggestion, the chancery office for the diocese of Rome appointed Don Battista as spiritual advisor to the students of the University of Rome where there was a chapter of FUCI, the Federation of Italian Catholic University Students. Thus he entered, in his own words expressed years later, into "that cage of lions which the university students of yesterday were: they were not as reflective, as thoughtful as those of today." He welcomed the appointment as would any priest who spends much of his day behind a desk dealing with reports and not directly with human beings. His concept of his office was typical. There would be no mere strident confrontation of himself and of his students with those who opposed or laughed at them, no struggle for ascendancy with the university as battleground. Rather he quietly and effectively opened to his students what it meant to be a human being, showing them how Christianity deepens and enriches man's every faculty, and how every true Christian witnesses to the truth which is in him.

Long years afterward, Monsignor Sergio Pignedoli, who knew Don Battista in those days and who would later become his auxiliary in Milan, was to write: "The great prestige that he enjoyed in the eyes of his students, both in his articulation of their spiritual problems and, more important, in his ability to resolve them, was centered in his assured and total concept of Christianity . . . for him its essence lay in the interior formation of conscience." Yet he would have had scant success had he not known how to enter the students' lives, to laugh and joke with them. This he did with an ease which suprised those who were already contributing to the myth of his coldness and aloofness.

From his quarters at the Academy of Diplomacy he moved to a house on the Via Aurelia. Every minute free from his duties at the Vatican found him with the students, and they responded to his devotion first with caution and then with affection. They stood somewhat in awe of him. His knowledge of the writings of Maritain, Bergson, Spengler, Thomas Mann, the Church Fathers, was staggeringly impressive to their young eyes. He was particularly concerned that these young people, most of them from the middle and upper classes, should not live sealed off in their comfortable lives from the squalor and misery which abounded in Italy. Every week he led them to one of the most forsaken areas of Rome, the Porta Metronia, to touch and smell poverty and to respond as Christians to the need of their fellow men after the example of Saint Vincent de Paul, in whose name they were organized.

In 1925, the scope of his activity was widened with his appointment as national assistant to the Federation of Italian Catholic University Students. He retained his chaplaincy at the University of Rome, but the area of his concern was extended to the whole of the Italian Peninsula. These were difficult and sensitive days for FUCI. Founded thirty years before, it seemed to be lacking in purposeful direction, in danger of becoming exhortatory and pious instead of intellectually militant. The Fascists were now strongly entrenched in the country, and the Catholic federation was a natural target for their attacks since it was made up of thousands of young Italians opposed to Fascism, although possessing membership in GUF, Fascist University Youth,[7] and not unwilling, in the way of youth, to add emphasis to principle by occasional resort to scuffling.

There were also internal difficulties for the Catholic student organization. 1925 was a Holy Year in the Catholic world, and FUCI, meeting in national congress at Bologna, sent a telegram of homage to the King, unaware of the significance of this move in the tense and delicate situation of Church-State relations in Italy. Young people are not given to weighing all the consequences of their actions, and the members of FUCI who voted the homage were unaware of, or at least gave little thought to, the fact that the Roman Question was still a living, burning issue in Italy and at the Vatican, and that already tentative steps were being taken to resolve it. Anything which tended to intrude on the negotiations, no matter how casually, was bound to cause concern at the Vatican, determined after more than fifty years to put an end to the impasse. It was felt that the directors of FUCI should have been more sensitive. As a consequence of internal difficulties, a change of leadership was decided; Don Battista was appointed assistant and a new president was appointed in the person of a young man, Igino Righetti, barely twenty, who was to become as close a friend to Don Battista as anyone in his life.

The two succeeded to their posts immediately, and Don Battista was on hand to greet the members of the Bologna congress when they arrived in Rome to obtain the Holy Year indulgences and, if possible, to be received by the Pope. It is said that Pius XI, to evidence his displeasure at the telegram of homage to the King, refused to receive them, and it was Don Battista who had to announce the decision. They had all gathered at the Church of Saint Philip Neri, not far from the Vatican, prepared to march in procession to hail the Holy

[7] Made necessary by the social and economic restrictions imposed by the Fascists on those not joining their organizations.

Father. When they were told that there would be no reception, the young people sat stunned. One of the chaplains called out: "There are some occasions when the *Te Deum* should be sung, and others when the *De Profundis* is called for!" And Don Battista, standing near the tomb of St. Philip, intoned the *Te Deum.*

This incident indicates the difficult situation in which Don Battista had been placed. He was on the staff of the Vatican Secretariat of State and he was leader, together with Righetti, of the Catholic students of Italy. From one side came exhortations to caution, to reserve; from the other the impetus to action, to witness. It was the first important act of diplomacy which Montini was to effect: the reconciliation in his own life of these two currents, as well as the guiding of the student organization between the Scylla of Vatican admonition and the Charybdis of youthful impetuosity. Righetti was as one with Montini in his thinking. Born in Rimini, where he had founded a small journal, the *Ariminum,* he once wrote: "To live dangerously is a program which too many have set for themselves. Sacred Scripture tells us, on the contrary, that he who loves danger shall perish in it." Yet it seemed almost impossible not to live dangerously in those days.

The headquarters for FUCI in Rome were in the Piazza Sant'Agostino. The first issue of their newspaper, *La Sapienza* (Wisdom), a weekly, appeared in May, 1925. It already reflected the Righetti-Montini emphasis that FUCI become a militantly intellectual élite. To this publication Father Montini contributed the first of what would be a regular series of articles on the spiritual and intellectual challenges facing the young in those already distant days. "To observe, seek, study, this is the life of the children of light," he wrote in his first article. This and subsequent articles were impressive for the scope of ideas and problems which he presented to the young men and women of FUCI. He was not content with vague generalizations; he took his office and his young people seriously, an attitude reflected in these first writings in *Sapienza* and in *Azione Fucina,* which grew out of *Sapienza.*

Monsignor Geremia Pacchioni, who was close to Montini and Righetti, is quoted as saying: "Whenever we had our meetings, I was the one to go to the Vatican to pick up Montini. It was a big problem because they let him go always with the greatest reluctance. And also because wherever we went chaos followed—the Fascists followed us everywhere. Very often our meetings began in one city and ended in another."

The greatest disturbance took place at Macerata in 1926. The meeting at Macerata was planned to celebrate the thirtieth anniversary of FUCI's founding. It was to take place on August 27, 28, 29, and 30, the last day to be one of pilgrimage to Assisi. The editorial in the August 25th issue of *Sapienza* in urging its members to attend, said: "This will not be a meeting of songs and banquets. There is a heaviness and challenge in the air which imposes on us the obligation of a correct and austere gathering. FUCI wants to live—it must live. This organization must ever be dedicated to the intellectual apostolate, because to proclaim programs of action is nothing if we are not above all perfected by Christian virtue."

On the eve of the meeting, representatives from Genoa and Turin were assaulted by Fascist thugs, but the first day of the reunion itself went smoothly until, at the close of the session, the Fucini, as they were called, led by Montini and Righetti, marched to the university of the city to lay a wreath on the memorial to students fallen in the war. When the Fucini sought to leave the university, singing their hymn, they were attacked. Fascist youths, singing their own militant, "To arms, we are Fascists!" grabbed the FUCI flags and the battle was on. At first the national police stood by, then moved in leisurely. Seven Fucini were hurt; two were arrested, one of them a priest. No Fascists. Protests were made to the authorities by those in charge, including Montini. A story is told that when the Fascist governor complained to Don Battista that a young Black Shirt had received a serious head wound, the chaplain said, "Your Excellency, it really was not our boy's fault. The Fascist was tugging so hard at a flag being held in the air that finally the student simply could not help letting it come down on the other chap's head."

The Fucini withdrew from Macerata and went to Assisi, where in the town of the gentle Saint Francis even the Fascists were somewhat more subdued. From Assisi they went to Rome, this time to be received warmly by Pope Pius. It is told that the eye of the Holy Father, who prided himself on being informed about everything, fell on one of the students who was still quite heavily bandaged as a result of the fracas at Macerata. He asked about the young man's injury and listened as Montini and Righetti explained what had happened; then, turning to poor Monsignor Pizzardo, with annoyance showing in his heavy voice, the Pope asked: "And why don't you tell me about these things too?" [8]

After the Lateran Treaty of 1929, the tension between the Fucini and the Fascists subsided, but in 1931 it exploded again. The meetings of FUCI were raided, their halls burned, the students assaulted, and finally all Catholic youth organizations were suppressed by the government. Pius XI reacted with his famous encyclical *Non abbiamo bisogno,* and at one point the Holy See invited all those at the head of youth groups to take refuge in the Vatican. The struggle for the youth of any country can be a bitter one. In June of that year, Montini and Righetti decided to suspend all public meetings but to continue to meet secretly. This they did for a few months. A student of the time later wrote: "We had no doubt that our chaplain was one with us. We felt that a kind of

[8] The story is probably apocryphal.

fraternal friendship united us, a friendship cemented both in the hours of joy and in the hours of testing."

In October, Mussolini intervened personally, and public meetings of the Catholic student organization were resumed, but the Fascist Party stepped up its pressure and persecution, desirous of suppressing FUCI and leaving only their own youth organization, GUF. One strategem was to bypass FUCI as being irrelevant by assigning chaplains to GUF. Montini's strategy was along lines of non-collaboration, of passive resistance, of preparing for the future when there would be no Fascism. "If we can't march with banners flying," he said "let us work in silence."

He was accused by some of not taking a strong enough stand, of not being committed, of being too moderate, while the austerity which he invited the students to share as they prepared themselves for the future was not at all to the liking of the old guard in the organization who remembered the days of food, laughter and song, of camaraderie based on mere "togetherness"; there was for them something too principled, too reasoned, too calculated, almost too austere, in Montini's approach. And also a disciplined lay élite was a source of uneasiness to many.

But Don Battista was his father's son, and his brother Ludovico remembers that "when we were boys, our father used to say constantly, 'We must prepare ourselves to see the light. No easy truces for us. We must know what shoes we will wear; and when we are of age, off we will go!' " His father referred to the days he knew would come when the Church and Catholics would be free in Italy; his patience and good cheer must have irritated the extremists as much on one side as on the other. So, too, did his son's at this stage as it would later.

There lives today on the outskirts of Brescia a man who thirty-five years ago was one of the priests most hated and feared by the Italian Fascists. His name is Father Giulio Bevilacqua, a member of the Congregation of the Oratory, and he is eighty-three years old. Before his transfer to Rome in 1928, he was involved in constant polemics with the Fascists. The party newspaper, *Popolo di Brescia,* attacked him in an article appearing in 1926, and when his reply in an article entitled "Why I Cannot Be a Fascist" appeared in *Il Cittadino,* the newspaper once directed by Don Battista's father, the latter paper was suspended.

When he was removed to Rome, Father Bevilacqua was met by Father Montini, and for five years they lived together in an apartment on the Via Terme delle Daciane, on the Aventine. The old man says: "I used to say to him: do less work—less, not more, do you hear? Leave a little for the others to do. Don't be up every night until two o'clock; it's bad for your health." But the advice did no good. Referring to Father Montini's work with the students, Father Bevilacqua adds: "He gathered around him a true aristocracy of faith and culture. He knew how to use ordinary language with the vigor of truth showing through, and his voice was warm and intimate . . . the voice of a person who knew how to take part in a dialogue. . . . He spoke to the young with a faith nourished by the treasures of the gospels and the liturgy. And this faith in God manifested itself always in the whole man, because Don Battista loved the creative human spirit under its every aspect—art, thought, culture, science. He was everything to the boys, following them in their activities of each new day with unflagging freshness and imagination."

On March 15, 1933 Monsignor Montini received a letter from Archbishop Pizzardo which read in part: "In consideration of the increasing work of your important office in the Secretariat of State, you have repeatedly requested that I obtain from the Holy Father permission for you to withdraw from your assignment as ecclesiastical assistant to the Catholic

University Students. . . . The Pope . . . has graciously consented to allow you to dedicate all of your outstanding gifts to the delicate tasks of the Secretariat of State. . . . In informing you of this I cannot conceal my regret in seeing you leave a post which you have held for eight years and discharged with true love and devotion."

Azione Fucina, the FUCI bulletin, in reprinting the whole letter, comments: "Monsignor Montini, in giving us the copy of the letter here reprinted, has expressed a formal desire that it not be accompanied by any comment, because only silence can express the sentiments of his heart at this moment. We cannot, however, fail to reveal that we will remain always closely united to him, because we will always feel ourselves guided by that same love for the Church of Jesus Christ and of his Vicar which pervaded and has been unforgettably manifested to us in the work Monsignor Montini has devoted for eight years to our association. To speak of gratitude is superfluous." Monsignor Guido Anichini, who succeeded Montini, wrote years later in his book *Fifty Years of FUCI:*[9] "Certain orders must be accepted with serenity, knowing as one does that superiors have their just and broad perspectives in such matters." Thus closed a chapter, a change made not without pain, but one accepted with as much generosity as would be the change to Milan twenty-one years later.

Speaking of him years later, Archbishop Pignedoli said: "There is (in him) a natural and ever-present nostalgia for everything having to do with university life and its spiritual and cultural problems. A prime quality which Monsignor Montini possessed is fundamental for assisting people of any age, but of first importance for the young—confidence. He himself looks at life with the confidence of the young; he sees even the most difficult problems with a characteristic freshness of eye and heart."

[9] Rome: Editrice Studium [n.d.].

Later the cardinal of Milan would say about these days: "For me it was a discovery. If I know anything I owe it all to these dear friends of years past, because they were for me a stimulus, a living lesson which I could not have received either from books or even from the example, shining under every aspect, of the world of priests."

Montini was never to lose his interest in the Catholic student organization. In 1936, he assisted in setting up the famous "Seminars of Camaldoli," weeks of study for men from FUCI who were later to be numbered among the leaders of the postwar Christian Democratic Party. Montini's recommendation to them was: sociology, sociology, and more sociology. On June 25, 1943, the day Mussolini fell, the Code of Camaldoli was proclaimed, and set forth the basis for a Christian social order in Italy.

Montini was not there; he was at the Vatican. Righetti was not there—he had died in 1939, at the age of thirty-five, his last request that his unborn baby, if a boy, be named Giovanni Battista Righetti-Montini. Together they had founded the small publishing house, Studium, brought up to date and revised the magazine, *Studium,* giving it a Roman setting and control after long years of identity with Bologna.[10] Together they had recast the program of FUCI on more intellectual lines, tightened and strengthened its organization, fought its battles and drawn close together in the sharing of hopes and difficulties. Together they saw grow out of the national congress of FUCI held in Cagliari, Sardinia, in the summer of

[10] *Studium,* the FUCI review, and its bulletin, *Azione Fucina,* never contained anything of Fascism in them, at most expressions of Italian patriotic sentiment. *"Studium* never put a grain of incense on the altar of Fascism. It maintained a certain cultural level at a time when the rest of Catholic Action was content to preach and give itself to devotional practices." Richard A. Webster, "The Rebirth of the Christian Democratic Party in Italy," in *Il Mulino,* Bologna, August, 1959, p. 26.

1932, the Association of Catholic University Graduates which sought with notable success to give witness in professional and social life to what its members as students had first learned as theory.

In an introduction to a book on Righetti,[11] Montini wrote: "He remains almost as if carved in the memory of his friends who will not find anyone to replace him, and they will always feel the need of turning to him in memory, not only to feel themselves young and good, as is the need of those who are getting on in years and who have had the good fortune in the years of their conscience's awakening to find a companion, a teacher of rare merit who gave them understanding and guided them through adolescence into maturity, but also to relive conversations, cherished and persuasive as few could be."

During the period of their association, Monsignor Montini, teaching the history of pontifical diplomacy at the Academy of Diplomacy, found time also to publish three small volumes: *The Way of Christ, Introduction to the Study of Christ,* and *A University Conscience.* All these were the fruit of his meditation on the role of the Saviour in the lives of the young, and they clearly show that in those days of political tension the emphasis of the still youthful but now balding monsignor was not on better and more subtle political infighting, but on giving a more personal witness to the Master. It was this same desire which found him organizing week-end retreats in the Basilica of Saint Paul Outside the Walls where the Benedictine Abbot Schuster (who was to be his predecessor in the see of Milan) welcomed the youths who came.

Monsignor Montini preached every Sunday in the Church of the Sapienza in Rome; he spent hours hearing confessions, and his charity to the poor grew to be a legend among the poor themselves. In 1933, still in touch with "his boys" who were

[11] Augusto Naroni, *Igino Righetti* (Rome: Editrice Studium, Rome n.d.).

now graduated, he founded together with them a unit of the Saint Vincent de Paul Society which held meetings and worked from the Church of Saint Anne, the little parish church of Vatican City. The area of their apostolate was the squalid, depressed section of Primavalle. Blessed are they who go to the poor in the name of Christ, he told them.

Those who thought they saw the whole man in his Vatican diplomatic setting saw one facet alone. If they failed to see the priest they did not see Montini, for it was this that marked everything he did. It was this quality of his priestliness, directing all his other talents, which caused him in his thirty-seventh year to be recognized by his superiors as one who could make an outstanding contribution to the diplomatic service of the Holy See.

3.   Vatican Beginnings

Those sensitive to their times and to the currents of those times knew in 1933 that they were no longer living in a world where, in spite of wars and the upheaval of continents, business could go on as usual and Christianity could remain as it had for centuries. The violent disruption of society caused by the First World War had brought about the collapse of such cultural structures as the belief in progress toward a better world and the triumph of reason over brutality, into which Christianity had fitted naturally and comfortably. With the props taken away, it was slowly being revealed that while the average modern man still professed certain traditional beliefs, they had long ago been emptied of their inner reality, and that pseudo-spirituality or naked nihilism had gradually possessed men's souls.

Europe for centuries had been ravaged not only physically by war but spiritually by the secularist thought born with the Renaissance, which had assumed control at the time of the French Revolution and whose final harvest was now being realized. Holy Russia was firmly in the grip of atheistic Communism, an uneasy truce existed between the Church and Fascism in Italy, and in Germany the confused Catholic

46

Centre Party had, in 1932, voted with the Nazis to make Hermann Göring the first Nazi president of the Reichstag, and in this year would vote for the "enabling act," effectively throttling the Republic and making Hitler dictator. Mussolini was already planning expansion in Africa, of which the rape of Ethiopia would be a part; Spain was building to the crisis of its civil war, a rehearsal for the war Hitler would launch against Poland in 1939. The United States, mired in depression, was hearing its new President, Franklin Delano Roosevelt vibrantly reassure his country that it had nothing to fear but fear itself.

At this juncture in world history, Monsignor Montini would arrive each morning in the courtyard of San Damaso in the Vatican, walk or ride on the slow, water-propelled elevator to the third floor of the palace, pass through the Hall of Maps, saluted by the guards, and enter the Secretariat of State to deal with the quota of problems assigned to him. The world of his service was quiet, almost serene, even though it was aware of the most sensitive currents or convulsive eruptions in the Church and in the world. "It is calm and tranquil," he would say years later, "because it wishes to be. Because its supreme purpose is to seek for peace, to create peace!" [1]

Although as *minutante* more and more important assignments were being given to him, and although his opinions and advice were followed in many projects and areas of research, Monsignor Montini was still one of many in the service of the Secretariat, not yet in the top echelon. He was to serve under three Secretaries of State, each in his way to contribute to his formation as a diplomat.

The first was Cardinal Pietro Gasparri, a brilliant jurist of farmer stock, nicknamed *"il Contadino,"* the peasant. He had

---

[1] Cardinal Merry del Val, Secretary of State to Pius X, when asked what were the guiding principles of Vatican diplomacy, replied, "The New Testament."

a gruff geniality, the quick mind and wit of the unselfconscious peasantry, ready to relax and make a joke, but unflagging and meticulous in every detail having to do with his office. Only in his dress was he indifferent to detail, his *zucchetto* askew, snuff stains on his cassock. He had received the red hat from Pope Pius X in recognition of his services in the project of codifying canon law. A man of great diplomatic adaptability, he served as Secretary of State under two pontificates, that of Benedict XV and of Pius XI. It was he who represented the Vatican in the settlement of the Roman Question, and who, as must all Secretaries of State, had articulated perfectly the mind of the Pontiff, Pius XI, in these delicate negotiations. "Almost all Cardinal Secretaries of State in modern times," as Sir Alec Randall writes, "have one thing in common: that it is impossible to say just where the influence of the Secretary of State came in. . . . A Cardinal Secretary of State is essentially self effacing in relation to the Pope he serves." [2] The Pope whom Gasparri served until 1930, and who was to advance Monsignor Montini "was a man of strict discipline and uncompromising austerity, aloof, an independent man, even an unyielding one, with little pliancy in his nature. He kept his own counsel and admitted few to his thinking." [3]

The man chosen by Pius XI to replace Cardinal Gasparri on his retirement as Secretary of State would himself be described in much the same words, but to these would be added the adjectives "baffling," "brilliant," "mercurial." This was Cardinal Eugenio Pacelli, a man of exquisite figure and manner, a linguist, still in his fifties, who had distinguished himself as nuncio to Bavaria and later in Berlin, and who now was at the peak of his powers and seemingly of attain-

[2] "The Pope's 'Alter Ego,' " in *The Tablet* (London), May 4, 1963.
[3] Alec Randall, *Vatican Assignment* (London: Wm. Heinemann, Ltd., 1956).

ment. He was to draw young Montini, whose elegance, intelligence and reserve attracted him, into closer ties of work and responsibility, so that even at this time it came to be said, exaggeratedly, that Monsignor Montini's very being and personality had been absorbed into that of Pacelli.

The final Secretary of State under whom Montini would serve succeeded Cardinal Pacelli when the latter became Pope Pius XII in 1939. Luigi Maglione was a prelate of great charm and dignity, former nuncio to Berne and Paris, proud of his Neopolitan heritage, explosive as southern Italians can be, but trained through the years to subdue and channel his natural self-assertiveness. He was appointed Secretary, it was said, because the new Pope, although preferring in those crucial days of 1939 to keep in his own hands the handling of the Church's diplomatic affairs, wished to please some of the cardinals who had elected him and who wished to see Maglione honored. When, in fact, Maglione died in 1944, he was not replaced.

In 1937, and still under the pontificate of Pius XI, Monsignor Montini was named Sostituto of the Secretariat of State, succeeding Monsignor Domenico Tardini, who in turn replaced Archbishop Giuseppe Pizzardo as head of the Section of Extraordinary Affairs, Pizzardo having been named cardinal. Thus thirteen years after being called to the Secretariat by the then Sostituto, Pizzardo, Monsignor Montini succeeded to the post, a rise to which the word meteoric may in this case be applied. And thus, too, his name is first linked with that of Domenico Tardini. Together they would act as Undersecretaries of State while a Cardinal Secretary held office, but from 1944 to 1954 they would serve together under Pius XII, acting as his own Secretary of State.

Two more dissimilar types could not at first be imagined. Domenico Tardini was a Roman, and he never lost his Roman wit nor his impulsive, ironic, colloquial way of talking; his observations, scarcely diplomatic at times, were to become the delight of Rome. Short and stocky, his hair close cropped and grizzly, walking with a stoop, his face drawn and dyspeptic, lacking in elegance, gruff with his subordinates, he was to work in tandem with the tall, erect monsignor from Brescia, already noted for his punctilio and reserve, in a perfect complement of type and talent. They possessed an instinctive affection and respect for one another, because in each there was a total lack of self-seeking. In both cases the office sought the man for the excellence he possessed.

As Sostituto (a word which cannot be adequately translated by Substitute; it is best understood as the title of one of the two Undersecretaries), Monsignor Montini's duty as head of the Section of Ordinary Affairs was to handle, with the assistance of his staff, informal day-to-day relations between the Vatican and dioceses, governments, and private individuals in areas which did not fall under the competence of one of the Roman congregations or of Monsignor Tardini's Section of Extraordinary Ecclesiastical Affairs, which dealt with the formal relationships between the Church and governments. The ordinary business of the Church which the Pope might wish to discharge by means of his Secretariat of State fell to the section under Monsignor Montini. As a section, the first section under Tardini was traditionally the more important, and its Italian character and personnel were jealously maintained by him during his tenure. Monsignor Montini was always, on the contrary, to welcome the addition of personnel of other than Italian background, and the second section which he led today owes to him the international character which distinguishes it.

In May of 1938, Monsignor Montini accompanied the papal legate, Cardinal Pacelli, to the Eucharistic Congress in Budapest, a mark of the special place he already possessed in the affection and esteem of Pacelli. He was not often able to indulge his love for travel during those Vatican years, but the visit to Budapest, the vision of the city alight with torches, the Eucharistic procession down the Danube, the hundreds of thousands on their knees before their Lord, moved him strongly, then and later, as Budapest underwent the passion for which this congress seems almost to have been the prelude.

He sent his family a photograph of himself in Budapest, smilingly crossing the street before the royal palace in the company of Bishop Tredici (later to be one of the co-consecrators when Montini became archbishop of Milan), the collar high and white, the arm swinging jauntily, the silver-buckled shoes skirting a puddle of water. His father sent the photograph to his sister Bettina, and wrote on it: "I am sure that you too will be consoled to see the smiling face of our dear little son. He begins his vacation at the end of August."

Vacations were about to become the rarest of Monsignor Montini's experiences, memories almost, as the fateful year 1939 dawned. At the age of eighty-one, the Pope who had started life as a librarian scholar and finished it as the fighting Pope, died. His last wish, it was said, was that his successor be the one who was closest to him and best suited for the Church in the age of war, the winter of the Church just dawning—his Cardinal Secretary of State, Pacelli. But Secretaries of State are notoriously unlikely candidates; they have taken too many positions; they have irritated lord cardinals and lord princes; governments have been admonished by them and in turn have not been amused. And when to all this is added the weight of the incantation, "He who enters the Conclave a Pope exits a cardinal," it seemed clear that Pacelli could not possibly be elected.

Nevertheless Eugenio Pacelli was promptly chosen on the third ballot in one of the shortest conclaves in history. He took the name Pius in memory and honor of his predecessor and began the reign which would begin in war, would witness peace, and bring the Papacy, through the personal vigor and indefatigable witness of the Pope himself, to that peak of prestige from which the gentle John, his successor, would smile on the world and speak to it in such a way that suddenly it would seem wonderfully possible for men, all men, to love one another again in a kind of new Eden. The age of Pacelli made the age of Roncalli possible.

Beside Pius XII, throughout most of his reign, until suddenly he was appointed to Milan, Monsignor Montini was to be a part of the greatness of that pontificate. Many affairs of state which Pius XI had directed from a small private office with the aid of two assistants were now placed under the Secretariat of State and personally under Monsignor Montini. He would eclipse in closeness to the Pope and identity with him his colleague Tardini, and yet Tardini would remain in Rome in 1954 while Montini departed for Milan and later would become Secretary of State under John XXIII. Monsignor Montini was never to be Secretary of State: he would share the office for two years with the ever present Tardini, from 1952 to 1954, but an office shared is simply that, and he would leave the Secretariat without being named to join the distinguished Secretaries of State of the modern Church: Rampolla, Merry Del Val, Gasparri and Pacelli.

The "prophecy of Malachy" had foretold a pontiff who would be a *Pastor Angelicus,* and Pius XII's first efforts as pastor were in the direction of preventing the war which everyone knew was coming and which the nations of the world seemed to be awaiting in a kind of fatalistic apathy. The memory of Julius II who rode out to battle was evoked, but Pius was no Julius. "They have given us a Pope of peace and what we need is a Pope of war!" He spoke movingly, passionately for peace; his voice, like that of Benedict, was not heard. His beloved Italy waited calculatingly and then moved to join Germany, and all of Europe was in flames. The Vatican, a sovereign State since the Lateran Treaty of 1929, was to test and prove that sovereignty as well as its complete neutrality in the following war years. They were years, too, in which the true testing and proving of Monsignor Montini would be made, as the Pope gave into his hands the mounting and directing of the massive relief work of the Vatican.

A service for the prisoners of war was instituted by Monsignor Montini, the Vatican Radio employed to bring information concerning them to their loved ones, and he was also to be instrumental in setting up an office for the resettlement of the thousands who had been removed from their own countries to concentration camps. No phase of mercy or assistance, immediate and personal as it might be, was overlooked by the monsignor who worked eighteen hours a day, matching hour for hour the Holy Father whose schedule of work was already legendary.

To his office each day came prelates and ambassadors, generals and journalists—to it too came the frightened people who filled Europe and who filtered through Rome in these early years of the 40's. Such people were Aldo Mopurgo, his wife, his mother, and their little son Augusto, aged four. They were Jews, and in 1942 Jews in Europe went in fear of their lives. The Mopurgos were stranded in Rome, their only hope being escape from Europe. They were advised to seek help at the Vatican—and the man who greeted them warmly and offered it was Monsignor Montini. The Mopurgos now live in Kew Gardens, Long Island, New York, and they remember that day vividly. "At the Vatican I was introduced to Monsignor Montini," says Mr. Mopurgo. "What a man! What a heart! He was the easiest man in the world to talk to, and he made me feel very good because he was so very warm and understanding. We couldn't work and we were afraid for our lives. We wanted to get out of Europe. He gave us new hope. He told us exactly what to do. He was very kind and very efficient." Through Monsignor Montini they obtained a visa to go to Ecuador, but when they tried to cross the Spanish border from France it was closed by the Spanish authorities. Their luggage was in Spain, and they were in despair. It was winter, and there seemed to be no hope.

"My husband decided to rush back to Rome and see the only man we could turn to—our Monsignor Montini," says Mrs. Mopurgo. "He gave my husband an introduction to General Franco's brother-in-law and soon we had the necessary permission from the Spanish embassy."

The Mopurgos stayed in Ecuador until 1946, when they entered the United States and became citizens in 1951. Mr. Mopurgo's mother died in 1962, and little Augusto, who fled across Europe in winter at the age of four, his only crime that he was a Jew, is now in Italy as an architect for the American Archaeological Excavations of Princeton. One human drama, one family—given hope by the slim monsignor with the enormous eyes who could make the great and the simple feel in conversation with him that only they mattered and that his only task of the day was to talk to them and, if possible, assist them.

In only one arena was the Vatican not neutral—that of human suffering. During the war thousands of Jewish refugees were assisted by the Holy See; they found shelter in churches and institutions which, although outside Vatican City itself, were considered extensions of the Vatican by reason of "extraterritoriality" and thus immune to search and seizure. According to one Jewish leader familiar with the background, no less than 15,000 Jews were sheltered at Castelgandolfo, the summer home of the Pope. Throughout Rome, priests and nuns, often at great personal risk, smuggled Jews to places of sanctuary in churches, monasteries and other institutions. More than 180 places of refuge were made available in Rome and secret asylum given to more than 7,000 refugee Jews. "Rome became one great cloister and all in it were safe." When ransom in gold could not be raised by the Jewish community in Rome, Pope Pius XII personally sent the sum needed. The worst excesses of anti-Semitism never took root in Italy. After the war the Grand Rabbis of Rome and Budapest would personally thank the Pope for his efforts on behalf of their people.

But after the war too there would be voices raised to question the policy, or the lack of it, on the part of the Holy See, toward the deportation and mass murder of Jews throughout Europe with the aim of the extermination of the race desired by the Third Reich. If only, it was whispered, the Pope had taken drastic action, excommunicated Hitler, or repudiated the concordat between the Vatican and Germany, if only he had protested in the name of morality and humanity, he could have stopped it all.

It is in this context that the pontificate of Pius XII is an illustration of the specific difficulties facing a supranational institution confronting a world made up of competing national sovereignties. There is a limit to the power of the Papacy. The Pope is a spiritual sovereign, not a political power in the modern sense ("How many divisions does the Pope have?" Joseph Stalin was to ask), incapable of protecting his children and their shepherds from persecution within their own lands. "The days are long past when a Pope could by his authority stop a war, bring about a truce, or change a government's action by excommunicating its rulers, or when nations could declare themselves subject to the Pope because this guaranteed their independence." [4] Pope Pius was poignantly aware of this even if his postwar critics were not.

"There is evidence that he felt himself in an agonizing

[4] Alec Randall in *The Listener*, London, June 27, 1963, p. 1067.

dilemma. He was acutely aware of the fact that energetic protests had driven the ruthless and wicked man who dominated
most of Europe to even more terrible extremes." [5] The Pope's
correspondence with Bishop (later Cardinal) Preysing of Berlin demonstrates his true convictions. Writing on February 27,
1943, to commend the bishop for his declarations denouncing
the inhumanities of the National Socialist dictatorship, Pope
Pius said: "We are grateful, Venerable Brother, for the clear
and plain words which you have addressed under divers circumstances to your faithful, and through them to public opinion. We are thinking among others of your exposition of June
28, 1942, of the Christian concept of law; of your declaration on All Souls' Day, last November, regarding the right of
all men to life and love; We think particularly of your pastoral letter of Advent circulated in the ecclesiastical provinces
of West Germany, upon the rights of God, of the individual
and of the family."

The pastoral letter to which the Pope referred was Bishop
Preysing's reply to Hitler's decision to exterminate the Jews.
Cardinal Frings and the future Cardinal von Galen had it
adopted by all the bishops of Western Germany and read
from the pulpit in every parish. It said in part: "All the fundamental rights of man—the right to life, to bodily integrity, to
liberty, to property, to a marriage which does not depend on
the arbitrary will of the State—cannot be denied to those
not of our blood or who do not speak our language. . . . To
deny these rights, or to act with cruelty against our fellow
men is an injustice not only to the foreigner but also to our
own people."

In his letter to Bishop Preysing, Pius XII said of the
Berlin Catholics: "As chief Pastor of the faithful, we are
anxious to see your Catholics preserve their convictions and
their faith pure from all compromises with principles and

[5] *Op. cit.*

acts which are in contradiction to the law of God and the spirit of Christ, and often even turn them into derision. We have been consoled to learn that Catholics, especially those of Berlin, have shown much charity toward the oppressed non-Aryans, and in this connection We address a word of paternal gratitude and deep sympathy to Monsignor Lightenberg, who is now in prison." [6]

"There is no doubt," says Sir D'Arcy Osborne, "in fact His Holiness said as much to me on one occasion, that he believed he had condemned Nazi atrocities in a letter he himself had written, in his wartime Christmas messages and other speeches." "There was no doubt," continues the British wartime minister to the Holy See, "of his convictions and intentions but there was admittedly no clear and unequivocal condemnation. . . . Were not the Germans, including Catholic Gemans, so hypnotized and morally enslaved by Hitler as to be impervious to any warning or appeal?" Osborne says in the same context: ". . . the language of his addresses was often so prolix and obscure that it was difficult to extract his meaning from its extraneous verbal envelope (I have been told that his style was based on a marriage between Cicero and Bossuet)." [7]

The dilemma was inescapable. And because there are here all the elements of the classic tragedy of a good man confronting evil and knowing the excruciating pain of being unable to confound it, it called for dramatization. A young German, Rolf Hochhuth, brought his play, *Der Stellvertreter*, to the Berlin stage in February, 1963, and plans were made for presentations to follow in London, New York, and Paris.

[6] Monsignor Lightenberg, provost of the Berlin cathedral chapter, was a leading spirit in an organization which Bishop Preysing had created to aid Catholics of Jewish origin. He died in the convoy on his way to a concentration camp.

[7] D'Arcy Osborne, in London *Times*, May 20, 1963.

"The Vicar (der Stellvertreter)," says George Steiner in his article in the London *Sunday Times* for May 5, 1963, entitled "Papal Policy and Mass Murder," inquires with unbelieving cold fury into one "of the most abject episodes of modern history: the refusal of the Vatican to intervene against Hitler's slaughter of the Jewish people." Steiner asks a series of inflammatory questions: "Why did Pope Pius XII make only the most perfunctory of protests when Jewish families were dragged into Gestapo vans under his very windows? . . . What mesh of cowardice, indifference or high policy lay behind the fact (glowingly noted by Hitler's envoy to the Holy See) that the Pope 'though urged to do so by various parties' had avoided any 'trenchant pronouncement against the deportation of the Jews'?" He quotes Mauriac: " 'We did not have the consolation of hearing the Successor of the Galilean, Simon Petrus, condemn with unequivocal plain words and not with mere diplomatic hints, the crucifixion of innumerable kindred of the Lord's.' " "The Nazis feared the possibility of Papal and Catholic action," says Steiner. "The King of Denmark put on a yellow star. The Vicar of Christ did not. . . . The Vatican, informed by Polish clergy of what was happening hour by hour in the ovens and bunkers of Belsen, assured them that prayers were being said for 'our Jewish brothers.' " "Why this evasion," asks Steiner, "why this terrible silence?"

Hochhuth, [8] in his at times wildly imaginative reconstruc-

___

[8] "Rolf Hochhuth . . . a Protestant of thirty-two years of age, belonged formerly to a Nazi youth organization. 'I was fourteen in 1945,' he said, 'and the total collapse of Germany shook me profoundly. I could not help thinking this: What would you have done had you been of an age to act? This led me to study what the supreme representative of the Christian idea had done in regard to all those crimes.' . . . He affirms that his play is not anti-Catholic. 'It is too Christian for one to think this,' he says, and on several occasions he has paid homage to the

tion of history, believes the answer lies in the coldly complex, antisocial and essentially diplomatic temperament of Pius XII, and under him the Vatican's specific view of the Second World War. In *Der Stellvertreter*, Pius XII sees Bolshevism as the final supreme evil. Hitler is a passing menace; limited defeat might even render him a useful citizen. The slaughtered Jews may represent part of God's mystical design; He will make good their agony. Soviet victory would mean the end of Christianity. Individually the Pope appears as a man of deep mercy, but as head of the Church militant he cannot risk an open fight with Hitler. There is a confrontation in the play between the Pope and the young Jesuit Riccardo Fontana, and Fontana flees in horror from the Pope's lesson in statecraft. He dies in Auschwitz, taunted by the "Doctor of Auschwitz" who tells him that the Church, refusing to act now, will at a future safe date canonize him to her credit. "No speck of ash from the ovens of Belsen will be allowed to stain the white garment of Pius XII." The play ends in despair.

From his prison, the young Jesuit Alfred Delp soon to be executed by the Nazis, had written some years before: "The Vatican and the Church are to be considered. So far as concrete and visible influence goes, the attitude of the Vatican is not what it was. . . . Of course it will be shown eventually that the Pope did his duty and more, that he offered peace . . . that he dispensed alms and was tireless in his work on behalf of prisoners of war, displaced persons and so on—all this we know and posterity will have documentary evidence in plenty to show the full extent of the papal effort. But to a large extent all this good work may be taken for granted and also to a large extent it leads nowhere and has no real hope of

---

innumerable Catholic priests who defended the Jews."—*Informations catholiques internationales*, April 1, 1963.

achieving anything. That is the real root of the trouble—among all the protagonists in the tragic drama of the modern world there is not one who fundamentally cares in the least what the Church says or does. We overrated the Church's political machine and let it run on long after its essential driving power had ceased to function. It makes absolutely no difference so far as the beneficial influence of the Church is concerned whether a state maintains diplomatic relations with the Vatican or not. The only thing that really matters is the inherent power of the Church as a religious force in the countries concerned." [9]

While Pope Pius may not have been as forceful as hindsight might urge, he was incapable of a morally unworthy action, not to speak of any calculated policy in the matter. The German bishops, following a meeting held March 4-6, 1963, published a statement paying tribute to the memory of Pope Pius XII, to his efforts to avoid war and bring about peace, and to his aid to suffering men and peoples. "We therefore find it particularly scandalous," they declared, "that it is among the German people that the action of Pope Pius is falsely represented and his memory profaned." But his best defense has been written by the man who saw him wrestle with the indecision to which he was prone,[10] determined to protect his prospects as a possible mediator, that he might assist in putting an end to the sufferings of humanity. He was not asked—and herein, as Vicar of the Prince of Peace, lay his greatest suffering. The following letter written by the cardinal archbishop of Milan, one of the last he was to write before entering the conclave which elected him Pope, is from the man who knew Pius XII best at this time, and knew also of the agonies a man can suffer though he be dressed in the

[9] *The Prison Meditations of Father Alfred Delp* (New York: Herder and Herder, 1963).

[10] Cardinal Tardini in his book *Pio XII* is the authority for this.

white of innocence, live in a storied palace, be the judge of prelates and princes, and a successor to one who himself suffered the pain of indecision ("Simon, Simon, I have prayed for you that Satan not sift you as wheat").

The letter written by Cardinal Montini to the editor of the London *Tablet,* and published in its issue of June 29, 1963, reads as follows:

Dear Sir,—It gave me much pleasure to read the article entitled "Pius XII and the Jews," which appeared in your excellent periodical on May 11th, 1963: it was a most welcome defence not only of Pope Pius XII, of venerated memory, and of the Holy See, but also of historical truth and sound logic, not to speak of commonsense.

It is not my intention here to examine the question raised by the author and the producer, Rolf Hochhuth and Erwin Piscator respectively, of the play *Der Stellvertreter* ("The Vicar"): namely, whether it was Pius XII's duty to condemn in some public and spectacular way the massacres of the Jews during the last war. Much, to be sure, might still be said on this point, even after the very clear and cogent article in *L'Osservatore Romano* of April 5th; for the thesis of Herr Hochhuth's play—that, to quote Mr. George Steiner's review in the *Sunday Times* of May 5th, "We are all accomplices to that which leaves us indifferent"—bears no relation whatever to the personality or the work of Pope Pius XII. I cannot myself conceive how anyone could bring such a charge (let alone make it the subject of a play) against a Pontiff who might well, had he wished, have declared with a clear conscience to the whole world: "No effort on our part was lacking, nothing that anxious solicitude could suggest was left untried to prevent the horrors of mass deportation and exile; and when despite our just expectations this proved impossible, we set ourselves to do everything in our power to mitigate, at least, the cruelties of a state of affairs imposed by brute force." But history—a very different thing from such artificial manipulation of facts to fit a preconceived idea as we see in *Der Stellvertreter*—will vindicate the conduct of Pius XII when confronted by the criminal excesses of the Nazi regime:

history will show how vigilant, persistent, disinterested and courageous that conduct must be judged to have been, when viewed in its true context, in the concrete conditions of that time.

For my part I conceive it my duty to contribute to the task of clarifying and purifying men's judgment on the historical reality in question—so distorted in the representational pseudo-reality of Hochhuth's play—by pointing out that the character given to Pius XII in this play (to judge from the reviews in the Press) does not represent the man as he really was: in fact, it entirely misrepresents him. I am in a position to assert this because it was my good fortune to be drawn into close contact with Pius XII during his pontificate, serving him day by day, from 1937, when he was still Secretary of State, to 1954: throughout, that is, the whole period of the world war.

It is true that the precise scope of my duties did not include foreign affairs ("extraordinary" affairs, as they are called in the language of the Roman Curia); but Pius XII's goodness towards me personally, and the nature itself of my work as "Sostituto" in the Secretariat of State, gave me access to the mind and, I would add, to the heart of this great Pope. The image of Pius XII which Hochhuth presents, or is said to present, is a false one. For example, it is utterly false to tax Pius with cowardice: both his natural temperament and the consciousness that he had of the authority and the mission entrusted to him speak clearly against such an accusation. I could cite a host of particular facts to drive this point home, facts that would prove that the frail and gentle exterior of Pius XII, and the sustained refinement and moderation of his language, concealed —if they did not, rather, reveal—a noble and virile character capable of taking very firm decisions and of adopting, fearlessly, positions that entailed considerable risk.

Nor is it true that he was a heartless solitary. On the contrary, he was a man of exquisite sensibility and the most delicate human sympathies. True, he did love solitude: his richly cultivated mind, his unusual capacity for thought and study led him to avoid all useless distractions, every unnecessary relaxation; but he was quite the reverse of a man shut away from life and indifferent to people and events around him. Rather, it was his constant desire to be informed of everything. He wished to enter fully into the history of his own afflicted time: with a deep sense that he himself was a part of that history, he wished to participate fully in it, to share its sufferings in his own heart and soul. Let me cite, in this connexion, the words of a well-qualified witness, Sir D'Arcy Osborne, the British Minister to the Holy See who, when the Germans occupied Rome, was obliged to live confined in the Vatican City. Writing to *The Times* on May 20th, Sir D'Arcy said: "Pius XII was the most warmly humane, kindly, generous, sympathetic (and, incidentally, saintly) character that it has been my privilege to meet in the course of a long life."

Again, it is not true to say that Pope Pius XII's conduct was inspired by a calculating political opportunism. It would be just as true—and as slanderous—to assert that his government of the Church was motivated by considerations of material advantage.

As for his omitting to take up a position of violent opposition to Hitler in order to save the lives of those millions of Jews slaughtered by the Nazis, this will be readily understood by anyone who avoids Hochhuth's mistake of trying to assess what could have been effectively and responsibly done then, in those appalling conditions of war and Nazi oppression, by the standard of what would be feasible in normal conditions—or in some hypothetical conditions arbitrarily invented by a young playwright's imagination. An attitude of protest and condemnation such as this young man blames the Pope for not having adopted would have been not only futile but harmful: that is the long and the short of the matter. The thesis of *Der Stellvertreter* betrays an inadequate grasp of psychological, political and historical realities. But then the author was concerned above all to write an interesting play.

Let us suppose that Pius XII had done what Hochhuth blames him for not doing. His action would have led to such reprisals and devastations that Hochhuth himself, the war being over and he now possessed of a better historical, political and moral judgment, would have been able to write another play, far more realistic and far more interesting than the one that he has in fact so cleverly but also so ineptly put together: a play, that is, about the *Stellvertreter* who, through political exhibitionism or psychological myopia, would have been guilty of unleashing on the already tormented world still greater calamities involving innumerable innocent victims, let alone himself.

It would be as well if the creative imagination of playwrights insufficiently endowed with historical discernment (and possibly, though please God it is not so, with ordinary human integrity) would forebear from trifling with subjects of this kind and with historical personages whom some of us have known. In the present case the real drama, and tragedy, is not what the playwright imagines it to be: it is the tragedy of one who tries to impute to a Pope who was acutely aware both of his own moral obligations and of historical reality—and was moreover a very loyal as well as impartial friend to the people of Germany—the horrible crimes of German Nazism.

Let some men say what they will, Pius XII's reputation as a true Vicar of Christ, as one who tried, so far as he could, fully and courageously to carry out the mission entrusted to him, will not be affected. But what is the gain to art and culture when the theatre lends itself to injustice of this sort?

With my sincere respects, devotedly yours,

✠G. B. CARDINAL MONTINI
Archbishop of Milan

Throughout the war the Vatican maintained its relations with both the Axis and Allied powers, the representatives of the latter housed in the Vatican,[11] the former until the declining years of the war free to go between the Vatican and the city of Rome, closed to their confrères who had become the enemy. Monsignor Montini dealt with impeccable cordiality and neutrality with all the representatives. During the larger receptions in the Vatican all representatives of the diplomatic corps accredited to the Vatican were present, and by reason of seniority the ambassador of Germany, Dr. Diego von Bergen, and the British minister, Sir Francis D'Arcy Osborne,

[11] Cf. Thomas B. Morgan, *The Listening Post* (New York: G. P. Putnam's Sons, 1944), p. 207.

would have found themselves sitting together. Monsignor Montini chose to sit between them, dividing his attention impartially, his every smile and gesture in one direction repeated in the other.

Mr. Myron Taylor, personal representative of President Roosevelt to the person of the Holy Father during the war wrote: ". . . the two principal Under Secretaries of State were Monsignor Domenico Tardini and Monsignor Giovanni B. Montini on both of whom it was always possible to depend for sympathetic and intelligent consideration of problems, whether burdensome or not." [12]

One of the Pope's greatest anxieties after Italy's entry into the war was the possibility that Rome might be subjected to aerial attack. For months he and his staff tried through diplomatic channels to persuade the Italian government to demilitarize target areas and proclaim Rome an open city. On May 18, 1943, he addressed a personal plea to President Roosevelt expressing the hope that the people of Italy would be given consideration and that their many treasured shrines of religion and art would be spared from ruin. The President replied by pledging that Allied airmen "to the extent humanly possible" would refrain from bombing purely civilian objectives, but the Pope's redoubled efforts to have Rome declared an open city were not at that time successful on either side.

On July 19, 1943, at 11 A.M., American planes carrying out an assault on railroad junctions in the periphery of Rome, bombed a section of the city in which the ancient Church of Saint Lawrence Outside the Walls was located. Many of the bombs fell on the surrounding civilian district, a crowded sector chiefly inhabited by workers, and on a hospital, religious buildings, and on one of the largest cemeteries in Rome.

From the windows of his study, where he was receiving

[12] *Wartime Correspondence between President Roosevelt and Pope Pius XII* (Macmillan: New York, 1947), p. 7.

official visitors, Pius XII could see the raid, which lasted for two hours. Soon after it began, he cancelled his remaining appointments and stood watching as he recited the prayers for the dying. Very shortly after the bombing was over he was in the area, accompanied by Monsignor Montini, consoling the wounded and weeping people, moving among them, careless of the dirt and blood on his cassock. He had directed Monsignor Montini to bring all the cash he could obtain, about two million lire, and the latter distributed the money to those most gravely in need. They found that the Basilica of Saint Lawrence had been hit several times; the roof had fallen in and the façade and vestibule were destroyed; in the neighboring cemetery, bombs had torn up the graves and wrecked among others the tombs of the Pontiff's own family, the Pacellis. Deeply affected, the Pope climbed up on the rubble of the basilica to pray. "Up to the last day of Our life," he said some years later, "We will remember this sorrowful occasion."

On returning to the Vatican he wrote at once to the President of the United States: "We have had to witness the harrowing scene of death leaping from the skies and stalking pitilessly through unsuspecting homes, striking down women and children; and in person We have visited the gaping ruins of that ancient and priceless papal basilica of Saint Lawrence, one of the most treasured and loved sanctuaries of the Romans. . . . We feel it Our duty to voice a particular prayer and hope that all may recognize that a city whose every district, in some districts every street, has its irreplaceable monuments of faith or art and Christian culture, cannot be attacked without inflicting an incomparable loss on the patrimony of religion and civilization."

The next day in a letter addressed to Cardinal Francesco Marchetti-Selvaggiani, vicar general of Rome, Pope Pius in even stronger terms recalled his repeated appeals to both groups of belligerents "to respect the inviolability of peaceful monuments of faith and civilization." This letter, published in *Osservatore Romano,* said that the "authority with which We, although unworthy, are invested, the recognition of our thorough impartiality and liberality toward all, apart from nationality and religion, would have given us at least the consolation that both the belligerent parties would have lent an ear to our mediation on behalf of Rome."

No official protest was made to the Allies but Pope Pius renewed his appeals for the proclamation of an open city. The American President indicated his approval but pointed out that Mussolini had so far resisted every demand to demilitarize Rome. The city was bombed for the second time on August 13, 1943, and as before, the Pope and Monsignor Montini were among the first on the scene in the San Giovanni district near the basilica of Saint John Lateran where the bombs had fallen, giving comfort to the wounded, praying for the dead, and distributing alms. After this raid, through the representations of the Pope acting directly and through his Secretariat of State with the powers on both sides, Rome was declared an open city and Pope Pius XII received a title which as a Roman was particularly dear to him: *Defensor Civitatis*—Defender of the City.

4. "Cloister of Ciphers and Secrets"

When the Secretary of State, Cardinal Maglione, died in 1944, and Pius XII appointed no successor to him from the College of Cardinals, it was obvious that the Pope was content with what had been the working arrangement for some time: acting as his own Secretary of State with the assistance of Montini and Tardini. The arrangement was to be criticized as it continued through the years. With all their ability, knowledge, and helpfulness, it was felt that the two could not in all circumstances fill the position of a fully authorized Cardinal Secretary of State. Access by members of the diplomatic corps to the Pope grew increasingly difficult, and grumbling was heard concerning excessive centralization and insufficient contact, in matters of detail, with the outside world. The Pope, especially after the Holy Year of 1950, became more isolated from both diplomats and cardinals, lavishing his time and energies on countless audiences to all classes of people.

Thus it was to Monsignor Montini that diplomats and cardinals came, to his small waiting room with its uncomfortable gilt chairs, the damasked-wall salon, the large office with its desk piled high with papers ("these are the cards I play with all day," he would say deprecatingly), and to him they would say what they wished to have communicated to the Holy Father.

"The paradox about Montini, the diplomat," it was said, "lies in the apparent lack of diplomacy, the seemingly unself-conscious willingness to speak openly and frankly." Yet a colleague of those days testifies that no word left the lips of the Sostituto without its having been fitted carefully to the thought he sought to express; no unguarded word, no careless phrase, yet always the willingness to enter into dialogue and say as much as he could and as much as his visitor desired without doing violence to his office and loyalty to the Holy Father. "He is . . . a man who, speaking with whoever goes to seek him out, does not shut himself off, as so many do and as he himself has a right to do, in a meandering tour of the subjects which are his proper competence, but he willingly ranges far beyond. He has interests and curiosities and experiences in the widest fields of culture, he always has some information he wants from his visitor in these fields, and his own judgments and observations in areas far removed from his everyday activities are always personal and reasoned."

Endlessly seeking to accommodate, to reconcile, to pacify and assist, advancing the views of a government or a superior, any diplomat may emerge without the hardness, the conviction at the core of his being, which would make him, should he be called, a leader rather than the leader's interpreter. Translators, no matter how brilliant, do not necessarily, when they turn to writing books, produce works of genius. Monsignor Montini was for the years he worked under Pius XII an interpreter, a translator into word and action of the mind and heart of the Holy Father. But the role as he conceived it was essentially a creative one, demanding a sensitivity to nuance and intention which would articulate by organization, by word, by letter, the fully formed or half-expressed wishes of the Pope.

Popes do not rule by inspiration. Theirs is the way of men, aided by grace, of using human means with the assistance of men whose brilliance and loyalty make them worthy of intimacy and trust. Pius XII had at his disposition a Curia of talented and devoted men, yet it was to one man that he turned most often. The reason cannot be sought in the one often adduced: that in their thinking on all questions they were perfectly and intuitively identified. There is reason to believe that the thinking of Pope Pius XII on the world and on the Church was more perfectly shared by Monsignor Tardini, a perspective, in some areas, of limited dimensions, less modern and comprehensive than Monsignor Montini's, even though—it must be insisted—no other Pope gave to the modern world a body of teaching on religious and ethical questions equal to that of Pius XII.

But as the perfect servitor of the Pope, Montini chose to be a shadow, as Pacelli had been a shadow of Pius XI, meticulously implementing the policy of the Pontiff whatever be the personal reservations as to its wisdom, never uttering a personal opinion or committing himself on any public issues.[1] "Pius XII was an exacting master. Reserved, cautious, brusquely obstinate, outwardly mild but easily irritated, he demanded of all who served him that they keep him informed, not advised." [2]

Perfect obedience does not mean the prostration of the heart and mind; the one who serves and obeys continues to be a man, with his own obligation to truth and the vision of how it must be discovered and implemented. Monsignor Montini served the Pope and truth in perfect harmony for fifteen years.

[1] Dante defines the true counselor as "one who discerns, wills aright, and accepts."

[2] Alec Randall, in London *Tablet,* May 4, 1963.

Shortly before Monsignor Montini's parents died (the father in 1943, the mother a year later) the Pope said to them: "Your son possesses every priestly quality in the highest possible degree." It was to Montini, the priest, not the diplomat or servitor, that the prayerful, ascetic, even holy Pope, pointed when he sought to tell the parents what it was he most esteemed in their son. Every good priest respects the integrity of his fellow priests in their witness; if Pius XII sensed reserves of thought and action in his Sostituto, he did not ask that they be opened to him or violated. Thus in harmony and mutual respect they worked for the Church. The right eye of the Pope, the Roman press called him, and the irrepressible Romans would say: "Why go to the *Monte* (Mountain) when things can be more quickly done by going to *Montini* (little Mountain)?"

In May, 1945, Monsignor Montini celebrated the twenty-fifth anniversary of his ordination as a priest, and Pius XII wrote him in part: "Since we are aware that those who esteem your high qualities, and their number is legion, are preparing to celebrate this date, we wish to anticipate the celebration with this Our letter, We who for so long and better than any other know your outstanding gifts, your notable talents, your diligence and your piety." Accompanying the letter was the gift of a handsome chalice, and Monsignor Montini used it in celebrating his anniversary Mass in the Chiesa Nuova of Saint Philip Neri.

The postwar years saw the work of the Secretariat intensify in the direction of assisting in the relocation of the millions rendered homeless and stateless by the war. These were the years of anguish for the Church in Eastern Europe, "the Church of Silence," as it would become and would be named by Pius XII, with the prosecutions of prelates such as Mindszenty, Stepinac, and Beran. In order to highlight the injustice of their sentencing, the Vatican through the Secretariat of State presented a complete picture of the true roles which these men, now accused of treason and crimes against the state, had played in the life of their countries. Montini was mentioned in the trials which sought to discredit churchmen in Czechoslovakia and Hungary. In the August 3, 1949 issue of the Czechoslovak Communist paper *Rude Pravo*, an article charges that the head of an "Organization X," had decided to make a martyr of Archbishop Beran because the organization was displeased by the relaxing of East-West tensions. "The members of the organization, who were linked in some mysterious way with . . . the general of the Jesuits and Monsignor Montini, were directing sabotage, espionage and various other disturbances in countries that refused to submit to Capitalism." [3]

"After the imprisonment of Cardinal Mindszenty, many of his responsibilities were assumed by Archbishop Josef Groesz of Kalocsa, whose duty it was to keep in contact with the Holy See and resist all pressure for the establishment of a national Church. He was arrested therefore in May 1951 and brought in for sentencing the following month. With the same mystifying calm (as shown by Mindszenty) . . . he confessed to everything required of him. . . . Archbishop Groesz involved Pope Pius XII, Cardinal Spellman and Monsignor Montini of the Vatican Secretariat of State in a fantastic plot to make himself the head of the State with the title Homo Regius." [4]

In these postwar years Monsignor Montini, always deeply interested in social questions, took a leading part in the founding of the Pontifical Work of Assistance (to the poor and dispossessed), the Association of Christian Workers (ACLI),

---

[3] Robert I. Gannon, *The Cardinal Spellman Story* (New York: Doubleday, 1962), p. 346.

[4] *Op. cit.*, p. 340. These fantasies reflect, perhaps, a persistent nervousness on the part of Communist-dominated countries concerning the influence of America on the Vatican.

and of the Women's Italian Center (CIF). He supported strongly the priest-worker movement in France, by which priests sought to witness to Christian principles in dechristianized areas of life by living and working among the Christless masses. Many of these priests were subverted by the very milieu they sought to change, and the defection of many among them was a shocking and sobering experience for this prelate, so sympathetic to modern trends and experiments.

Monsignor Montini supported the concept of the priest-worker movement with an audacity and enthusiasm which contrasted sharply with the suspicion and even hostility with which it was regarded in certain quarters in Rome. When its activity was sharply curtailed he was in agreement that new protection and directives had to be provided, but he never wavered in support of its basic concept: to give witness to Christ in those places where His name was no longer known. Some years later in Milan he said to a group of French priests: "France is the animating spirit of life in the Church. Her books are read everywhere. When a heresy breaks out somewhere else no one knows anything about it, but if it is in France all the world speaks of it. I have often said to French bishops: the whole world expects from the French people a solution from the Church's point of view. . . . If the submission (of the priest-workers) had been total, I believe you would have saved the institution." [5]

Italy, in 1948, held its first general election following the war, with the Communist Party strongly organized and heavily financed, the Christian Democratic Party making its first appearance, the Monarchists hoping somehow to retain the royal house so long identified with now discredited Fascism. It is from this period that Italian conservatives began categorizing Montini as "progressive" or "of the Left," their feeling being that the decline of the Italian monarchy in 1946 could

[5] *Informations catholiques internationales,* July 1, 1963, p. 20.

have been prevented by him had he asserted himself strongly with the Pope who, it was said, was wavering. But the Allies in 1946 had no intention of allowing the tarnished monarchy to confront the growing power of Communism in Italy, and anti-Fascist Italians saw the future of Italy as associated with the United States and Britain, headed at this time by the Democratic Party and the Labor Party respectively.

In 1950, the organizing of the Holy Year was largely the charge of Monsignor Montini as, in 1953, was that of the Marian Year. The intention of peace in the Holy Year was officially articulated by Monsignor Montini in May, 1949. "The Holy Year," he said, "is part of the present Pontiff's line of conduct; it is intended as a prolongation, an application, of the program—in everyday language we say politics—of the Holy See." This was the hope, but Monsignor Montini was sufficiently a realist to see the chasm between hope and actuality. The world had come to think of peace, he said, as merely a cessation of battle, a failure to resist. Not this, not the abandonment of principle, not the desire to enjoy life and the compromise making this possible, and certainly not the enforced peace of totalitarian regimes—none of these was peace. The Holy Year, he urged, was not merely to express aspirations toward peace, but provide inspiration for action. It would, no doubt, quicken the spirit of religion which, genuinely embraced, would contribute to the peace of the world by turning men's thoughts to the Fatherhood of God. Even at this time, Monsignor Montini struck an ecumenical note by adding that the Holy See expected "a powerful effect upon all men of good faith, not only Catholics."

Of great interest to Monsignor Montini was the visit which he made between August 20 and September 9, 1951, to Canada and the United States. This visit was the subject of some speculation in the American press, although the coverage given his visit, which was termed "unofficial" was negligible.

The New York Times ventured the explanation that there were papal objections to the Japanese peace treaty which Montini had come to the United States to express, but this was officially denied by Monsignor Montini, who described his first trip to North America as a holiday tour. He flew from London to Montreal and while in Canada visited a number of Catholic prelates and institutions, the shrines of Saint Anne de Beaupré and Cap de Madeleine, also Ottawa, Kingston and Ontario. In Ottawa he lunched with the then prime minister, Saint Laurent, and one of his stops was at a jamboree of 3,000 Boy Scouts at Vandreuil near Quebec.

He entered the United States through Niagara Falls, N.Y., and was greeted at the border by the late Bishop John F. O'Hara, C.S.C., of Buffalo, who later became cardinal archbishop of Philadelphia. From Buffalo he flew to Washington, D.C., where he was met at the airport by the then apostolic delegate to the United States, Archbishop Amleto Cicognani, now cardinal and secretary of State of Pope Paul VI. In Washington he spent four days visiting such historic sites as Mount Vernon, the home of George Washington; toured the headquarters of the National Catholic Welfare Conference, the central coordinating headquarters of the U.S. hierarchy, and met the staff at a reception to which executives of the Federal government, the diplomatic corps and of national labor unions were invited. In St. Louis he was the guest of Archbishop (now Cardinal) Ritter; next he swung west to Denver, then to Chicago, where his host was the late Cardinal Stritch. While in the latter's see city, he quietly mingled on Sunday, September 2, with the congregations in several churches, including two for Negro Catholics. In Detroit he stayed with its archbishop, the late Cardinal Mooney, and asked to visit the assembly lines of one of the big auto factories. He had a personal reason for visiting Pittsburgh; Monsignor Walter S. Carroll, head of the English language section of the Secretariat of State, with whom he had worked for nine years, had died suddenly in Washington in 1950, and Montini came to visit his family and pray at his grave. Back on the East coast, he stopped in New York where he was the guest of Francis Cardinal Spellman, and under his guidance saw many Catholic institutions as well as tourist sights in and around the City. On September 9, he recrossed the Atlantic, and made a brief visit to Ireland on his way back to Rome.

The routine which Monsignor Montini followed for years began at six in the morning with his meditation, Mass and thanksgiving in the Chapel of Julius II, followed by a breakfast of coffee and milk and bread served by his faithful housekeeper, Maria. He was in his office at about eight and his first appointment of the morning on alternate days was with the Holy Father. Appointments and paperwork kept him at his desk until two o'clock and after. The Holy Father usually took a walk in the Vatican gardens at about three, and this was often the hour when Monsignor Montini took his lunch—invariably of soup, grilled meat and vegetable, fruit and a glass of wine—and after it a short siesta. He would read his breviary, and at six o'clock be back in the office until nine or nine-thirty. The Holy Father usually went to bed after one in the morning, and Monsignor Montini kept his timetable as well; he was on call day or night, and if the Pope needed him at any hour the monsignor was ready. He was never far from the phone which connected directly with the office of the Holy Father, and he grew accustomed to its ring and to the soft voice saying, *"È qui Pacelli* (Pacelli here)." He took no holiday for years, and only in 1950 had he agreed for the first time to take a month off, spending two weeks at a Fiuggi spa and the others in Concesio.

The world of Monsignor Montini, which was rather a window on the world, was one in which the long perspective was taken, a perspective in which history is reckoned by eras rather than years, "a cloister of ciphers and secrets," but in its less sensational reality a place of sober and dedicated work. Responsible to a sensitive and meticulous man, he was in turn sensitive and meticulous in his day-to-day dealings with his staff, demanding but just, gentle for the most part but capable of eye-flashing disapproval when work or attitude did not meet his high standards. His "Relatively immediately," spoken softly or written in his careful hand on work assigned, had a galvanic effect on the slower moving staff men. He was impatient of pietistic platitudes. "Too many barks of Peter, too many fishers of souls!" he wrote dryly on an address prepared by a subordinate and submitted to him for approval.

He was not lavish with praise for work well done—work should be well done—but he showed his appreciation by the warmth with which he welcomed those who came to him with personal problems. A knock at his office door, a moment to listen to the soft-spoken *"Avanti*—come in," and the visitor entered the office, bare and efficient, its only disorder the piles of documents and papers filling the desk and spilling over onto adjacent tables. He was appreciative of brief, concise explanations and grateful to anyone who would be quick and be gone, but he never showed impatience with the prolix or hesitant, sitting quietly while his visitor spoke, his bright eyes fixed on his face. "With his eyes," said Maria, his housekeeper for many years until he left Rome and she was sent back to her native Abruzzi with a sewing machine, sewing lessons, and a bicycle as gifts, "with his eyes he could read your soul. Sometimes he would fix me with a glance and say, 'Maria, tell me the truth!' and I would tell him the truth because I loved him —and also because of those eyes!"

The eyes, somewhat disconcerting at first, are penetrating without being curiously probing, reflecting both the intelligence and warmth of the man. His patience and "unflappability" were legends in the Secretariat. "Only once," said a colleague, "did I ever see him lose control and get excited; only once, and that was on the 10th of June, 1940, the day Italy entered the war." His schedule of work, his care of detail, his courtesy and efficiency were at once the inspiration and despair of those who sought to emulate him and who were obliged to admit ruefully that they possessed neither the stamina nor inner drive of this totally dedicated man. The man who was to succeed him in his office, Monsignor (now Archbishop) Angelo dell' Acqua, himself a model of hard work and genial efficiency, said of his predecessor's schedule of work: "He demonstrated his abnegation and love of the Church, his dedication to duty illuminated by a great simplicity of life, a life of exceptional goodness and of continuing unselfishness, which earned him first our admiration and then our total affection." "He treated us," said a minor employee of the Vatican, "as if we were the most important of diplomats."

On January 12, 1953, Pope Pius XII convened a secret consistory of the cardinals in order to reveal to them the names of those he intended to raise to the cardinalate in a future public consistory. In the course of the meeting the Pope said: "There is one further matter which we cannot pass over in silence. It was our intention to raise to the Sacred College the two distinguished prelates who preside, each in his own Section, over the Secretariat of State, and their names were the first entered on the list of Cardinals-elect already prepared by Us. However, these two prelates, giving palpable evidence of their virtue, have so insistently requested that they be dispensed from accepting so high a dignity that We have considered it opportune to accept their repeated petitions and desires in this matter. But in doing so We have also wished to reward their future in some manner; and in fact, as you know,

We have given them a higher title which better and more fully corresponds to the field of their hardworking activity."

The apostolic brief formally creating the two monsignori Pro-Secretaries of State gave them precedence immediately behind the cardinals, and preceding patriarchs, archbishops and bishops; they were also given most of the privileges of cardinals listed in the Code of Canon Law. Monsignor Montini's tasks and his relationship to the Pope remained the same. When the delighted members of his staff went to greet him in his new role, he received them all with a smile and handshake and spoke beautifully, not of his new distinction, but of the joy of service to the Holy Father. It is not the servant but the service that matters, was the theme of his little talk as it was the theme of his life in the Secretariat. Deprived of the opportunity of doing the priestly work of preaching and hearing confessions, of talking to the young about Christ, of being a priest with his people, Monsignor Montini, secretly and prodigally, was a priest to the people in the charity which he distributed during his years in the Vatican. "We exist for others, not ourselves," he once said, "and what we possess is not for ourselves but for them."

His only passion of acquisition centered in books, and his apartment in the Vatican was lined with them: books on sociology, theology, literature, biography, choice books to satisfy the hunger he felt for renewal in mind and spirit after the draining hours spent serving others. He was a voracious reader of newspapers, as became the son of a journalist, an acute observer of trends, critical of journalistic intemperance and wildly speculative pondering and pontificating in print. In his address to journalists after his election to the Papacy he would say: "For this coverage (of Pope John's death and the conclave), which was on the whole so dignified and reverent, We owe you Our praise and Our gratitude. We believe that

Our praise and gratitude correspond to the praise and gratitude of your numberless readers. . . . Should We dilute the expression of Our gratitude because of any flights of fancy, inaccuracies, or anything unsuitable that may have been noticed in reports and interpretations of this event, too pertinent to Our person and over-controlled by public opinion? We will be indulgent toward those arbiters of journalism—and alas, they are not so few—and instead fix Our eyes on the aggregate value of your service of disseminating information; in general We have seen it to be considerate and well disposed toward Our humble person, and serious and respectful toward the Holy See, so We willingly give it the reward of Our public recognition and of Our gratitude."

In 1954 the health of the Holy Father gave cause for concern. Always impatient with physical infirmities, Pius XII drove himself to work against the advice of doctors, at seventy-eight adhering to the schedule which had been his for years. He seemed more dependent than ever on Monsignor Montini. Yet in November of that year the Pope, in a move which caused surprise and speculation in Vatican circles, named Monsignor Montini archbishop of Milan in succession to Cardinal Schuster. Monsignor Montini was, the Pope said gracefully, his "gift to the people of Milan."

Monsignor Montini was stunned and overwhelmed. To the Pope he said, "Holy Father, do you think I am capable of this charge?" And the Pope gave him an embrace as his answer. The apostolic letter of appointment written by the Holy Father to his Pro-Secretary said: ". . . You, O beloved son, appeared to Us the person most indicated [for the post] because by an almost daily intimacy We know your excellence and talents, your strength of soul and your sincere piety joined to zeal for the salvation of souls. Thus in the long years in which you have been close to Us in dedicating yourself to the care of ecclesiastical matters, not only have you merited well of the Apostolic See but you have also had a means of gaining much experience of men and their affairs, so much so as to appear to Us to be the one best prepared to assume the spiritual government of that metropolis." A curial cardinal who knew Montini well said of him at this time: "There are those who are equal to him in intellect, but I have met none who are his spiritual superiors. None!"

There were tears in Monsignor Montini's eyes as he made his farewells to the Secretariat and to the diplomatic corps. The entire corps turned out for the farewell ceremony, and in its name the French ambassador, Count Vladimir d'Ormesson, spoke of the strong impression made on them all by the Holy Father's gesture of sacrifice in naming Monsignor Montini to Milan. To Montini he said: "Monsignor, in the very heart of Catholicism and in the service of a great Pope, you have passed years of intensive and magnificent work; but you have also passed years of heavy import in the history of poor humanity. Some among us have been able to appreciate, in the worst moments of the torment in which we have all lived, the constant delicacy of your heart, your spirit of justice and of charity. . . . We who came here so often . . . to set before you many of the questions which preoccupied us, how could we have failed to be aware of the generous understanding, the keen intuition, the balance of mind and the inexhaustible desire to find the just solution in all matters which we have encountered in you? . . . Permit me to add that what we have respected and most loved in you is that behind the diplomatic official we have always found the priest. Be assured, Monsignor, that in our eyes it is this which is most important."

Monsignor Montini was visibly moved as he rose to address the diplomatic corps. He thanked them for their kindness, their courtesy, their delicacy. He recalled to their minds what they had been through together during the war: "How can we forget those Christmas Masses, those gatherings of all the diplomats of countries at war with one another, who during that sacred night filled with human and divine mystery, seemed to forget the conflict and to find it a natural thing to be close to one another in celebrating the peace, the fraternity and the love of Christian civilization?" Then, with a smile, remembering the Holy Year and the importunities by which the members of the corps had been besieged by visitors from their countries: ". . . Holy Year with its great and spectacular moments, during which the diplomatic corps exercised, even to the point of heroism, the virtue of Roman hospitality!" And then seriously: "Is it not true that the diplomatic relations with the Holy See, which honor the countries you represent, have always been on both sides inspired by the most sincere loyalty?"

He told them that in his going nothing would be changed: "In those who succeed me here you will always have what I have ever sought to offer you: the highest measure of esteem, the highest recognition, the firmest and most devout intention of working with you for the good of the world." Monsignor Montini then accepted from the corps the gift of a magnificent episcopal ring, shook the hand of each member for the last time, and spoke to each a word of gratitude and affection.

On the 12th of December as a light drizzle fell on Rome, in the baroque splendor of St. Peter's, the least baroque of Roman prelates lay face down on the floor of the sanctuary as he had on the day of his ordination to the priesthood, and heard the Sistine Choir in the name of the thousands present beseech God and His saints to bless and sanctify him in his episcopal office, to confirm him in grace that he might serve the Milanese[6] as he had served the sovereign Pontiff, with

[6] Thousands of Milanese in St. Peter's for the ceremony broke into applause for their new archbishop, forgetting that only the Pope is applauded in the Basilica.

total devotion. The Holy Father himself had wished to consecrate the new archbishop and had given him his pectoral cross, but he now lay seriously ill in the adjoining palace, and Monsignor Montini received the fullness of the priesthood from the bearded Frenchman, Cardinal Tisserant, dean of the College of Cardinals, with co-consecrators the bishop of Brescia, Giacinto Tredici, and the vicar capitular of Milan, Domenico Bernareggi, titular bishop of Famagosta.

Nevertheless the courageous Pope was not to be absent. At a moment in the ceremony, over loud-speakers installed in the basilica, the low, clear voice of the Pontiff was heard speaking from his apartment. He declared himself to be spiritually present at this episcopal consecration which, because of his affection for the one being consecrated, he had reserved to himself, but that Providence had not allowed him to fulfill his intention. He went on: "It is indeed consoling for the Father who has not been able to impose his hands while invoking the Holy Spirit, to raise them at this moment to bless his faithful collaborator, one who has today become his brother in the episcopacy."

Brother to Pope and bishops, father to the faithful of Milan who awaited with pride and anticipation the prelate whom the Pope was sending them, Archbishop Montini prepared to leave Rome, its memories and associations. The way in which he spent his Christmas night that year is revealing. In the Secretariat of State he had been quite secretly a moving force behind the work done by his friend Don Carlo Gnocchi in assisting children who had lost limbs or been disfigured in explosions during the war and afterward from unexploded bombs and mines. A center for them had been established in Rome at the Foro Italico, and Montini helped support it directly and through appeals to others for assistance. Don Gnocchi had also given shelter to young victims of polio, at Monsignor Montini's insistence, after Montini, in 1952, had visited a summer colony established for them at Ostia. He said afterward, "I was literally assaulted by the mothers of these young ones, overcome with the anguish of not knowing where to bring their children after their brief stay near the sea. The children afflicted by polio in Italy alone number some sixty thousand, and I could not forget those eyes full of maternal pleading. I could not forget what I had seen—the arms and legs of these children like thin, dry branches. Never in my life would I be able to forget!"

After this visit to Ostia he had turned to Don Gnocchi, a vibrant, totally dedicated man; few words were necessary between them. A section of Don Gnocchi's institute for youth was set aside for these young victims, and it was to them that Montini came to spend his first Christmas night as archbishop of the mighty see of Milan. As they awaited the archbishop's arrival, Father Gnocchi and a visitor were going through the mail piled on the priest's desk. The "useless letters," as Don Gnocchi called them, those containing only praise of his work, went immediately into the wastebasket; those containing more substantial evidence of support were laid aside. At one point Don Gnocchi opened a letter from an anonymous citizen of Milan praising the archbishop and himself for the work they had done together; Father Gnocchi tore it up and threw it into the wastebasket with the remark, "That's not worth much." But looking at the basket a few minutes later, his sharp eyes spotted a fragment of paper carrying the words, "one million lire" (about $1,500).

When Archbishop Montini arrived he found Father Gnocchi and the visitor on their knees on the floor, the contents of the wastebasket all around them, frantically looking for the other pieces of the check. With a chuckle and the remark, "Next time, Don Carlo, be more careful," the archbishop dropped to his knees and searched with them until the last piece had been found. Going out afterward he found all the little ones gathered to meet him; one small girl, a polio victim, her legs twisted, wanted to accompany him and, putting her hand in his, tried to walk painfully beside him. The archbishop bent down, picked her up and carried her in his arms, and there were tears in his eyes. For the little sufferers who filled the chapel he said his three Masses that night—his last Christmas in Rome.

As the time for his departure drew near he wrote in a letter to the Pope: "To say what are my sentiments at the moment of leaving this blessed home is not possible. But quieting the whirlwind of memories, of impressions and of thoughts . . . I feel the overwhelming need to tell Your Holiness of my intense filial gratitude for the favors, whose very number and magnitude I can never count nor measure, which have been bestowed on me by the paternal, generous, ever renewed and ever loving goodness of Your Holiness."

"Archbishop Montini leaves Rome with nothing, nothing except what he carries with him of our appreciation and love," said a Roman newspaper on the day of his departure. And so he went; sitting in the railroad carriage on a cold January day, a shawl tucked around him to keep him warm, his possessions other than his books contained in a suitcase borrowed from his brother Ludovico, his thoughts no longer in Rome but in the Milan which awaited him. He remembered the question he had asked the Pope when he received his appointment: "Holy Father, do you think I am capable of this charge?" And he remembered and was consoled by the answer the Holy Father had given him.

5. "And So I Came to Milan"

Saint Augustine

In the middle of the great plain of Lombardy stands Milan, the financial, commercial, literary and cultural pivot of Italy. The region of which it is the heart and center was once the battlefield of Europe; fed by Italy's largest river, the Po, it is one of Europe's richest regions, covering 7.6 per cent of Italy's national territory but containing over 15 per cent of its inhabitants. The city itself has a population of 1,581,000, but in the sprawling suburbs and clustering villages and towns of the commune are another 1,569,000 people. The Milanese reputation for business enterprise goes back to the twelfth century when its merchants and bankers made Lombard Street in London a symbol of commerce and finance. Industrial, fast moving, creative and sophisticated, Milan lacks the warmth and color and charm of most Italian cities, and, somewhat self-consciously and defensively, projects a verve and pace which makes it, more than other Italian cities, identical in mood and problems with other great metropolitan centers of the world.

In its thinking as in its commerce, Milan has always, especially in modern times, looked across the Alps to find its cultural and political challenge. The eighteenth-century Enlightenment took root there; Napoleon was anointed and crowned himself king of Italy in the cathedral, itself a symbol of Milanese ultramontane thinking; and the Risorgimento found ready welcome. It is a city proud of its present, aware of its past, a very symbol of modern urban civilization, "rich, clean, productive, full of diversions and amenities, but soulless and leaning to neurosis and despair." In this it is a reflection of the restlessness and disenchantment which pervade the whole of Italy today. "Western 'social progress,' which has everywhere produced unsatisfactory emancipation and a complete urbanization of the soul, is a relatively recent force in Italy. Finding themselves committed to the visible benefits and the concealed contradictions of the modern world, the Italians, remarkably naïve where they are not exceptionally cunning, have experienced shocks of revulsion and alarm at every social level." [1]

But the greatness of Milan today reflects only dimly the greatness which has been hers at various times through the centuries. From Milan, in 313, Constantine issued his edict of toleration which made of the outcast Christian Church a respectable one. Here, in 390, the Bishop Ambrose, former Roman prefect of the city, by acclamation made the spiritual leader of the Milanese, stood before the door of his basilica and barred entrance to Theodosius, Emperor of the West, until he had done penance for the massacre of 7,000 at Salonica. The tormented Augustine was converted here. Here the Renaissance flowered, and to this city, in 1564, sent from Rome by his uncle Pope Paul IV, came the twenty-six-year-old Cardinal Charles Borromeo, a man "whom Jews might bless and Protestants adore," to reform a people and a Church in a see where no archbishop had resided for over eighty years. Ambrose and Charles—these names enclose Milan in more than a thousand years of her history, the one standing at the

[1] John J. Navone, in *The Commonweal,* March 15, 1963.

entrance to its medieval era, his back turned to the crumbling Empire: the other, Borromeo, standing at its close, both consecrating by their sanctity a Church which in her liturgy remembers Ambrose,[2] and which in her life still reflects the dynamism of the tall, thin, ugly young man from Rome who restored her pride and practice to the ancient Church of Milan.

Nearly sixteen hundred years after Ambrose and four hundred after Carlo Borromeo, their successor, another "man from Rome," Giovanni Battista Montini, was preparing, on January 5, 1954, to enter his archdiocese to take on the most challenging assignment in all Italy. Another predecessor in Milan, Achille Ratti, later Pius XI, had said: "It is easier to be Pope than archbishop of Milan." The archdiocese, sprawling, vast, and complex, with over three million Catholics, heavily industrial but agricultural too, with social and religious problems of enormous intricacy, a top Communist regional party to combat and reconcile, with the backwash of the war adding to and confusing the perspective, presented Archbishop Montini with a challenge which dwarfed any other in his life. The quiet corridors of the Vatican, the genteel encounters, the diplomatically and religiously aseptic life had been left behind, and he would have to be at the top of his powers, endlessly creative and exhaustively engaged, if his people and their problems were to yield to him. "He who knows Milan knows the world of the twentieth century." He came *in nomine Domini,* in the name of the Lord, but others had come in that

[2] The Ambrosian rite, disputed in its origin but generally thought to be Roman, has certain distinguishing characteristics: a different arrangement of the Kyrie; an offertory in the cathedral of bread and wine by the lay people; the Credo sung just before the Preface; no bells at the Consecration; the breaking of the Host just before the Pater Noster; the Agnus Dei used only at requiem Masses. The sequence of color of the vestments is also different, with black used for Lent. Most feasts have a proper Preface.

same name and had been overwhelmed by difficulty and indifference. If Milan was, as the French ambassador to the
Vatican had said, "cut to his measure," it still remained for
him to prove that he was not merely "a diplomat who cele-
brates Mass," but one who could touch hearts and move not
only those who awaited him with joy but the thousands for
whom his coming was a matter of supreme unconcern.

Archbishop Montini reached the town of Lodi, in the province of Emilia, adjoining Lombardy, at a few minutes after
four o'clock in the afternoon of the day on which he left
Rome. The *rapido* train on which he traveled made an un-
scheduled stop for the archbishop to leave the train, and
when he descended he was met by prelates of the archdiocese
and representatives of the provincial and city governments
who would have the honor of accompanying him into his
archdiocese. He walked quickly along the special carpet laid
for him and into the station hung with draperies hastily assembled from dusty cupboards, for it was years since Lodi
had received so distinguished a visitor. The welcome over, the
archbishop left the station, and as he did a group of railroad
workers, shunted behind barricades with other curious or devout, called out to him, "Archbishop, give us your blessing!"
And the archbishop's quick eyes sought them out; he smiled
and traced a blessing over them, and he was in the car heading
out of Lodi.

The procession crossed into Lombardy over the Lambro
River. Once on Lombard soil, the archbishop stopped the car,
and kneeling on the damp, slushy pavement, his hat laid carefully beside him, he prayed to the Virgin: "Under thy protection, O holy Mother of God . . ." and, having said a prayer
to the Holy Spirit, he leaned forward and reverently kissed
the land of Lombardy. Dusk was falling, the only illumina-
tion provided by the headlights of the cars, throwing into relief the kneeling archbishop and those surrounding him—

amazement, alarm, concern and delight flitting over their faces, their hands extended as if to assist or prevent him. When he rose to his feet the archbishop opened his arms in a wide embrace, but his words, "And now . . ." were drowned by the roar of the motors. That his gesture was unexpected is clear, yet it was a typical Montinian gesture, born of emotion and his keen sense of symbolism, and it sped before him into Milan to the intense gratification of the Milanese. They knew of the brilliance and fame of their new archbishop, but they had had as yet little knowledge of those personal characteristics which render one *simpatico,* a word which is a synthesis of the appealing qualities which Italians find important, even in archbishops.

Archbishop Montini spent the first two nights which preceded his taking formal possession of his archdiocese in the town of Rho, a few miles from Milan. There he was the guest of the Oblate Fathers in their college attached to the Sanctuary of the Virgin of Sorrows, founded in 1755. A crowd was on hand to greet him and to keep him late into the night appearing on the balcony of his room to bless them. January 5th he observed as a day of retreat.

At two o'clock on the feast of the Epiphany, the archbishop left Rho, telling the people with gentle charm that he could happily spend the rest of his days there. His journey was a short one, bringing him in half an hour to the historic church of Sant'Eustorgio within the city limits of Milan, the church from which the cortege of a new archbishop, in earlier days mounted on a white mule, traditionally proceeded through the streets to the cathedral. Sant'Eustorgio is the church which claims, with greater pride than accuracy, to possess the relics of the Three Magi. A great banner, now hung from its façade, welcomed the archbishop: "From the Basilica of the Magi in Saint Eustorgio may the star of Bethlehem guide the way of His Excellency, the Most Reverend Giovanni Battista Montini, come in the name of the Lord on the day of Epiphany among his people, to lead them in their meeting with the Divine." On the threshold of the church the archbishop was met by the mayor of Milan who presented to him a crucifix which he kissed reverently. After entering the church for a short adoration, he went to the presbytery for the donning of his pontifical robes and the presentation of his rochet to the pastor, another tradition. What was not a tradition but a gesture, simply and beautifully expressed, was a written and personal invitation to 1,200 of the city's poor to be his guests at dinner that day.

As the 140th archbishop of Milan made his entrance into his see city, the day was biting cold and a driving sleet was falling, but he chose to ride in an open car, the mayor of Milan beside him, the rain forming puddles on his hat and sliding off onto his shoulders and lap. "I want the people to see me," he said. Before and behind him on horseback rode the uniformed *carabinieri*. Through the ugly outskirts of the city the procession wound slowly, through acres of cement and blocks of flats, new streets like gashes opening on every side. It was a cheerless, almost desolate sight,[3] the only warmth provided by the people huddled under umbrellas or peering through windows from the comfort of their houses, waving and clapping as their archbishop waved back or raised his hand in blessing.

When the procession reached the Cathedral in the center of the city, the great square in front was packed with people, their umbrellas bobbing and bumping as they jostled one another to catch a glimpse of the archbishop, by now thoroughly drenched. He seemed oblivious to his damp condition, lingering on the steps of the cathedral, taking off his glasses to dry them, blessing the people once again. Inside the immense

[3] Months later Archbishop Montini said: "Milan appeared to me as an immense, hostile forest."

Duomo, hung with draperies and tapestries, its vaulted heights resounding with the music of welcome, the archbishop made his adoration before the Blessed Sacrament, and then mounted the handsome, massive pulpit in the cathedral of Ambrose and Charles. He stood for a moment, mitred and silent, flanked by candle-bearing acolytes, a gothic figure in the gloom which the hundreds of lights and tapers could not wholly dissipate.

Thirty thousand people waited for him to speak his first words. His sermon was long, well developed and articulated. He spoke of his last meeting with Pope Pius: "The Pope was then ill. When I presumed to ask a directive for my future ministry, His Holiness with a profound and paternal accent— which I now echo—said to me, 'Preserve the deposit,' that is, of the Apostolic Roman Catholic faith." In this sermon the new archbishop touched on labor: "May this field which here surrounds me become truly Christian. It will be my care to cooperate so that instead of a field of battle, labor will become a terrain of sincere and peaceful human encounter. . . . Wherever there is suffering or injustice or legitimate aspiration for social improvement there will be the frank and solid defense of a pastor and a father."

There were words from Pope Pius XII for him and his people on this day: "On him We invoke from God, under the auspices of the great father of the Ambrosian Church, the spirit of his admirable predecessor, Charles Borromeo. Like San Carlo, who was given to the Lombard metropolis by a Pope who considered him a fruitful collaborator, so too may the new pastor . . . give to his flock what the Shepherd of shepherds and the souls entrusted to him expect from his actions and from his life. May he be the glory of his children; may his children be his crown!"

The archbishop celebrated his first Mass in the Milan cathedral in the Ambrosian rite, and then, through ranks of torch-bearing youths, he rode to the archiepiscopal palace while the hymn *Christus vincit, Christus regnat* rang out in the gelid air.

The words spoken by the archbishop in his cathedral had been words expressing awareness and a spirit of conciliation and love. It remained to see what the new archbishop of Milan would do.

Archbishop Montini was a man with a plan. His instinct and training rebelled against whatever temptation presented itself to get caught up in a flurry of activity in which service would be counterfeited by mere episcopal busyness. He intended to base his activity on a true appreciation of conditions in the archdiocese, not the conventional stereotyped perspective but one reflecting his people in their lives and in their needs. Mere words would not do—but neither would action devoid of informed direction. "Our ordinary error—which the Lord will forgive us because we have little time, little resources and few talents, but which objectively is an error—is empiricism, the doing of something for the sake of doing something. Those are wrong who say, 'Let's get busy on the apostolate,' almost as if the apostles worked haphazardly. The art of the apostolate is that of the fisherman; it is the art of adapting means to particular ends. For this reason it is necessary to be eminently experimental. . . ."

Not all of his experiments would work—but he would be endlessly creative in shaping them. If his archdiocese was industrial, then his mission was to workers and employees; if the city of Milan was a center of cultural creativity then the intellectuals, so many of them estranged—"too modern for the clericals, too Catholic for the secularists"—must be reached; if his people were without homes and schools and social services and churches, then these must be provided. If, in common with the other new Europeans born of the war, their materialistic dream was transcending their commitment to God, then they must be taught. New ways, new words, boldness were needed; the gospel must be preached to twentieth-century man in twentieth-century ways;[4] and it was not the twentieth-century way of Archbishop Montini to wait in his cathedral for his people to find him.

He was to write: "It is the priest who must make the move, not the people. . . . It is useless for him to ring his bell; nobody will listen to it. Instead it is for him to hear the sirens sounding from the factories, those temples of technical achievement where the modern world lives and breathes. It is for the priest to make of himself a missionary if he would have Christianity abide and become a new living leaven of civilization." And again: "If the pastor begins to move, if he goes out and seeks, if he calls, if he suggests—then he has a chance of succeeding."

His first significant public appearance and statement were made three days after he had taken possession of his cathedral. Although suffering from a cold he had caught on the day of his arrival, he had been out of his residence already, visiting hospitals, casually dropping by the apartment of two elderly women who, bedridden, had written him of their regret at not being able to welcome him. But it was in Sesto San Giovanni, the steel city of northern Italy, called "Little Stalin-

---

[4] "The Church faces the same tasks that nations and states and the Western world in general have to face—the problem of man, how he is to be housed and fed and how he can support himself. We need social and economic regeneration. And then man must be made aware of his true nature—in other words we need intellectual and religious regeneration. These are problems for the world and they are also problems for the world Church—far more so, for instance, than the question of liturgical reforms. If these problems are solved without us, or to our disadvantage, then the whole of Europe will be lost to the Church, even if every altar faces the people and Gregorian chant is the rule of every parish."—Alfred Delp, *The Prison Meditations, op. cit.*

grad" because of its formidable Communist apparatus, that he chose to identify himself and his mission with the workers of Lombardy.

"I begin here," he said, "my colloquy with the people of Milan. And since I do not wish that there ever be secrets between me and my children, I confess that in this moment I am realizing a dream which I have cherished for many years —to speak to real workers. I hope that my ministry here and elsewhere will give me the grace to resolve the equivocation that some may wish to bring between the Church and the working class. More than once it has been said that I would be the archbishop of the workers, but until this moment I have never replied to this affirmation. Well, here today I want to dissolve my reserve . . ." Then, turning to bless the cornerstone of a new community building for women and children, he said, "And now, with prayer, we place the first stone of what is to be a new Sesto San Giovanni, a new Milan—may they be Christian!"

The significance of Archbishop Montini's desire to be known above all as the "archbishop of the workers" lay not in its romantic or political implications,[5] but rather in his deep awareness of the truth of words spoken by a predecessor in the see of Milan. Achille Ratti had said: "The greatest scandal of the nineteenth century is that the Church should have lost the working class." Montini shared with Ratti the conviction that the loss was part of a larger failing: the Church's estrangement from the times. Recoiling from the shock of the Reformation, wounded and defensive, the Church had tended to seek its temporal shelter under the protection of the established European monarchies. Itself a holder of large temporal

---

[5] It was generally believed that it was Montini who had persuaded Pope Pius XII to swing the Church's active support behind the postwar liberals of the Christian Democratic parties in Europe with their concrete programs for Europe's social reform.

possessions in Italy, the Papacy of the nineteenth century was inclined to defend the established political orders at a time when they were doomed to collapse, and to look upon the secular democracies which replaced them as suspect and hostile. They were, in fact, largely indifferent to the Church, and the estrangement hurt most deeply those whom the Church and government should have cooperated in assisting.

In 1955, the Communists in Italy still boasted "a Communist cell for every church spire." That the Communists had not taken lightly the appointment of Montini to Milan was seen in the almost simultaneous assignment to Lombardy, as party director, of the number two man of the Communist Party in Italy, Pietro (the Cask) Secchia. Once described as the "perfect Bolshevik," the tough, gold-toothed, fifty-two-year-old Secchia, who had spent twelve years in Fascist jails, left the central Secretariat of the Communist headquarters on the "Street of the Dark Shops" in Rome to tighten the discipline and draw the battle lines against the sensitive, ascetic monsignor from the Vatican, the type of intellectual whom Secchia most despised.

Secchia was a formidable opponent, burly, fearless, committed; he had directed the drive which raised membership in the Italian Communist Party from 400,000 to more than 2,000,000. But Montini in his person and in his office was now the leader of over 3,000,000, many of them trying to live two faiths; his job was to persuade them that "Christianity will have the power to raise the people up anew, to bring about the return of justice, to elevate the working class." Such efforts, he would tell them, had been made by others, but they were based on economic motives or on hatred.

Earlier he had said: "Whoever has faith in the power of Christian charity has already within him the sound basis for social responsibility. . . . Charity can give birth to a modern world. If it has not yet appeared it is because we have not yet applied the eternal law of the gospel. . . ." "One of the greatest evils of our time is precisely this: that Christians are not Christian and that the mystery of newness and continuity communicated to them in the baptism of resurrection is not lived by them. In its place are compromise, inconsistency, lack of logic and infidelity. These are the miserable survivals of a vocation that should have embraced perfection, sanctity and Christian fullness."

Montini's appeal was to the gospel of Christ, Secchia's to the gospel of Lenin. A few days after Montini spoke at Sesto San Giovanni, Secchia made his first public speech. It was full of toughness and emotion. "Here in Milan," he told workers in a rubber factory, "Socialism was born and the fight for liberation began [he was referring to the 1945 partisan uprising which he had helped to organize]. . . . Here at Milan, therefore, must originate a great new example of unity and force . . . this is not the hour of resignation or laziness. . . . No fear, therefore! No facile hopes!" He knew his opponent; the lines were drawn, and over the next few years Montini's appeal and action were matched and contrasted and fought. There was to be no slackening of the Church's efforts, directed not so much at fighting Communism as making the gospel a living, dynamic force in men's lives.

Archbishop Montini sought to convert rather than to combat the Communists. In a pastoral letter written in 1956, he said: "May the imprudent and the unhappy who march behind the banner of Marxism know that there is Someone who loves them still, strongly, immensely, divinely. May they know that those who pursue in this world the mission of Christ crucified think of them, follow them, love them and await them in His name."

On January 8, 1957, *The New York Times* carried a feature article by its Rome correspondent, Arnaldo Cortesi. Under the headline "Pope's Ex-Aide Defeats Milan Red Chief," with the arresting subtitle "Pope's ex-aide credited with winning over workers in key industrial region," the article reported that the archbishop had won the first round. In shop steward elections in Lombard factories anticommunists won control for the first time in many plants and made great inroads in others.[6] Secchia was removed and relegated to a minor post in the Communist Party in Rome.

How had Montini done it? Americans, with no oppressed working class and with a traditional if lukewarm respect for religion, may have difficulty in understanding the gulf which still in the early 50's separated the "haves" from the "have-nots" in Europe not only economically but politically, socially and religiously as well. The appeal of the Communists was to class war; Montini's appeal was to the dignity of all men, of all labor, stressing the spirituality which creative and manual labor share. He sought to give them a vision and a hope of what the world could be like through the translation of Christian social principles into reality. He knew that a materially insecure proletariat is a plaything for any party that can provide bread or even promise it. *Primum vivere, deinde evangelizare*—this he knew was the idea behind the great social encyclicals. He spoke of peace to the workers, for themselves and their families; and, since they were men of good will, they listened. But much of this they had heard before; what made the difference?

Montini refused to see the world in which his people lived simply as the enemy, one to be fought and scorned and avoided. He had no illusions: "Modern labor is insensible to the voice of religion." He had none of the hostility of the priest

---

[6] The noncommunists gained control in the Fiat works, the Officine Mecchaniche brush and tractor plants, the Falck steel mills, and the Pirelli rubber factory, involving 60,000 workers. In 92 small factories noncommunists increased their union voting power from 8,701 to 13,803. The communists shrank from 21,463 to 17,893.

who is content to reject or damn all that interests the world. He wanted to remove every ambiguity affecting the relationship of the workers to the Church and answer the suspicion or accusation that the Church and big business are allies. He knew what was in their minds—that they had come to believe in his words "that religion distracts them . . . from their true social and economic interests, that religion lulls and deludes them . . . fixes them in a juridic and social system in which others live in abundance, in security, in pleasure and in privilege, while they, the workers live in hardship and subjection. . . . Hence class struggle, workers and employers locked in battle, both affected by eighteenth-century Enlightenment concepts of personal and class self-sufficiency without need for God or obligation to others. And when the Church sought to speak, the rich accused it of too much favoritism to the poor, the poor of favoring the rich. The rich dismiss the gospels for not giving sufficient importance to economic values, the poor dismiss them for maintaining that the poor are blessed."

To these objections, Archbishop Montini replied: "The drawing together of the world of labor and of religion can come about only on a spiritual level. . . . Also in this area of life great attention must be paid to two decisive and mysterious factors: human liberty and the intervention of divine grace. . . . The law of God ties us to itself, not to the past, and it obligates us to new ventures which we would wish were even better than those of the past. Out of its own perfection there arises from the law that hunger and thirst for justice that every Christian should feel. . . . Thus the problem of the equilibrium between the present state of things and that one that will emerge is brought into focus. Before this problem all good Catholics and those who bear the responsibility of pastors must be equally alert, neither to surrender to the mania for new ideas that which should be defended and conserved, nor to halt the progress of what is lawful and beneficial."

He spoke to them in their language about their interests: "We hear today that the world of labor is divided. Many battle against us; many march in other organizations. Nevertheless, they share many of your desires, your sacrifices, your aspirations. . . . You must have the boldness of those who possess the whole truth. Do not be afraid you are playing the losing cards. You are love, the future, success, victory. They are automatons. They crush their adversaries; if they won we would all be crushed. . . . But our victory will not damage others. . . . However, we do not want so much to win as to convince; we wish for the others to share our joy, our life, our liberty, our well-being, our future. We wish for them to be at peace with us. And we will pray for them and tell them, 'Brother, come with me if you have lost your way.' We do not want a selfish class struggle. Christ is with us all."

He spoke these words and similar ones, not in throne rooms, in ecclesiastical settings of baroque splendor, but in the grime and noise and sweat of factories. The Communists answered him with a bombing of his residence at two in the morning on January 5, 1956, when two pounds of dynamite were thrown through a window, shattering all the windows of the building, and a part of the walls. Archbishop Montini, still at his desk at that late hour, went on working—"The gesture of a madman" was his only comment.

The futile, exasperated attack spoke tellingly of the inroads the archbishop had made in two years. It had not been easy. He went to find the worker in his steel mill, his factory, his shop, his store; he went down into mines, into the fields. The dusty black Alfa Romeo was always on the road. The workers were not accustomed to see priests, let alone archbishops, walking ramps, climbing ladders, peering into furnaces, asking them about their work. Some responded with hostility, with booing; he continued to smile and move among them. One man held back because there was grease on his hand; Montini seized and held it as he asked him about his family. His thoughtfulness was instinctive. To some miners in Condoglia he remembered to send an accordion to cheer them in their isolation.

On his first Christmas in Milan the archbishop had chosen to say Mass, not in the splendor of his cathedral, but in a wood and tin shanty at Porto di Mare. He brought the mayor of Milan with him to show him that the "economic miracle" of Milan had stopped short of Porto di Mare. There was no electricity for him that night, but bonfires burned in the district in his honor.

The Communists sought to organize the opposition to him, to refuse him access to the assembly lines and shops where he seemed to spend a good part of his day. In one factory, management, too, disturbed by his outspokenness, tried to censor his talk before he delivered it. It came to be that when a visitor who called to see him was told that the archbishop was out, the question came back: "What factory is he visiting today?" Wherever he went he carried a portable Mass kit in a briefcase,[7] and he did not hesitate to celebrate Mass in factories and shops for men who had not been to church for twenty or thirty years. The democratic feeling and social mobility characteristic of the United States gives the American priest the opportunity of knowing the poor, the middle class, and the rich; his European peer is not so fortunate. Often drawn from a single social group, isolated from his people in terms of historical judgments no longer viable, he tends to live apart from them, to become on some levels incomprehensible to them, and since he is isolated he may be somewhat ignorant of the problems they confront in their daily living. The arch-

[7] The irreverent among the Milanese called him, not without affection, "the board chairman of Jesus Christ."

bishop was showing the way to his traditionally conservative priests, and the people were responding slowly but with increasing affection and admiration.[8]

Archbishop Montini had never forgotten the rows of worker flats as he had seen them the first day he rode into Milan, dreary warrens of deadening sameness. He knew that modern assembly line techniques tended to deaden all newness, all joy in men who felt nothing of themselves enriching their work or being enriched by it. It was necessary to restore to them a concept of the holiness of the work they did, to give a Christian purpose to their lives. "You are the first-born sons of the world of work because you give your brothers the tools with which they will work. No work is accomplished except with materials that have passed through your hands. . . . Does the man seeking to produce a particular form or function know that he has before him, almost springing forth from his hands, neither a simple mass of material nor an idol . . . but a mirror? Yes, a mirror—made by him from a ray of divine perfection. Does he know that when he works he is praying?" And again: "Work is great but it is not an end in itself; if it remained an end in itself, it would be a yoke, slavery and chastisement."

In a pastoral letter he said: "I should like to see the workers given every assistance—social, professional, religious. I should like them to realize not only the wrong done them by forcing on them a materialistic view of life, but that our own spiritual view of life has far more respect for them as persons and recognizes in them the boundless treasure of a soul that thinks

[8] In 1960, as cardinal, he went to Assisi to give a conference on the Papacy. Some workers came from Prato and were met by a priest who warned them that the theme would be beyond them. "We haven't come for that," they replied. "He (Cardinal Montini) is someone who really has our interests at heart—we only want to kiss his hand and then off we go!"

and prays and believes. I should like to see technical schools helping them to realize that there can be a vocation, a redemptive value, a religious dignity in human work. I should like their days of rest to be sacred and inviolable. I should like their public holidays to become marked with flowers and song and thought and prayer, and to be truly occasions for recreation of the spirit. I should like to see prayer once again linked with work, sustaining it, ennobling it, sanctifying it. The working people are on their way toward such a spiritual outlook and the Church of Christ looks forward to its attainment."

"I feel myself to be your friend, I understand so many of your thoughts," he said to the workmen of the Pirelli factory. "I also understand that you look at me with a silent question in your hearts. Now I have nothing to give you; I am empty-handed. But I know that precisely because you are workers, you seek for something which lies beyond your labor, beyond your salaries, beyond the material. You seek a little of the true life, a little happiness. And from this point of view I have immense treasures to give you: hope, the sense of human dignity, immense horizons of light. You have souls, and I have treasures with which to feed them."

Management did not escape his attention: "The wealthier classes should recognize the respect of the Church for private property in its essential forms, its constant, vigilant, often stern but always right and fatherly warnings on the moral and social dangers of selfish wealth, on the necessity of a more just distribution of economic goods, on the beauty of a disinterested and general contribution to the elevation of the working classes. The social doctrine of the Church has never denied the functions of private enterprise, provided this does not damage human dignity and the legitimate aspirations of those who take part in the productive process."

He was forthright. "The workers were not the first to

abandon religion," he told the workers of Sesto San Giovanni, "but the industrialists and economists of the last century, who dreamed of founding progress, civilization and peace without God and without Christ. Let us not say that religion is the opium of the people and that it contrives to extinguish their drive and hopes of rising in the world; on the contrary, religion is the light, the glory and the strength of such aspirations."

He was candid in pointing out that much of the social and political tension afflicting Italy lay outside the province of the Church and depended on the state of human relations between employers and employees. But Christian teachings had to be dusted off, refurbished and preached day in and day out, so that the protagonists in the drama might act out their roles in truth, and with a script which was ageless in its call to morality and justice. The adaptation was to be worked out between employer and employees in mutual respect and awareness of their Christian vocation.

His directness, his identification with the workers, his obvious affection for them, his sharply articulated social messages, his tireless pursuit of his people was in vivid contrast to the traditional picture of a prelate presiding grandly and somewhat remotely over a vast archdiocese. Archbishop Montini saw his work in Milan as part of a pattern, a mode of modern Church action which could fit other dioceses with equal ease. The archdiocese of Milan was a world in microcosm, urban and agricultural, with class divisions and social problems, embracing the believing, the indifferent, and the hostile, a Church in a twentieth-century world, until now geared in many aspects of its apostolate to eighteenth and nineteenth-century means. A re-formation of the Church's activities in areas of social progress, a commitment to the best of the world's values and the employment of the most modern techniques of communication were part of Montini's contribution to the life of the Milan archdiocese.

But was all this the proper sphere of religion? "An objection that one often hears made today," the archbishop said, "is directed by our secular and materialistic age against the Christian who seeks the kingdom of heaven; it is the legitimacy of claim and capacity of this same Christian to seek the kingdom of the earth which is contested. It may be asked if hope for things eternal should exclude the hope for temporal well-being. Are the two hopes incompatible? Did not the Master say that no man can serve two masters? It is a delicate question, which shapes the torment of our age: on the one side are those who would choose a wholly spiritual solution, challenging the Christian's right to concern himself with temporal things, demanding that he live a life of utopian angelism with certain Manichean overtones; on the other side are those who would have the Christian gather up the benefits of religion with those of the profane world, somewhat as we see done in the Old Testament. . . . The supreme precept for the Christian is love, together with concern for the concrete and human needs of his time, but he must also flee the totalitarian spirit of those who have no other hope than that founded on the things of this world."

This is the age of labels. In his impact on the life of Milan, and indeed of all Italy, in his daring innovations and undisguised words and actions there was nothing of the traditionalist about Montini except his witness, day in and day out, to the gospel. He could not be called a conservative; therefore he must be a progressive, a liberal—even a "leftist." In an Italy which still finds it difficult to believe that any action of the Church in the social sphere is divorced from political intention, it was said that in his political thinking Montini was left of center, how far to the left depending on the convic-

tions of the speaker. Shortly after being raised to the cardinalate, when he was in Concesio to inaugurate and bless a new
hall attached to the Church of Sant'Antonio, he was enthusi-
astically hailed by someone with the shout: "Long live the
priest of the Left!" The cardinal was obviously surprised and
not pleasantly. Later, speaking to the parish priest, Don Luigi
Bosio, he referred to the shouted greeting of the parishioner:
"But what is this business about, 'a priest of the Left?' Priest
of the workers, yes, but not of the Left."

Archbishop Montini was prompt in reorganizing the diocesan structure in order to give direction and continuity to the
impetus his words were creating. He revitalized the Ambrosian Social Institute, giving it the task of establishing schools
of social formation (they now number twenty) with first two-
year and then three-year courses of intensive study and practical application. He founded the bulletin *Relazione Sociale,* entrusting it to a group of university students and giving them
total autonomy as to its form and matter. His priests were not
forgotten. "We must all become competent [in the field of
social action]," he said. "Even as we know how to explain,
for example, the doctrine of the sacraments and of prayer, so
too we should be able to explain this new chapter which has
come to be inserted in Christian teaching. It is not enough to
practice the charity of almsgiving and of prayer; it is necessary to become involved in this 'social charity.' "

To both his priests and his people he insisted on the importance of correct liturgical observance. "There are still
those," he said, "who consider the liturgical renewal as an
optional matter, or as one of the numerous devotional currents to which a person may adhere or not as he chooses." He
went on to remark that sadly enough the mentality still exists
"which thinks that the liturgical movement is a troublesome
attempt at reformation, of doubtful orthodoxy; or a petrified,

external ritualism which has to do merely with rubrics; or an archaeological fad, formalistic and 'arty'; or else a product of the cloister ill adapted to the people of our world; or finally, a preconceived opposition to piety and popular devotions." And by both word and example he vigorously combatted these ideas.

He also pointed out that the Catholic Church is a missionary Church and that the vitality of parishes and dioceses should be channeled into missionary activity. Again with the archbishop pointing the way, a mission staffed by priests and sisters from Milan and supported by Milanese funds was founded at Kariba in Southern Rhodesia and a second at Chirundu, also in Rhodesia.

In order to study and coordinate the activity of his see, the archbishop founded the office "Pastorale Sociale" in his chancery under the direction of Father Cesare Pagani. Its purpose was realized in guiding and encouraging the various Catholic organizations of workers as well as offering guidance and counsel at times when strikes convulsed the labor world of Milan. For immigrant workers there was the diocesan center for immigrants, to offer spiritual assistance and to cooperate with the city of Milan in integrating them into the working life of the city. Seven out of ten of these immigrants came not from the south but from the rural dioceses of Lombardy (Pavia, Cremona, Mantua) and from the Veneto; the archbishop was especially desirous of obtaining priests from these regions to be with them. Another of his activities was to establish an association for aid to persons released from jail. In 1955, a statistical bureau was established to tabulate and card index the parishes of the archdiocese.

On his arrival in Milan, Archbishop Montini knew that the influence of the powerful Communist-controlled General Confederation of Workers, with its three million members in Italy, must be neutralized. Italian Catholics had formed ACLI, the Association of Catholic Italian Workers, and with his encouragement this association became particularly vigorous in the province of Milan, with nearly 50,000 members out of a national membership of over a million, which now plays a leading role in the noncommunist Free Federation of Labor. Nearly a quarter of the Milanese members take educational courses in the modern five-story city headquarters, one of fourteen provincial centers, and the Lombard ACLI operates five rest homes for workers in the mountains and at the seaside.

For his clergy the archbishop founded a school of social formation. It numbers today a hundred priests among its students, and is attached to the Toniolo Social Institute of the Catholic University of Milan, through which it issues a degree after two years of study and the presentation of a thesis. A summer school at La Mendola, summer seat of the university, holds social seminars for the young. A new review, *Diocesi di Milano,* was added to the diocesan daily, *L'Italia.* The cultural life of the city was served by the founding of the Academy of San Carlo which later Pope John XXIII from his sickbed was to praise with a message saying that it was the realization of a dream long fostered by him. In all these activities Archbishop Montini's method could thus be described: challenge by word, arouse by example, consolidate by action.

In the last year of the war, four big Allied bombings had destroyed a third of Milan, but with almost Teutonic speed and efficiency it had all been rebuilt. Giant apartment buildings had sprouted to care for the dispossessed and for the thousands who streamed northward from the impoverished and depressed south. Archbishop Montini's predecessor, Cardinal Schuster, had founded the Domus Ambrosiana to deal with the problem of those thousands too poor to find homes other than in hovels which they constructed themselves from their scavenging of rubbish heaps. Through this organization, Archbishop Montini had an entire village constructed at

Rovagnasco, southeast of Milan, where more than three thousand people were given modern apartments with at least four rooms.

The organization known as Caritas Ambrosiana distributed the charity of the archdiocese, and the archbishop's "Office of Charity" was established to provide free medical and legal advice for his people. For the children of the underprivileged there were summer colonies in the mountains and by the sea; they were cared for in ten houses. He refused to allow the charity of the archdiocese, of the Church, to become depersonalized, bureaucratic. Each year at Christmas he went to the giant *Monte di Pietà,* a kind of official pawnshop, and redeemed the objects left there during the year by people in need; they were his Christmas presents to them. And always there were his visits—unofficial, unannounced—to the orphanages, to the sick, to those without homes, and to the poorest of his poor, living in their shanties. "For the poor," he said, "we must have a special reverence, a particular solicitude. They are the mirror of Christ, indeed almost His living sacrament. They are both the inspiration and the object of our practice of charity. They are our brothers whose needs . . . impose on us an obligation. They become an annoyance to us if we flee them, a joy if we care for them. . . . They are our companions on our journey."

In 1955, Milan was without churches for over 300,000 of her population. Thousands of people were arriving each year, drawn by the prosperity and higher wages of the Milan area, and the archbishop felt responsible for each one of them. The *Osservatore Romano* called this need "his predominant pastoral anxiety." "We must call to your attention," he said to the people of his archdiocese, "the great and urgent problem of new churches for the city of Milan and for the new districts which are growing everywhere." It cannot be allowed, he told them, that people should take root in a city without a church where their spirits could be fed. Hundreds of thousands, he said, lacked religious assistance; if something were not done immediately and positively the moral and civic tradition of the Italian people was threatened with deformation and decay.

He was the first to show the way, donating what little he had of worth: his most precious pectoral cross, and a ring "of a certain value," as he said in a letter accompanying it. The late Enrico Mattei, something of a political gray eminence in Italy but a devoted member of the Milan archdiocese, was named to head the committee for the new churches. Various church groups and associations of workers, industrialists, shopkeepers and craftsmen took over the financing of the individual churches built beyond the city's ancient Spanish walls, with the Italian government subsidizing one-fifth of the cost.

Often the archbishop would go incognito to the outer reaches of the city to see for himself what was needed, to study the suggestions for solution, and to see the people as they really lived. The plan he formulated for Milan and the other cities of the archdiocese involved the building of new parishes in new areas, also subdividing those grown too large; according to local circumstances and needs. He insisted that the parishes encompass a sense of community and that people feel themselves members of a spiritual family. The churches must therefore be adapted not only to a perfect expression of liturgical worship, but insofar as possible be centers of a Christian community, each gathered around its pastor.

During his eight years in Milan, Archbishop Montini blessed and consecrated seventy-two churches, and on the eve of his departure for the conclave after the death of Pope John XXIII, another nineteen were under construction; in addition thirty-two chapels were built. "A church must be more than a house of prayer," he said. "It must have a children's home, a sports field, a recreation center, a cinema, a library, a place where neighbors can discuss community problems." A church which serves as a model of the archbishop's desire to make each parish the heart of neighborhood life is that of Saint Agnes, located in an area of the city where immigrants from the south and other low-paid workers live. In addition to the church, the parish contains a school for 800 children, an apprentice training center, a vocational school for 300 young workers. There is a dormitory and a dining room for 150 boarders, an athletic club, a cinema, a dispensary and an ambulance service for accident victims in the neighborhood.

But the most interesting feature of the archbishop's plan to provide services to his people and to break down their spiritual isolation, was the building of eight central chapels in the blocks of cooperative flats which flank the city, and his urging of architects to include chapels in their plans. The tenants were to pay each month for the maintenance of the chapel and other expenses involved in having a chapel in the building. In some buildings and clusters of buildings there are a hundred families, in others close to a thousand, and the archbishop realized it would be easier for the priest to come to the people than to persuade them to go to the church. When he conceived this partial solution, the archbishop commented on "a new and profane mentality . . . where many no longer pray, where Christian doctrine is not taught and the sacraments are not administered. It is a problem of public welfare."

His response to the problem became the blueprint of activity for the Italian Peninsula. Speaking of the explosion of buildings "conceived and activated," he pointed out drily, "on an anti-economic plan," he said: "No other type of building has, as do these, a popular, collective, truly social origin, and no other is more open to the people, to all the people, of our new suburbs. These buildings are not therefore only decorative monuments in the perspective, often oppressive and monotonous, of today's urban living: they are truly houses of the people, for their consolation, for their peace, for their faith and for their growth in goodness."

The archbishop's "concern for the concrete and human needs" of his people had expressed itself in material ways: first, in what he had called "social charity"; secondly, in the building of churches. Their "growth in goodness" had always been the central motive. It would now become the object of a massive frontal attack for which the cardinal had been long preparing.

Pope Paul VI

ANSA

*Giuditta Alghisi **Montini***
mother of Pope Paul

ANSA

Giorgio Montini
***Pope Paul's** father*

ANSA

House in which Pope Paul was born

Giovanni Battista Montini in the arms of his grandmother

The three Montini children
Giovanni Battista in center

Young Montini, 1916, with two friends
about to leave for the front
Photograph taken at the Institute Cesare Arici

Father Montini
at the time of his ordination

Monsignor Montini with university student, 1942

ANSA

Monsignor Montini at his desk in the Vatican Secretariat of State

ANSA

UPI

*The Archbishop of Milan kisses the ground
of his new archdiocese*

Archbishop Montini with Pope Pius XII in 1956

Cardinal Montini visits a coal mine
at Collio Val Trompia

*Cardinal Montini and President Eisenhower
meet at Notre Dame University, 1960*

*Cardinals Montini and Cushing
in press room of Daughters of St. Paul, Boston*

Cardinal Montini and Pope John XXIII
shortly before the Pope's death

*Cardinal Montini
arriving in Rome to visit
the dying Pope*

Cardinals Montini and Spellman during the Conclave

UPI

Unique photograph of newly-elected Pope and College of Cardinals shortly after his election

*Eugène Cardinal Tisserant, Dean of the Sacred College,
voices homage of the Cardinals to newly-elected Pope*

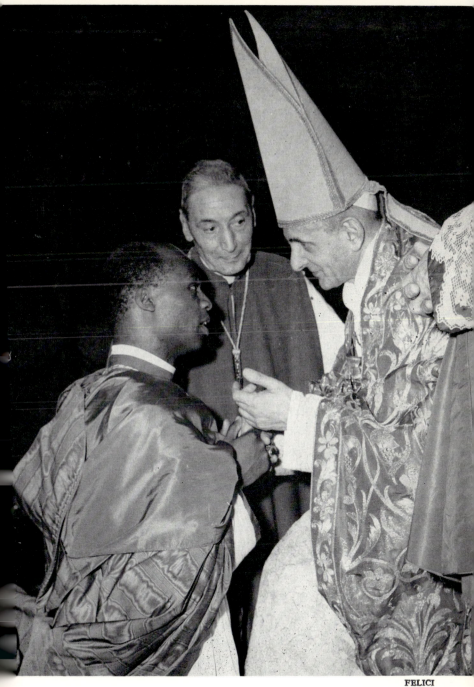

Pope Paul VI greets Cardinal Rugambwa of Tanganyika
Archbishop Enrico Dante, papal master of ceremonies, in background

The Pope greets Bishop Vladimir Kotliarov,

head of Russian Orthodox delegation to the Pontiff's coronation. Others in picture are Russian Archpriest

Vitaly Borovoy and Anglican Church delegate, Bishop John Moorman, of Ripon

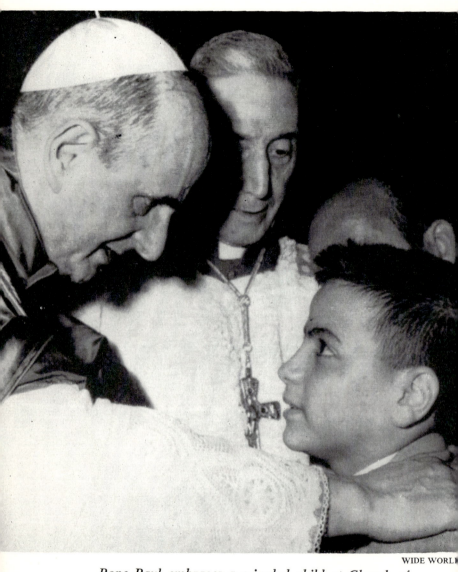

*Pope Paul embraces a crippled child at Church of
SS. Ambrose and Charles, June 29, 1963*

6. Mission to Milan

*"For you and in your serv-
ice I am a bishop; but with
you I am a Christian. Bishop
is the title of a charge assumed; Christian is the name
of a grace received. A dan-
gerous title, a salutary name.
Wearied in a charge which
is personal to us, we repose
in a benefit which is common to us all."*

Saint Augustine

In the early days of November, 1957, posters by the hundreds
of thousands suddenly appeared on every viewable surface in
Milan, five years in preparation, revealing better than any-
to the 24th of November, a thousand voices will speak to you
of God." It was the announcement of the Great Mission of
Milan, five years in preparation, revealing better than any
other of Archbishop Montini's actions his powers of organization and the vision he had of his own mission.

113

All that had gone before—the exhausting travel, the un-flagging witness in person and in word, the slow building up of confidence and expectation in his people, the social reor-ganization of the diocese, the construction of churches and schools—all of it was in vain unless his people, each in his own life, possessed a personal relationship to God. One and a half million Milanese, almost all at least nominally Catholic, but many still morally and spiritually uprooted by the war of a decade before, distracted by their material preoccupations, disturbed by the claims of Communism, resentful still of real or imagined clerical injustices and indifference of the past,[1] with a religious sense suffering from progressive attenuation —these were his people. Having sought to provide for their physical well-being by massive programs of building and of charity, he sought to equal his activity in those spheres and even surpass it in a monumental spiritual solicitation of the city of Ambrose and of Charles.

The idea of the Mission was first conceived at a meeting of the council of pastors of the city, and presented to the arch-bishop in April of 1955. From the beginning it was deter-mined to limit the Mission to the city parishes, since concen-

---

[1] "A church that makes demands in the name of a peremptory God no longer carries weight in a world of changing values. The new gen-eration is separated from the clear conclusions of our traditional theol-ogy by a great mountain of boredom and disillusion thrown up by past experience. We have destroyed man's confidence in us by the way we live. We cannot expect two thousand years of history to be an unmixed blessing and recommendation—history can be a handicap too. But re-cently the man turning to the Church for enlightenment has all too often found only a tired man to receive him—a man who then had the dishonesty to hide his fatigue under pious words and fervent ges-tures. At some future date the honest historian will have some bitter things to say about the contribution made by the churches to the crea-tion of the mass mind, of collectivism, dictatorship and so on."—Alfred Delp, *Prison Meditations, op. cit.*

tration of effort and total awareness of it by the community were felt to be important psychological factors in inducing people, first out of curiosity and then from devotion, to attend. Said the archbishop: "Milan is good, intelligent and generous, open to spiritual progress; I think it would be hard to find another city with as open a face and heart as Milan."

The theme of the Mission would be a fundamental, easily grasped cornerstone concept, basic but forgotten by a world grown poor in spiritual insight: that God is our Creator and our Father; God is Providence; God became incarnate and entered humbly into the mainstream of man's history to save man; He dwells with us still in His Church. "The scope, the immediate target at which we aim, is a rebirth of the sense of religion in the consciences of the people," said the archbishop. "It will be a message preached to all the people without distinction, but it will be directed above all to those who, although baptized, have lost the sense of mystery and of involvement with God in His Church—the estranged."

Archbishop Montini personally directed the mounting of the Mission from the first preparatory meetings. Four commissions were established: one for the press and publicity, one for finance, one for preaching (each preacher was given a directive with the theme developed in seven meditations and seven moral instructions prepared by the faculty of the major seminary of the archdiocese and presented in modern crisp terms) and one for organization. Each parish had its own committee; courses in theology for lay people were made available. The archbishop would settle for nothing less than saturation of the city, and he drove the committees, leading, suggesting, calling them to meetings, writing memoranda in his neat script. No modern means adaptable for preaching the gospel were ignored; no area of human life and endeavor overlooked.

There were words of caution. In June of 1957, speaking to the future preachers of the Mission, the archbishop said: "We will seek to be most respectful also toward those who profess atheism. We will employ no sarcasm; there will be no setting of one group against the other." The archbishop also warned the preachers that there were to be no overtones of politics in their preaching. But there was fear already abroad that the Mission was to be revolutionary. Many of the factories refused permission for the preachers to speak to their employees. From the other side, the Communist daily of Milan, noting the growing interest and excitement of the city as the day of the Mission approached, stated: "The preaching will set forth to the poor a vision of their heavenly country so that the rich will not be disturbed in the possession of their heaven on earth. In addition to discrimination between the rich and the poor, there is now added the distinction between the good poor who are Catholics, and the bad poor who are not. This preaching does not defend the daily bread of men, but the wealth of those of whom Christ said that it is easier for a camel to pass through the eye of a needle than for a rich man to enter heaven. Doesn't this show that the fight can't always be made on the side of the big industrialists, even if they are the ones who some time ago besought the Pope to make Montini a cardinal?"

Finally the day of this "extraordinary event," this "prophetic moment" came on November 4. 1,288 preachers were mobilized, among them 2 cardinals, 24 archbishops and bishops, 600 diocesan priests and 597 belonging to various religious orders, and 65 seminarians. From Bologna, accompanying their cardinal, Giacomo Lercaro, came the twenty "flying friars" and with them their trucks equipped with altars, confessionals and loudspeakers. Led by Montini, preaching, exhorting, ranging everywhere in the city, they reached out in the first week to thirty-one hospitals, clinics and homes, wherever there were sick and elderly. "Go forth and speak," said the archbishop to the preachers. "Your lips are opened.

Preach the gospel to every living creature . . . open the churches! Open houses and courtyards, schools and barracks. . . . Open every doorway and, above all, open every heart to God!"

The second week of the Mission was for the women, the third for the men, but all three weeks found the preachers going into factories, schools, cinemas, preaching on street corners, wherever the people were. "Abandon yourselves to the Mission with faith," the archbishop pleaded. To the youth of the city he said, "Before all others, may you come—the most original and sincere understanding of what we are trying to do can be yours—because it is youth which is the bearer of ideas. Come!" There were special programs for special vocations—for artists, lawyers, ballerinas, bartenders, bus-drivers, policemen, professors, radio and television workers, social workers, soldiers, students, taxi-drivers. Cardinal Siri of Genoa preached to the industrialists, Cardinal Lercaro to the workers and intellectuals. The Vatican Radio broadcast Montini's sermons every night; the *Osservatore Romano* ran daily reports on the Mission's programs; and the Pope promised a message for the Mission's close.

For three weeks Milan was a city under siege, and the archbishop was the field commander of the troops. In and out of department stores, into banks, the stock exchange, the inevitable factories, visiting thirty churches a day, he exhorted and pleaded: "Come to our Mission and hear us. What are we talking about? The usual things? Yes, but do you really know them? The same old story? Yes, but better say, the eternal story. Useless matters? No, useful as bread and as air itself." And always there was the special pleading to the fallen away: "We are determined to place those estranged from us in the first position of our activity and our prayer. . . . If there is a voice which can reach you, those of you who have left the Church, the first will be one which asks pardon of you. Yes, we of you. . . . When we see one who has fallen away there is much remorse. Why is this brother estranged from us? Because he has not been sufficiently loved." There was nothing in Montini's manner or words of what Merton calls "baroque glamorizing of the mysteries of faith," no dramatic banalities, no false glitter of new apologetic techniques.

Of such massive effort the question was asked: what are the results? The Mission, for all of its publicity, for all of its preparation and agony of activity, was a seed, the word of God falling quietly into hearts. Its effects could be measured in a variety of ways, none especially revelatory, but its need, the insights it provided, the huge human dimensions of the effort, witnessed to the burden laid on the shoulders of all whose responsibility it is to preach the gospel. To call it a "display of fireworks, dazzling but short lived," [2] is to miss the point of its challenge to men's consciences, a challenge which is resolved interiorly and without publicity.

"With regard to the ordination of priests, Holy Father, no care whatever is taken." Thus did the cardinalitial committee on reform report to Pope Paul III eight years before the Council of Trent. "The most ignorant men," they said, "and sprung from the dregs of society, and themselves depraved, mere youths, are everywhere admitted to Holy Orders." As Philip Hughes has pointed out in his *Church in Crisis,* there is here revealed one of the great mysteries of medieval Catholicism, not that there were bad priests, but that the Church never faced up to the training and educating of the rank and file of parish clergy. It was a failure which the Council of Trent dealt with vigorously, but in Europe especially it helped feed an attitude of disdain and outright opposition to the diocesan clergy which has persisted in various forms to this day, and which in turn, joining other influences, has in some countries

[2] Tanneguy Quenétain in *Realités,* May 1962, p. 50.

served to make of the parish priest a somewhat defensive, isolated figure, limited in influence and access to his flock, a situation which would be incomprehensible in an American parish.

Archbishop Montini had written: "The modern world has looked at the priest with eyes inflamed with hostile sarcasm and blinded by a utilitarian approach. The heir of the long-dead Middle Ages, the ally of selfish conservatism, the high priest of a silenced litany, the stranger in life: this is the priest. The clergy . . . has felt the repelling aversion of society in the midst of the new needs of the century. The clergy started its self-examination. . . ."

The archbishop loved priests as he loved his own priesthood. As spiritual leader of the Milan archdiocese, he was assisted by over two thousand priests; Milan is one of the few dioceses in Western Europe where spiritual vitality is evidenced by sufficient vocations.[3] He looked upon his priests as collaborators and sought from the beginning to establish a natural ease in his relations with them, abhorring the impersonal and legalistic attitude which makes a relationship between priest and bishop rather one between priest and ecclesiastical authority. His was a spirit of brotherhood, a scorning of the merely juridical.

Every year on Holy Thursday a letter was issued by the archbishop to his priests in order that he might, as Christ with his apostles, spend the day in a form of union with them. Each Thursday morning was reserved for visits from his priests; no appointment was necessary and they would leave his office with a hearty *"Grazie, carissimo"* ringing in their ears, warmed by contact, renewed by his encouragement and understanding. The priest, he told them, must be an artist, a skilled worker, the indispensable physician, expert in the sub-

[3] Recruitment in Italy is a serious problem. In 1875, there were 150,000 priests for 26 million people; in 1963, 83,000 for 60 million.

tle and profound phenomena of the spirit, a man of learning, a man who can talk, a man of taste, of tact, of sensibility, of finesse and of force.

He was not only the superior but the teacher of his priests, and the seminaries in which they were trained were his special concern. The major seminary at Venegono, in the foothills of the Alps near Lake Como, built in the monumental Milanese style, was a model of its kind. In Italy, the cultural currents of the nation are in the main areligious and anticlerical. Seminary students, moreover, are often deprived of a vital cultural climate during their formation, which isolates them further from the life of their country. The major seminary of Milan, with a library of 190,000 volumes, under Montini subscribed to over 200 foreign and Italian publications. The four-year course in theology leads to a pontifical degree, and the three-year course preceding it in philosophy, literature, languages, science and mathematics obliges the students to take the state examinations each year, assuring them of training on a par with other professions. The theology students take a two-year course in sociology and an additional one in religious sociology. Visiting specialists lecture on psychology, psychiatry, labor conditions, the films, etc. There is a one-week course for all priests on current problems, soon expected to be lengthened to a one-month residence at the seminary for periodic mental retooling. The diocese receives a high proportion of delayed vocations, workers among them, with about ten each year coming directly from the university and others from technical schools.

At the seminary of pastoral theology, established by Cardinal Schuster at the request of Pius XII in 1952, young priests take courses in religious sociology, catechetics, preaching and popular apologetics. There are lay professors who teach special subjects; the classes are open and informal, with lectures always followed by discussion. On weekends the priests go back to their parishes for pastoral work. All of the dioceses which are suffragan to Milan were invited by Montini to use the facilities of this highly specialized and thoroughly modern seminary.

The perspective on the formation of priests in the Milan archdiocese under Montini tended, without it being a conscious purpose, to dissipate much of the anticlericalism of the Italians. It has been pointed out that where there is anticlericalism there must first be clericalism: "This factor implies that those who make ecclesiastical decisions often tend to see the problems, tasks, risks and achievements of the Christian life solely from the perspective of the priest as an ecclesiastical official. It results in denying to God's creation its proper ontological value. This is what Père Congar has called the inability to see the values involved in the secular as secular. This tendency is increased by the false extension of the monastic outlook . . . which sees the secular only as the object of ascetic exercises. . . . Clericalism . . . combines with formalism and authoritarianism to impose its own view upon the laity, who, trained under clerical influence, are passive, although often demurring, in the face of such attitudes." [4]

Nietzsche wrote of priests "to darken the sky, to extinguish the sun, to make joy suspect and hope worthless, to lame the diligent hand—these are things which they have always known excellently how to do." Christ called them the salt of the earth, and yet Bernanos calls hatred of the priest one of the most profound of human emotions and also one of the least understood. "There is no doubt," he says in *Monsieur Ouine*, "that it is as old as the human race itself." Montini's charge to his seminarians and priests was a positive one: to witness in the world while remaining men not of the world—a sensitive charge. The priest who, in order to protect his priest-

[4] Thomas F. O'Dea, *American Catholic Dilemma* (New York: Sheed & Ward, 1958), p. 159.

hood, would see the world simply as an enemy, as a contradiction of all he stands for, would have little effect on it; he would generate repugnance and hostility instead of love. "The priest who merely rejects or damns all that interests the world, whose attitude varies from hostility to indifference will, in turn, be rejected by the world, and yet the world expects more of the priest than that he should show some understanding of it and be ready to meet it; it rejects those priests who can give it only what is human; it expects from them that other thing, for even his enemies see in the priest a higher power." [5]

"A true, a good, a human, a saintly priesthood," Archbishop Montini said, "would save the world. The mission of the spirit cannot be contested. Even atheism has its own agitators, ideally devoted to its cause. . . . The capacity to express the ineffable truths that surround us, to approach without profanation the mystery that envelops the universe, to give a meaning to material things, an interior language to the spirit and a resounding voice to man's labor, to his sorrow, to his love—this capacity is nothing but prayer, a prayer that must be true as light, a prayer that like light is poetry and reality as well. All this *is* priesthood. And this capacity is still alive in the heart of the twentieth century."

The training received in the seminaries of the Milan archdiocese gave the men educated there insights into men and their situation which made it increasingly possible for them to identify with their progressive archbishop, and the change in mood and fervor in Milan was observed and marveled at by the Milanese themselves. [6]

[5] Josef Sellmain, *The Priest in the World* (London: Burns, Oates, 1954), p. 219.

[6] A recent study by Joseph H. Fichter, S.J., "Anticlericalism in American Catholic Culture" (*The Critic,* Feb.-March 1963, p. 15) makes the interesting point: "Where both priests and people are liberal and progressive, the practice of the faith is high. Where the clergy are

During his eight years in Milan, Archbishop Montini addressed eight pastoral letters to the faithful of his archdiocese, the first issued in 1956; its theme, Jesus Christ. There followed: The Religious Sense, Liturgical Education, The Meaning of Easter, The Christian Family, The Moral Sense, The Council (Vatican II), and his final letter, The Christian and Temporal Welfare. They are distinguished not only by erudition, by research and knowledge to which the numerous footnotes alone attest, but by the grasp the archbishop reveals of the problems and anxieties of his people, many living divided lives in a divided world. There is a vigorous affirmation of the perennial efficacy of the Christian gospel, tempered by sympathetic comprehension of the world as it is; an attempt to effect a fusion in his people's lives of their Christian faith and the good which is in the world. In these letters the archbishop sees the world, despite its perils, as the stage on which the drama of man's salvation is mounted, and thus one which in its way is holy and full of mystery. A vigorous and complete faith expressed through vitality of worship is the answer held out to those who seek for peace and purposiveness in the century of anxiety.

In addition to the pastoral letters there were the pastoral visitations made to every parish in the archdiocese. The archbishop was intensely aware that it is in and through the parish that the people are instructed and sacramentalized, and that

---

traditionalists and the people are progressive the practice of the faith is low. Where both clergy and people are conservative, religious practices are middling. . . . The most important conclusion . . . is the fact that the liberal laity has a tendency to be pro-clergy, while the conservative laity tends to be anti-clergy. On every item that could be used in our study as an index of lay attitudes toward the clergy, the liberal laymen are more favorable to the priests than are conservative laymen. . . . The kinds of lay people who are constantly cited as being restless and disturbed about the position of the laity—these are the best friends the priests and Church have."

they in turn enrich society by the fervor and vigor of their Christian lives. He sought, therefore, to assure that every parish was well administered by the clergy, and that the people were served in all their needs. In his eight years as archbishop, he was able to make a thorough visitation of 649 parishes out of a total of 822, an extraordinary and exhausting accomplishment against the background of his other obligations and activities. The visit to each parish was also the occasion for the administration of the sacrament of Confirmation, an opportunity to meet the people, to talk to the children and ask them questions about their faith. To one little boy who told him, in answer to his question, that God made us to know, love and serve Him, the archbishop said: "Very good indeed! You know more than a philosopher."

The archbishop's attitude toward Catholic education was revealed in an address delivered in 1958 in Milan at the interregional meeting of the Italian Federation of Church Schools. After greeting those present and encouraging them to do all in their power to perfect their pedagogical methods, he said in part: "We must remember above all else that the best defense of our schools is their excellence. If the schools are sound and good, if they provide direction as well as education, if they give satisfaction to parents and to society, they are well defended, and to this defense ecclesiastical authority will give its approval and support. . . . We might be tempted to think that after so much effort and the construction of so many buildings, our schools have reached a final standard, and that we could say we have done everything in our power, that we have reached the peak of efficiency; consequently, that there is nothing more to be done. The reply to this is that, on the contrary, we must believe in the progressive improvement of our schools, not in a spirit of dissatisfaction with the schools of the past but because the improvement of our schools is part of a broader transformation in the life of the people.

. . . The culture that is permeating even the least educated classes has stirred up consciences, opened up horizons, changed customs, created a new mentality, so that if our schools wish to keep abreast of the times, they must be willing to change.

"Other countries have done much to improve their schools . . ." he continued. "We have far to go. The first point is this: we must put an end to poorly conducted schools which struggle for existence, their aim not sound pedagogy but the keeping alive of a community, or providing for the maintenance of other institutions of the Catholic world. Our schools in the hands of responsible and experienced religious congregations or ecclesiastical authorities must not be mediocre; they must strive for perfection in every detail. Our schools must know how to really educate, how to form strong souls, form the consciences of those for whom the Christian way of life is not a veneer and who lead a true interior life, who demonstrate the manner in which we must live today in order to give witness to Christ and to serve society by loving our neighbor.

"Our schools are attended by children whose parents sometimes undo what the school does; we must not overlook this problem. . . . I believe there should be a little more discipline, more insistence on study, more submission on the part of pupils to authority. I take the liberty of suggesting that relations between teacher and pupil be more personal. To be successful, education must be the result of a dialogue and of the meeting of one soul with another. We must do everything possible to provide, especially for our colleges, spiritual directors who are truly learned, truly reasonable, and able to instill dynamic and strong principles into the minds of the students. . . . A school which stresses only scholarship imparts instruction but leaves souls dissatisfied and indifferent. . . .

"Having said this, we hope that our schools will be transformed, improved, perfected, not in a spirit of rivalry but in a spirit of collaboration with other schools, including public or State schools. . . . These are my sentiments regarding the service you are rendering the Church, and I am not only asking you for greater sacrifices and great efforts, but wish to express my hope for your greater success and your greater rewards."

Archbishop Montini's affection for youth continued undiminished during his years in Milan. An indication of his interest was the founding in 1957 of the Overseas College attached to the university, especially for Catholic students from underdeveloped countries. Indians, Africans, South Americans, Syrians and Indonesians were among those granted the opportunity of a free education. The archbishop's interest was again personal, not merely administrative. Each year it was his custom to invite the students to his home for dinner on the feast of the Epiphany. He chose the day, he told them, as being the feast significant of the universality of the Church, and he said, "it could not be passed better than in the company of representatives of the peoples of the world."

He knew of the students' nostalgia for home, and told them that as their father he wanted to be with them and if possible diminish somewhat their loneliness, at least for a day. Of each he would ask his name and country, and each was surprised at the archbishop's knowledge of their country, large or small —the world of the Vatican had been an informative one! He spoke to them in Italian, in French, in English or in Spanish and laughed with them if he made a mistake. He gave each a book; the first year, two large volumes on Saint Paul, and in successive years books on Milan and other subjects. He posed uncomplainingly for snapshots, and it was his custom to give each foreign student cards of blessing signed for his family and for his bishop.

On October 9, 1958, the Pope of Peace, Pius XII, died, wracked with illness and exhausted by years. Archbishop Montini flew to Rome to pray at his bier. The College of Cardinals which met to elect a successor to the dead Pope was a reduced one; there had been no consistory since 1953, and only 53 gathered in the Sistine Chapel to elect the one who would follow a Pontiff who had reigned for eighteen years. The archbishop of Milan, which is traditionally a see headed by a cardinal, was not among them. He had been an archbishop for almost five years, easily the best known of Italy's prelates, his words and actions observed and quoted in the world press, mentioned as a possible successor to the man he had served for so many years—but he was not a cardinal and it is from the College of Cardinals that the Popes are elected. For four hundred years they have been Italian; for the most part, leaders of the large Italian sees such as Florence, Palermo, Naples, Turin, Bologna and Venice. The conclave was brief;[7] the choice fell to the short, rotund patriarch of Venice, the benign, unknown seventy-eight-year Angelo Roncalli. And the most famous and short-lived reign in modern papal history began.

The new Pope was not long in calling a secret consistory to replenish the depleted College which had elected him. On December 15, 1958, twenty-three prelates were named by him to receive the cardinal's hat—the first name on the list was that of the archbishop of Milan. This time he would not refuse because, unlike the offer made in 1953, this was also a gesture of affection toward the archdiocese which he led. Milan exploded with pride and joy. It was no secret that the Milanese had, since Montini's appointment to be their archbishop, waited with increasingly ill-concealed impatience for Pius XII to recognize his one-time closest collaborator and their city. But

[7] It is said that Archbishop Montini received at least one vote in the conclave.

Pius died without naming his "beloved son" to a seat in the senate of the Church. John XXIII corrected the oversight with a graciousness and purposiveness which was not lost on those who weigh the winds of the Vatican.

As apostolic delegate in Bulgaria and Turkey, later as nuncio in Paris, John XXIII had often reported to Montini in the Secretariat of State. In the absence of a Cardinal Secretary of State, the then Sostituto and later Pro-Secretary was, together with Tardini, a superior of Roncalli's, and the affection and esteem which characterized their infrequent meetings as archbishop of Milan and patriarch of Venice dated from those earlier days.[8] It had been thought that the new Pope would call Montini from Milan to be his Secretary of State, but it was the other half of the Montini-Tardini combination who was named. Montini was to stay in his pivotal position in Lombardy, working and preaching and traveling in ways which would have been severely limited had he been back in the Curia.

Cardinal Montini was formally elevated to the cardinalate by Pope John XXIII at a public consistory in Saint Peter's Basilica on December 18, 1958, the first in the long list of new cardinals which included his former colleague in the Secretariat of State, Monsignor Domenico Tardini, and the apostolic delegate to the United States, Archbishop Amleto Cicognani. Among the thirteen Italian and ten non-Italian cardinals elevated at this time, men from eight nations were represented; two were from the United States—Archbishop Richard Cushing of Boston and Archbishop John O'Hara of Philadelphia. Cardinals Antonio Barbieri of Uruguay and

[8] An interesting incident is related in a French paper, describing Monsignor Roncalli's preparations, in 1944, for a flight back to Rome from Ankara in an old army plane. In answering the line on the questionnaire: "In case of accident, please notify ———" he wrote, not the name of a relative, but the words: "Monsignor Montini, Vatican."

José Garibi y Rivera of Mexico were the first ever to be appointed from their countries. Pope John had described them all as having "in pontifical missions, at the head of dioceses or in the Roman Curia, spent themselves actively, zealously and prudently, and thus greatly contributed to the progress of the Christian religion." There were those among them who because of their own activities or the growing importance of the sees they governed had become prominent in recent times, and several of these were distinguished by their youth. Bishop Julius Doepner of Berlin (later of Munich) was at 45 the youngest cardinal; Bishop Franz König of Vienna, was only 53.

Before returning to Milan, Cardinal Montini took possession of his titular church in Rome—SS. Sylvester and Martin on the Esquiline Hill—a church under the direction of the Carmelites and built in eighteenth-century style. There had been a church on the spot dedicated to the two saints ever since the time of Pope Sergius II (844-847), and even prior to this there was one on the site dedicated to Saint Martin of Tours in the time of Pope Symmachus (498-514). Charles Borromeo had SS. Sylvester and Martin as his titular church; it had also been the titular church of Cardinal Achille Ratti and of Cardinal Ildefonso Schuster. Cardinal Montini now truly belonged to Milan.

7. Portrait of a Cardinal

The new cardinal's pace continued unabated. His daily routine was an exhausting one. By six-thirty every morning he was up and on his way to chapel, through his private study where two photographs—his mother's and his father's—faced his desk together with three small pictures in Byzantine style. His Mass was served by his secretary, Don Macchi, and he in turn served the secretary's Mass. He finished matins, lauds, and prime of his daily office before breakfast, which he ate as he scanned all of the Milanese newspapers. The cardinal had a standing order at one of the newsstands near his residence for any extraordinary editions to be brought to him immediately. On days when he had no pastoral visits planned, he received his vicar general promptly at nine-thirty, followed by the other audiences of the day. These would continue until one or two in the afternoon.[1]

[1] "I could not ask of him (Ambrose) what I wished as I wished, for I was kept from any face to face conversation with him by the throng of men with their own troubles, whose infirmities he served. The very little time he was not with these he was refreshing either his body with necessary food or his mind with reading. . . . No one was forbidden to approach him. . . ." *The Confessions of St. Augustin.* Tr. by F. J. Sheed (New York: Sheed & Ward, 1943), pp. 107-8.

The impression made by the cardinal on his visitors was memorable. At sixty-one the abrasive effects of his Vatican service and five years in Milan were visible. He showed the quiet patience and deep-etched tolerance of humanity and its importunities to be found in men who have given exhaustively of themselves and are in consequence devoid of any human posturing or pretense. For years he had lived the life of another man, and no matter how lovingly and willingly he had served, the diminution of his own will and desires, thousands of times confected, had given him a discipline and dignity of impressive dimensions.

His gentleness was apparent. His hands, long and thin and curiously white, the veins high and bluely visible, rested delicately on the black of his cassock or on the desk as he listened to his visitor; they did not, in a kind of episcopal self-consciousness, play with the pectoral cross. His eyes, full of reserve and yet alive, meditatively studied the visitor as they chatted. For most Italians it is the hands that provide nuance to the words. In the cardinal it was the eyes—bright, gray-green, changing color with his mood. His voice was low, with a gently grating undertone, perfectly modulated.

His person could be called confusing. He had always been slim, but without angularity. There was an economy about his person, words and gestures which seemed a human articulation of Mies van der Rohe's architectural principle: "Less is more." His smile was not served by the straightness of his lips; it seemed somewhat wintry, but there were always the eyes to reveal the warmth and light of the man.

After dinner, his main meal of the day, he would take a short nap.[2] He would finish his breviary in the chapel of his residence and promptly at four-thirty he was at his desk again.

[2] Later, after his election, he caused consternation at the Vatican court by saying that he had lost the Roman habit of siesta while in Milan.

He preferred to write longhand, although on a table nearby was the white typewriter which had belonged to Pius XII. Supper was light, and was followed by a viewing of the news of the day on television. The rosary was recited together with the priests of his household, the cardinal preferring to say it with them as he walked up and down in the library or in the corridor lined with books.

At his desk in the library, Cardinal Montini then continued to work far into the night. Occasionally he would relax before the television set if a good comedy was being shown; his taste in music centered on Beethoven, Chopin and Mozart. But usually in his hours of relaxation he preferred to read. If he could be said to have any hobbies they were reading and traveling. Books were a passion with him,[3] and his residence was a veritable arsenal of them. Every month the director of the Saint Paul Bookshop would receive a list of the latest books desired by the cardinal. "How many books there are!" he said one day when visiting the bookstore. "One would need a long life and much time to read all that one would want"; he said it almost wistfully. His reading was far ranging. Years earlier he had translated Maritain's *Three Reformers* into Italian, and he retained his admiration for the gentle Frenchman whom he had come to know personally when the latter was French ambassador to the Vatican in the immediate postwar years. Thomas Mann, Camus, Bernanos, Congar, De Lubac, Charles Journet, Louis Bouyer, Danielou—these were his favorites. Jean Guitton of the French Academy had been long accustomed to sending Montini his books as they appeared. When Guitton sent him *The Church and the Gospel,* the cardinal wrote thanking him and said he had stayed up all night reading it.

He criticized writers who say that they need "to have ex-

---

[3] He had brought 90 cases of books with him to Milan, with many American treatises on sociology and economics among them.

perience of evil," and to a congress of Italian authors he said: "The temptation for knowledge of evil has a strong attraction. There are those who say that it is necessary to have experience of evil to write about good. This is not true. Above all things, keep yourself pure and do not be afraid to put great theses in your writings." His taste in art was conservative: "Artists," he said, "seem to have abandoned the idea of producing works which are intelligible," and critics "use language that requires a special knowledge in order to understand the meaning. . . . We, the audience, make pathetic efforts to understand at least something. We believed that the kingdom of art was beatitude, whereas today it is pain and confusion."

His usual hour for retiring was two in the morning. Four or five hours of sleep were enough for him, but his spareness of face and figure was due in large part to the rigor of the demanding life which he had lived ever since his ordination. The harsh Milan winter caused him much trouble with colds and influenza, but apart from these "annoyances," as he called them, his pace was that of a man many years his junior. It was now to quicken.

In June of 1960 the cardinal arrived in New York for his second visit to the United States in nine years; it was to be a brief stay of seven days. He had accepted the invitation of Notre Dame University to be the recipient, together with President Eisenhower, Dr. Tom Dooley and others, of an honorary degree at the annual commencement. The United States is not yet accustomed to European prelates of Montini's stature arriving for routine reasons, and the usual speculations were rife. The "real reason," it was adduced, lay in the need to reassure the American Church that a recent editorial in *Osservatore Romano* affirming the Church's "right and duty" to instruct the faithful on how to vote did not apply to this country since Marxism was not an issue. However, since editorials do not shape the thinking or action of the American Church in such delicate areas, and since the cardinal loved to travel, his presence here could be sought and found simply in his desire to see more of a country for which he had on many occasions expressed his admiration and to which he had been specially invited on this occasion by the president of a great university.

After celebrating an outdoor pontifical Mass for the graduates of Notre Dame and their guests on June 5th, Cardinal Montini spoke briefly and informally. "The university world is one of research and is, therefore, humble and attentive in the face of truth," he said. "The university world is one which teaches and, therefore, it serves and spreads the truth." Noting that it was Pentecost Sunday and that the message of Pentecost is the message of truth, the cardinal continued: "How fitting it would be on this day to study this fundamental aspect of our religion, and to clarify for ourselves the concept of the system of truth which Christianity creates in the world. Saint Augustine, freshly converted by Saint Ambrose, asked as his first desire to eliminate from himself the worst infirmity of the mind, the lack of confidence in arriving at the truth." And he told them that "the university must understand that the divine design of truth is for us a vocation, a blessing, a duty."

Later in the day, at the commencement exercises, the future Pope and the President of the United States[4] received their honorary doctor in law degrees from Notre Dame's president. The citation accompanying that of the cardinal saluted him as "a Prince of the Church who has brought the Christian vision to bear, with extraordinary practical success, on the harsh political and social realities of our time. Through his

---

[4] At this meeting with President Eisenhower, the cardinal offered him a statuette of an angel breaking chains. In writing later to thank him, the President said: "Dear Cardinal Montini, before leaving for the Far East I wish to thank you for the expressive statuette which you gave me at Notre Dame last Sunday. It can be a symbol of what I hope to realize on this trip and in my life. . . ."

long and brilliant career in the Vatican Secretariat of State, fulfilling even its highest duties, he came to know those realities well throughout the world, and he directed his great talent and energy to the intellectuals and the workers to renew among them powerfully the moral and spiritual leadership of the Church. . . ." The citation also noted that, "When Pope Pius XII named him Archbishop of Milan, the industrial center of Italy and a stronghold of Communism, he pledged himself to be 'the Archbishop of the workingman,' a pledge which he has fulfilled with inexhaustible apostolic vigor to the strengthening of the Christian world."

New York, Chicago, Boston, Philadelphia, and Washington were included in the cardinal's itinerary on this visit. He had arrived in New York, where he was met by Cardinal Spellman and the apostolic delegate to the United States, Archbishop Egidio Vagnozzi. On his trip to American cities he was accompanied by Frank Folsom, chairman of the executive board of the board of directors of the Radio Corporation of America. Boston gave him, in the words of *Time* magazine, "banners and hi-fied hymns," and while there he took part with Cardinal Cushing in a public ceremony at the Don Orione home for aged Italians. In Washington he was entertained at a dinner given in his honor by the apostolic delegate.

From the United States the cardinal continued on to Sao Paolo and Rio de Janeiro in Brazil. The President of Brazil, Juscelino Kubitschek hailed him as "one of the major figures of our time." The cardinal visited the *favelas* of Rio, and talked to government and church officials about conditions in this country and the explosive continent of South America. His memory of this visit was to be a long one.

From July 19 to August 10, 1962, the cardinal was again away from Milan, this time in Africa. His trip was brief, bringing him to Rhodesia, where he visited the two missions sponsored by his archdiocese, to South Africa, to Nigeria and to Ghana. He was the first cardinal from Europe to visit Africa and his trip gave him a perspective on the reality of Africa's problems and of its progress as its countries sought through their multiple political expressions to take their place in the world community of nations. It was the Church, struggling and vital, which he had come to see, and his visits were largely to missions, churches, seminaries, convents. The names of the towns and cities were like poetry to him—Kariba, Chirundu, Salisbury in Rhodesia; Johannesburg and Pretoria in South Africa; Lagos, Ibadan, Enugu in Nigeria; Accra and Tena in Ghana. Less poetic were the abject conditions resulting from discrimination which he found in certain of the countries and the poverty and illiteracy which, happily, he found everywhere being challenged. Monsignor Macchi, his secretary, remembers driving through Nigeria on the way to Ibadan and passing signs which read: "One God alone is a majority," "The greatest King is God," "Thank God today," "God is my way." And the cardinal would prod him: "Write it down! Write it down!" Everything was new—everything told a story.

The cardinal told his people on his return: "It was for me an extraordinary experience. Perhaps because it concerned the first visit of a European cardinal to their continent, perhaps for other motives, the reception was magnificent. I do not speak of the Italians at Kariba and of the numerous whites whom I met during the trip, but of the native populations: Christians of deep faith, demonstrated on many occasions. We visited many mission stations in South Africa and West Central Africa and were most favorably impressed. Indeed, we must say that the edification received from the religious spirit demonstrated by the Catholic communities we visited did not spare us some pain as we contrasted their fervor with that of our own people, who, while devout and faithful, have lost something of that intensity of faith, that totality of presence, that grace of manner, that beauty of song, that spontaneity of devotion which . . . we admired in the celebration of the sacred ceremonies, in the holy Masses and Communions of the flourishing African churches. We saw how the faith there is lived seriously, being the very center of life. We saw how ardent and dignified is the expression of faith, worship, prayer, devotion among these new Christians. We saw how the youth especially throng to the missionary churches. We heard the singing, full voiced and moving, of the entire community, and we witnessed the celebration in Latin of our festive Masses."

No other trip of his life had impressed Cardinal Montini as had this last one to Africa. He had visited the "locations" in Johannesburg and Pretoria, ridden in a canoe down the Niger with the sound of drums sending word of his coming ahead; he had heard the beauty of the Gregorian chant sung by Africans in their dirt-floor churches; he had seen vistas of natural beauty which overwhelmed him—but above all he had seen people in love with their faith, and he was profoundly influenced by it. On his return he went immediately to Pope John's summer residence at Castelgandolfo to make a two-hour report.

Cardinal Montini was never allowed to be simply the archbishop of Milan. His words and actions for years had been public coin throughout the world. Many who hailed him as a liberal demanded that his every word and action fall resoundingly into a category of highly elastic outline. This they refused to do. Conservatives tended to be critical—and yet on certain positions he was found in their ranks. Without wanting to be, he had become a symbol, and symbols are expected to be univocal; they do not allow of the alternation of attitude and action which through the years confused the symbol-makers. He defied categorization. He did so because he was the man he was, a dispassionate seeker after truth, and such a man is often of necessity ambivalent where the truth is concerned. Such ambivalence would find a natural repugnance in the doctrinaire, conservative or liberal. The doctrinaire liberal, for example, will embrace an idea as an idea, and tend to ignore the context of its implementation. The existential liberal, however, will subject it to scrutiny in the same context, and this latter will be affected by multiple influences.

Cardinal Montini had not been consecrated that he might become a symbol; he had been consecrated to be a pastor of souls. This gave a dimension to his actions in Milan which, while doing no violence to the naturally progressive inclination of his thought, provoked charges of inconsistency and indecisiveness. Pastoral responsibility involved the translating of ideas into actions—not all of them successful—and the context of translation modified at times his known positions. Thus the charge of inconsistency. A sensitive, complex thinker, he sought in translation to make the expression in action the right and complete one, since it was to affect his people. This demanded reflection, sometimes postponement, and always, time. Hence the charge of indecisiveness.

The cardinal's concern with social problems led some to assume too readily that he was leftist politically. His identification with the workers caused some disaffection among the intellectuals, especially since he preached openly his belief that the story of Europe's large-scale apostasy was primarily a tragedy of the intellectuals—those citizens of the eighteenth century who sought to create a self-sufficient society of their own and to reject God's revelation, their "wisdom" sifting down through the middle classes to the proletariat and preparing the ground for the Socialist and Marxist faiths. Yet he was an intellectual himself; the historical or philosophical error was his only target.

Politically the cardinal's sympathies seemed to be some-what left of center; yet he could, in 1960, warn against a flanking movement to the left of the Christian Democratic Party: a proposed alliance with Nenni's Socialists. He made the warning "with regret," and "considering the present state of affairs"—it was the context of the times, the danger of a materialistic overwhelming of the principles of the party or of its left wing which concerned him. "We will not fail to give you other instructions should the circumstances change," he told his priests.[5] So too with the priest-worker movement with which his name had been associated in Rome in its be-ginning years. The idea was considered valid and was en-couraged by him in the late 40's when the more conservative of the Curia urged caution or refusal of permission for the ex-periment. Yet years later in Milan he would voice his regrets and express caution with regard to such experiments through which spiritual considerations ran the danger of being en-gulfed by temporal demands. Again the context must be con-sidered. His speech in Rome, shortly before the opening of the Ecumenical Council, in which he "baptized" the Italian Risorgimento, which led to the creation of an Italian State independent of the Church, was called "flamingly liberal" and "stoutly anti-conservative." Rather, again it was an ob-jective evaluation of a situation stripped of nostalgic attach-ment and outmoded theology.

No one was more devoted to the concept of the freedom of the press. But in the context of his responsibilities as arch-

[5] When, in February 1962, an "eminent lay person" of the Milan archdiocese anonymously deprecated the "new suffering" caused the Church by the alliance of the Center left-wing with the Socialists in forming a government, the archdiocesan daily, *L'Italia,* sharply rebuked the critic, first for his anonymity and secondly for presuming to make his own reaction seem to be that of the Church—which apparently it was not.

bishop he became involved, in 1962, in a case which caused much comment. A bimonthly Milanese newspaper *Adesso*, founded by Father Primo Mazzolari, received a "private warning" from the Holy Office which asked it "to modify the spirit and orientation of the paper which blends so many professions of the Christian Faith with questionable ideas and attitudes." Cardinal Montini, in transmitting the *monitum*, added that since the paper had maintained the same attitude of ill-considered criticism of the hierarchy and regarding the authority of the laity, he himself felt obliged to agree, though with regret, with the reasons for such a warning. In addition he asked that the paper cease collaboration with two French reviews *Esprit* and *Témoignage Chrétien*. In replying to the cardinal, the director of the paper explained that the purpose of the paper was to discuss problems among an adult laity using "those gifts of God, intelligence and liberty."

Adesso decided to suspend publication with its issue of September 15, 1962, stating: "The paper cannot disavow the ideals of its origins and its sense of responsibility by an act of rebellion;[6] nor, on the other hand could it accept an unconditional obedience which would alter the reason for its existence as an interlocutor, and would have reduced it to an organ of the Curia, like so many others, whether armed or not with an imprimatur." The words of Cardinal Newman to W. G. Ward are fitting here: "There have always been differences of opinion in the Church and there always will be, and Christians would cease to have a spiritual and intellectual life at all if such disputes did not occur; for they are members of the

---

[6] "Things which are really useful end by getting done under God's will at the appointed time, and not at any other. If one seeks to do what is right in itself at the wrong time, one may become a heretic or a schismatic. . . . Inward brooding over insults is not patience, but memory with a glance at the future is prudence." Cardinal Newman, quoted by Sellmain, *op. cit.*, p. 216.

Church Militant. No human power can prevent them nor, if it attempted to do so, would it achieve anything but a wilderness which it could rechristen a 'peaceful landscape'! And when I reflect on the fact that no man, however hard he tried, could prevent these things, I do not feel any particular anxiety or disquiet about them. Man cannot do it and God does not desire it."

Again in 1962, Cardinal Montini drew world-wide attention to himself by his action in sending a telegram to the Spanish head of State asking clemency for a young student, Jorge Gonill Valls, and workers condemned, as the cardinal thought, to death by a Spanish court for an act of terrorism. His telegram to Generalissimo Franco read: "In name of Milanese Catholic students and my own, I ask your Excellency to show clemency students and workers condemned so that human lives may be saved and it made clear public order in Catholic country can be defended by methods differing from those which prevail in countries without faith and Christian tradition." The Spanish government replied coolly, indicating that the cardinal had been misinformed, that the offenders had been sentenced not to death but to prison. A spokesman for the Spanish Foreign Office said the procedure followed by the cardinal was "quite unusual in diplomacy." But this many-faceted man had not acted this time as a diplomat—he had reacted as a priest, a pastor, a lover of youth and of workers. The diplomat was eclipsed and the man shone through.

On the 25th of January, 1959, Pope John XXIII went to the Roman Basilica of Saint Paul Outside the Walls to commemorate the feast of the conversion of Saint Paul and to celebrate a Mass for Christian unity. Following it, in the quiet of the monastery adjoining the basilica, the Pope announced to the eighteen cardinals of the Roman Curia present his intention of holding a Council of the Universal Church, "to proclaim the truth, bring Christians closer to the faith, and contribute at the same time to peace and prosperity on earth." He painted for them a picture of a world in convulsion, a world of divided allegiances, of confused morality, a world seeking its destiny in fear and suspicion—a house divided against itself. The Church should, for only the twenty-first time in its two-thousand-year history, hold a Council and in and through it confront the world of its people and of its century. Then, very simply, he said to the cardinals: "I would like to have your advice." They sat silent before him. Not a word was spoken.

The Pope was later to call their silence "devout and impressive." Yet he was disappointed by the lack of response: "Humanly We could have expected that the cardinals, after hearing Our allocution, might have crowded around to express approval and good wishes." That they had not, deeply wounded the Pope, but it did not swerve him from his intention, which he had first expressed to his Secretary of State, Cardinal Tardini. It was the result, not of a carefully reasoned programme for his pontificate, but rather of a spontaneous idea[7] which came to him while talking one day to Tardini about the state of the world and the need of the Church to revitalize its witness. "A Council!"—he had exclaimed—and thus was born the most significant event of modern Christian history.

If the reaction of certain of the Roman cardinals and of segments of the Curia was cautious and restrained, that of the cardinal archbishop of Milan was not. "An historic event of immense grandeur," he wrote when the projected Council was announced, ". . . an event important for peace, for truth, for the spirit; important today for tomorrow, important for

[7] ". . . an inspiration felt in the humility of Our Heart as a sudden, unexpected direct touch." (John XXIII, Letter of April 24, 1959 to the Venetian clergy.)

the people and for human hearts; important for the whole Church, and for all humanity." The *Osservatore Romano* had buried the announcement of the Pope's call to council in the following day's edition, between two items of far less relevance, and the important *Civiltà Cattolica*, a Jesuit bimonthly with semi-official Vatican status, made no mention of the Council until four months later, on May 2. But between its announcement and its convening, Cardinal Montini delivered three major addresses on the Council, and his Lenten pastoral for 1962, *Pensiamo al Concilio* (Let Us Look at the Council), was the most significant of Italian episcopal statements on the subject.

The cardinal cleary was not to be among the "prophets of doom" who were uncomprehending of the Pope's desire to renew the Church.[8] Of the Council, the cardinal said in 1960: "All feel themselves to be on the eve of an extraordinary event. . . . We who have the faith sense obscurely but strongly that such an event has a connection with the mysterious and universal designs of God for the destiny of man, and that it has a particular relationship with the individual conscience of each one of us. . . . Something of the prophetic is abroad in our time . . ." The cardinal went on to say that the manner in which the Council had been conceived was

---

[8] In his address at the solemn opening of Vatican Council II, October 11, 1962, Pope John said: "In the daily exercise of Our pastoral office we sometimes have to listen, much to Our regret, to voices of persons who, although burning with zeal, are not endowed with too much discretion or measure. In these modern times they can see nothing but prevarication and ruin. They say that our era in comparison with past eras is getting worse, and they behave as though they had learned nothing from history, which is nonetheless the teacher of life. They behave as though at the time of former Councils everything was a full triumph for the Christian idea and for proper religious liberty. We feel We must disagree with these prophets of doom who are always forecasting disaster, as though the end of the world were at hand."

something of a surprise, especially for one who had some knowledge of how pontifical acts are conceived; most of them, he said, are born in the departments and offices of the Roman Curia, sometimes exclusively in the minds of those who immediately serve the head of the Church.[9] "But this announcement . . . has its origin in the unique and highly personal will of the Supreme Pontiff. He had no collaborator, no counselor. No one used pressure, no one promised results. And we are not here confronted by a despotic will . . . but rather by one which is naturally inclined to pastoral benevolence, which seeks the good in others and for others, and which promotes it with spontaneous dedication. . . . Without recourse to the theory of a charismatically preternatural impulse, we can safely say . . . that he knew and felt himself to exercise, with the prophetic virtue of his office, that supreme power to which the assistance of the Holy Spirit is promised, as guarantee, by Christ."

Cardinal Montini pointed out that there had been from time to time talk of another Council, "but no one dared to give such a possibility any real hope of foreseeable and concrete realization." He indicated that such thinking in part had its origin in a misinterpretation of what the definition of papal infallibility in the First Vatican Council had effected in the Church, namely the mistaken idea that the Bishop of Rome had absorbed and annulled the universal functions of the body of bishops.[10] The solemn dogmatic definition of the Assumption by Pius XII, preceding which he had consulted

[9] Cf. Xavier Rynne, *Letters from Vatican City* (New York: Farrar, Straus & Co., 1963), p. 25.

[10] The doctrine of the collegiality of the bishops was given little recognition by the preparatory theological commission in its schema on the Church prepared in 1961-62 under the chairmanship of Cardinal Ottaviani during the first session of the Council. Cardinal Montini's sharpest intervention criticized the failure.

the bishops of the world singly but not the entire body of bishops in collegiate assembly, seemed to lend some credence to such a distortion. But, the cardinal said, "The forecast that the epoch of Councils had come to an end was laid to rest by the spontaneous initiative of the Pope." The Council is, he continued, a solemn reunion of all the bishops of the world, one in which they participate by divine right. The authority of the Pope, convoking and confirming, is necessary for the Council to be truly ecumenical. But no matter what its importance to the Church, no Council is a permanent institution such as a parliament; it is not a synthesis of the whole Church; it does not transform the Church into a corporation represented and directed by a sovereign assembly to which the Pope himself is subject. "The Council is an episode in the life of the Church, a particular moment that calls forth the supreme authority of the Church; but it does not create that authority, it exercises it."

The cardinal quickly synthesized the Councils through the ages. Of Trent he said, "The Council of Reform . . . saved the dogma and the discipline of the Church but signalized the fatal separation of whole Christian peoples now designated by the sad name of Protestant." The Vatican Council defined the doctrine of the infallibility of the Pope but Montini approvingly quoted the statement of "eminent theologians" that "the problem of the reconciliation of the divine rights of the episcopacy with the divine rights of the Pope unhappily has not yet been thoroughly discussed. A well balanced theology of the Church demands above all that this question be posed. . . . Will this be the work of the Second Vatican Council? It is a secret hidden in the future." To these words the cardinal added: "Perhaps this secret will be disclosed in this much desired Vatican Council for which we are preparing. . . ." As the date of the Council approached, the cardinal stated: "We are thus at the threshold of the new Ecumenical Council, and we are naturally tempted to predict what it will be like. It is difficult to say. . . . Important events are transpiring around us; we must be vigilant, we must seek to understand the designs of God, the movement of history, the inspirations of the Spirit, the hour of responsibility."

In his addresses and pastoral letters, the cardinal returned more than once in those pre-Council days of great expectations with a quiet word of warning against overexpectation and too great a personalizing of the Council. "Each one of us has some imaginative concept of himself as a reformer of the Church, and naturally each hopes that the time has come for the realization of his dream. If the Council corresponds to the plans of God, it is difficult, no matter how fine our own plans, to see how it will respond to our exact desires." And again: "It is necessary to avoid fostering capricious desires which are arbitrary and strictly personal. It is not necessary that the Council correspond to our particular viewpoint; we ought rather enter into the general perspectives of the Council. To believe that the Council will be able to repair human fragility and immediately bring about perfection in the Church and in the world is an ingenuous dream. To hope that it will remedy the many inconvenient practices and also the many theoretical imperfections in Catholic life which each one meets with in his own experience as a member or observer . . . is to hope too much. . . . We must guard against thinking that the Council will decree radical and bewildering reforms in the present structure of the Church, such changes as to alter its appearance in time and to make it a wholly new institution. . . . The present juridical structure of the Church certainly has need of some renovation, but the Church cannot be substantially changed; [the present structure] is not the result of infidelity to the genuine mind of Christ . . . it is rather the result of an historical experience promoted by a rigorous intention of coherence and of fidelity to the spirit of the divine Founder. . . .

"The Council . . . will give revised programs on the discipline and on the worship of the Church; it will give directives and precepts in many sectors needful of correction, of bringing up to date, and of development. . . . The Council will not be measured purely by its good results juridically and ritually considered. It must be a moment of the ineffable presence of the loving and merciful action of God in His Church."

The cardinal did not hesitate to confront boldly the notion and the possibility of reform within the Church, and the need for it, a possibility and a need which many were denying in the "spotless Bride of Christ." "Reform has been through the centuries the renewing ferment of Catholic tradition." The cardinal pointed out that the Church can be seen under two aspects, divine and human, with the latter calling for periodic renewal. "Reform, therefore, is a perennial effort in the Church, which tends to bring the divine idea close to reality, and to put the human reality in touch with the divine." "The characteristic of this Council," the cardinal continued, "while aiming expressly at some notable reforms, derives from a desire to call forth the good rather than to flee from evil. Thanks to divine mercy, there are not in the Church today, errors, scandals, deviations, abuses. . . . Today the Church, always by the grace of God and the merit of so many good and holy Christians, is rather in a state of suffering and of weakness than in a state of scandal and decadence. The condition and aspect of the Church shows it as more wounded than sinning, more needful than unfaithful. . . . The Council will be, therefore, a Council of positive reforms, rather than of punitive ones; one of exhortation rather than of anathemas."

"The Church . . . intends through the forthcoming Council to come in contact with the world. This is a great act of charity. The Church will not think only of herself; the Church will think of all humanity. To this end she will seek to be sister and mother to men; she will seek to be poor, simple, humble and lovable in her language and manner . . . she will seek to make herself understood, and to give to the men of today the opportunity to hear her and to herself the opportunity to speak to men with ease in the language of today."

Referring to Christians separated from the unity of the Catholic Church, the cardinal said of the Council: "It will very probably not be able to solve this question. Perhaps we have not yet merited such a miracle. But the Ecumenical Council can prepare for this hoped for solution. Under this aspect it will be a Council of preparation, a Council of desire."

The cardinal, by his speeches and in his pastoral letters, sought to give the historical setting and the theological basis for the Council, in order that the generations who had lived their lives in a "council-less" period might know its significance by first understanding its context. His warning against vain and ephemeral hope seemed to be conditioned not by his personal lack of high expectations from the reforming Council, but rather by his wish to create a climate of objective, sober and prayerful appraisal. His words were addressed for the most part to the laity, and to them he held out hopes of a vigorous restatement and implementation from the Council of their high vocation in and to the Church. The words with regard to separated Christians, which occur again and again in his pre-Council addresses, are words of affection and sensitive appreciation of their role in witnessing to Christ. At the same time he expresses the caution of one who knows the dimensions of the gulf separating Christian bodies and who will not allow his enthusiasm to mislead and defeat the very cause he would advance.

In all his pre-Council speeches and writings, Cardinal Montini's affection for the great Pope who had called the

Council is marked, his sense of the Pope's prophetic destiny profound; "A great hope is kindled in the Church. Blessed is he who has made this light of hope shine forth!" The hunger of the world for the words and prayers of the Council was not unknown to the cardinal; repeatedly in his life in Milan he had witnessed to the need of the Church to speak in twentieth-century terms to a twentieth-century world grown indifferent to a Church which appeared in a way to be a magnificent anachronism. In Council the cardinal would show no patience toward those who sought to thwart this move into the century of the bomb, the century of anxiety, the century of everyman.

The cardinal's public role in the Council was to be a muted one.[11] He was named to the Central Commission, principal organ of preparation for the Council and to the technico-administrative commission as well as to the new and sensitive Secretariat of Extraordinary Affairs. He was one of a group of seven cardinals, four Italian, one American, one Western European, and one Central European,[12] commissioned to ex-

[11] It is reported that Cardinal Montini helped compose Pope John XXIII's remarkable opening address to the Council on October 11, 1962.

In the context of the cardinal's minor public contribution to the Council session, an article by the Abbé René Laurentin in *Le Figaro* (June 22-25) contains an interesting aside. The Abbé reports asking the cardinal's theologian during the first session, "Why doesn't your cardinal say more? We expect so much of him." The Abbé says he was later informed (not by the theologian in question) that the cardinal had been advised by John XXIII to remain in the background during the first session. The Abbé adds: *"La dernière vue à long terme du Pape qui vient de nous quitter a été d'écarter les obstacles sur les voies difficiles qu'il savait devoir être celles de l'élection de son successeur."*

[12] The Italians were Cardinals Cicognani, Siri, Confalioneri; the American, Cardinal Meyer of Chicago; the Western European, Cardinal Suenens of Malines-Brussels; the Central European, Cardinal Doepfner of Munich.

amine new questions raised or submitted by the Fathers of
the Council, apart from those already presented and inte-
grated in the various schema. It was noted that the average
age of the cardinals composing this Secretariat was a relatively young sixty-six, and that the presence of Montini,
Meyer, Doepfner and Suenens gave it a majority of progressive complexion.

Cardinal Montini went often to Rome in the days before
the opening of the Council, flying in one hour from Milan
and returning the same day when possible. During the days
that he was in Rome for the Council he alone of all the
Fathers of the Council was the guest of Pope John in the
Vatican. An apartment in the Archpriest's Palace was placed
at his disposal and it was he whose prerogative it was, as the
first cardinal named by Pope John, to celebrate on November 4, in the presence of the whole Council, the Mass for the
fourth anniversary of the Pope's coronation. He offered the
Mass in the Ambrosian rite of Milan, rarely if ever used before in the Basilica of Saint Peter. November 4th was also
the feast of Saint Charles Borromeo, a predecessor in the
see of Milan, who had vigorously reformed the Church of
Milan after the Council of Trent. In his sermon that day the
Pope recalled Borromeo's role at the Tridentine Council in
pacifying the disputing Fathers and his intervention which
brought it to a successful close. No such role had yet been
cast at this Council, although the differences which would
give vigorous life to its sessions were already evident.[13]

Cardinal Montini spoke briefly in the opening days of the
Council on the schema of the liturgy, and his voice was not

[13] Jean Guitton sees the two tendencies, Progressive/Conservative,
in the Council not as opposite but as parallel columns which end in a
magnificent Gothic arch. The Council cannot be conceived as a battlefield; the "triumph" of one tendency over the other he sees as incon-
ceivable and meaningless.

to be heard publicly again until December 5, when the schema on the Church was debated. The archbishop of Malines-Brussels, Cardinal Suenens, had spoken the previous day, criticizing the schema as presented to the Council, asking its revision and requesting a consideration of the Church in dialogue not only with itself but with the world, and a confrontation of the questions which the latter dialogue would raise. On December 5th, the cardinal of Milan rose to speak and he gave wholehearted support to Cardinal Suenens' suggestion. The Church, he said, is nothing by itself; the Church is Christ Himself, using us as His instruments to bring salvation to mankind. He called on the Fathers of the Council to restate the "mind and will of Christ" by defining the collegiality of the episcopate and by giving a truly ecumenical perspective to the Church. The less we insist on the rights of the Church, he said, the more chance we have of being heard. Thus, because of its intransigent and incomplete character, he urged that the schema on the Church be completely revised.

His intervention, the more dramatic for its singularity, was made against the background of his letter published in the Milan diocesan daily, *L'Italia*. In it he criticized the members of the Council who refused to follow its ecumenical and *aggiornamento* character, but more strikingly he blamed the Council's failure to make greater progress on those members of Curia who had prevented cooperation between the various commissions during the preparatory phase.[14]

The cardinal's position before and during the Council was one of enthusiastic endorsement of the idea of the Council, of the Pope's insistence that it be a Council in dialogue with the world, that it be one which would open windows in the Church. Each week while the Council was in session he wrote a letter to the people of his archdiocese to keep them in-

[14] Rynne, *op. cit.*, p. 227.

formed of the Council's progress. His pastoral concern was that they be involved through him who spoke in their name. He told them of the Council's slowness, of its uncertainty at times; of the excessive number of speakers who slowed its pace (necessary, he added, in an assembly of free men freely speaking). He was critical of some of the phases of its organization but enthusiastic about the climate of freedom which it was daily creating.[15]

That he himself was not so much to the forefront of the Council's public shapers and speakers as his personal and pastoral reputation would seem to warrant was less an indication of his reluctance to be committed than it was of a desire to allow men of similar thinking but of less international reputation to come forth and speak in other than Italian voices. His concern that the Church appear and actually be international was rewarded by the emergence of Dutch, Belgian, French, German, and American prelates as movers of the Church's majority will that *aggiornamento* be the cornerstone of the Council's deliberations. When it was necessary to speak, the Cardinal spoke; for the rest he was content to be a Father of the Council together with the other largely anonymous 2,600 bishops.

The first session closed on December 8. Pope John, whose health had given reason for serious preoccupation, was present to close the session and to send the bishops back to their dioceses with the exhortation to continue the Council's work before the convening of the second session on September 8, 1963. He also issued a directive which established a new coordinating commission to guide the Council's working commissions during its recess. Its function was to reduce the 70 schemata of the first session to 17, insuring their brevity and irenic tone. Headed by the Cardinal Secretary of State it was to continue through the second session and effect a speeding

[15] Letter of November 4.

up and more efficient handling of the work of the Council. The establishment of the steering committee was seen as an implementation of Cardinal Montini's desire, expressed long before the Council convened, for procedures on a more efficient basis. He had said of the material proposed for Council consideration: "It is a question of an immense body of material, excellent but heterogeneous and unequal, which would have evoked a courageous reduction and classification if one authority, one that was not merely extrinsic and disciplinary, had dominated the logical and organic preparation of these magnificent volumes [of schemata] and if one central architectural idea had polarized this considerable work."

The commissions of the Council would have nine months of hard work before them. Cardinal Montini was to be a part of that silent and hidden work as in Milan he prepared for the Christmas which would be his last as archbishop of that historic see.

8.   Sede Vacante

The death of a Pope has always provided a moment of drama in history. From the death of Peter on an upended cross, through the long series of Popes who were saints and Popes who were not, the world has watched down the centuries with varying attitudes of detachment and involvement as pontificates drew to an end and the men who made them prepared to meet the God whose servants they had been.

Most of the twenty-two Popes who into the fourteenth century bore the name of John reigned briefly and unspectacularly. The man who, in 1958, at the age of seventy-eight succeeded to the papal throne as John XXIII, the patriarch of Venice, Angelo Roncalli, seemed destined therefore by name and by years to a pontificate which would be short and decorous, unmarked by innovation, strong leadership or impact on the world. But by a goodness which quickly became legendary, by a boldness which affronted the few and delighted the many, he threw open his arms to all men and revolutionized a Church grown remote from the world it was meant to savor. He was a man in a hurry, impatient of anathemas, of cant and gloom, with a mind and spirit as young as his body was old, and the world, with unprecedented affection, wished for him long length of days as, at the age of eighty-two, he opened the Second Vatican Council, a symbol of the Second Spring which his pontificate had become to the Church.

In November of 1962, during the Council session, the Pope fell ill. He rallied and was able, seemingly with his customary vigor, to close the first session on December 8th. But there were signs that all was not well as the Pope entered 1963. Audiences were canceled and it was apparent everything was being done to conserve his strength. Increasingly he made reference to "sister death." On May 21st it was announced that President Kennedy had changed his plans for a 1964 visit to the Pope and would arrive in June. On May 22nd a general audience was canceled, and the Vatican, cautious while the world speculated, announced that the Pope was to take nine days of complete rest before Pentecost.

Then on May 26th came word of the Pope's serious illness, a malignancy, and the world's vigil began. Informed by his Secretary of State of the prayers being said for him, the Pope, according to the *Osservatore Romano,* replied: "As the whole world prays for the sick Pope, it is quite natural that an intention be given to this supplication; if God desires the sacrifice of the Pope's life, may it serve to bring down copious favors on the Ecumenical Council, on the holy Church, and on humanity which aspires to peace. If, on the other hand, it pleases God to prolong the Pontiff's service, may this bring a sanctification of the soul of the Pope, and of all those who work with him and suffer for the expansion of the Kingdom of Our Lord. . . ." Sounding more his own were the words he had spoken on his eighty-first birthday: "Any day is a good day to be born and a good day to die. I always think of that other shore and submit to the will of the Lord, whether he decides to keep me here or call me to Him." To his doctor he said:

"Do not worry too much about me, because my bags are packed and I am ready to leave, in fact very ready."

On Friday, May 31st, hope was abandoned for the Pope, whose strong heart continued to beat against the assault of his infection. He remained lucid, although in a state of extreme weakness. At one juncture he said: "On the point of leaving you I wish to thank the College of Cardinals; I am as a victim on the altar, a victim for the Church, for the Council and for peace." That night the Pope entered upon the agony which was to convulse his body for four days. He lapsed in and out of comas, wracked with a pain no sedative could kill. "My Jesus," he called out during one lucid interval, "free me now. I cannot endure it. Take me with you."

Thousands waited through the day and night in Saint Peter's square, while millions throughout the world watched and prayed with them. The Pope who had hailed the Council he had convened as a "New Pentecost" for the Church, lived through Pentecost Sunday and into Monday, the 3rd of June. At 7:45, as a Mass celebrated for him on the steps of St. Peter's basilica ended, the Holy Father, invoking the Blessed Virgin with the words, *"Mater mea . . ."* —my mother—died. He had been Pope for less than five years, the shortest reign in modern history since the twenty-month pontificate of Pius VIII, from 1828 to 1830.

When word reached Cardinal Montini in Milan, on May 31st, that the Pope's life was despaired of, he made plans to leave immediately for Rome—the Pope had asked for him. The plane on which he traveled that night was, by coincidence, the same carrying the three brothers and sister of the Holy Father, flying for the first time, to the bedside of their brother. Together they all drove from Rome's Fiumicino Airport to the Vatican. The cardinal spent only a brief time with Pope John who, during one of his rare moments of consciousness, recognized and spoke to him affectionately, his right hand grasping the cardinal's. It was the last time they were to meet.

Cardinal Montini returned to Milan on Saturday night, June 1st, in time to celebrate a midnight Mass for the dying Pope in the presence of 20,000 in the rainswept Vigorelli stadium. He spoke to the silent, prayerful crowd of how the Pope's word of peace had gone around the world as never before, and he stressed the need of an accurate understanding of the word: "Peace is not something which just happens; it is created, constructed." And he added, "We wish to make our own the Pope's great message, to make it an inspiration and program for our life."

On the next day, Pentecost Sunday, the cardinal, preaching in his cathedral said: "Blessed is the Pope who has given to us and to the world the evangelical example of the Good Shepherd. . . . Blessed is this Pope who has shown us that goodness is not weakness or slackness, not an equivocal irenism, that it entails no renunciation of the great rights of truth or duties of authority, but is rather the master virtue of him who represents Christ on earth. Blessed is the Pope who has made us see again that the authority of the Church is not an ambition to dominate, not aloofness from the community of the faithful, not a remote and custom-ridden paternalism. Blessed is this Pope who has enabled us to enjoy an hour of fatherhood and spiritual companionship—who has taught the world that humanity has need of nothing so much as love."

As he weighed the unprecedented outpouring of grief which convulsed the world on the day of the Pope's death, the cardinal reflected on the reason for a sorrow which the death of no Pope in his memory had generated. "Why do they mourn his death everywhere in the world? What marvel of spiritual convergence produces this thing without precedent in history? Everyone of us has felt the attraction of that personality, has

grasped that the sympathy that enveloped him was not a de-
lusion nor a fashionable whim; it was a secret revealing itself—a mystery which absorbed us, the mystery of two words
which, united in magic power, dazzled our eyes—the words,
truth and charity." Others in the Church were to voice more
conventional and qualified tributes, but the cardinal's had
nothing of the facile or automatic about it, and his words were
to speed around a world stunned by the loss of such a man as
John and fearful for a future without him.

With the death of Pope John, the centuries-old machinery
of the interregnum began to function. Ten minutes after the
death of the Pope, the 84-year-old Cardinal Camerlengo of
the Church, bishop of Palestrina and prefect of the Congregation of the Sacraments, Benedetto Aloisi Masella, bearing
the staff of office, had taken possession of the pontifical palace.
Entering the room where the Pope's body lay, the cardinal
bent close to the face of the Pontiff in a formal "recognition"
of death which is twelve centuries old. He then pronounced
the traditional formula: "The Pope is truly dead." He took
custody of the gold Fisherman's Ring used by the Pope in
signing documents and of his personal seal.[1] He ordered the
death knell to be sounded from the great bells of Saint Peter's,
and the Pope's body removed to an adjoining room, there to
lie in state. Later the papal apartments would be locked and
sealed. From that moment on until the election of the new
Pope, the provisory government of the Church rested in the
hands of the College of Cardinals whose authority was represented by Cardinal Masella.

---

[1] Later it was broken and the pieces buried with Pope John's body.
The Camerlengo's delegate, Monsignor Sargolini, was entrusted with
the obligation of obtaining all seals from the Apostolic Datary and
Apostolic Chancery.

The office of Cardinal Camerlengo, while much reduced in power through the centuries is still today, during the *sede vacante,* the highest authority in the Church. All other high Vatican officials lose their offices—the Cardinal Secretary of State, for example. Cardinal Masella had come to the office by way of election by the cardinals resident in Rome when Pius XII died in 1958. Pope Pius had allowed this office also to remain vacant during the latter years of his pontificate, and the hasty election of Cardinal Masella by his peers following the death of Pius had been confirmed by John upon his accession. While his government of the Church during the interregnum is limited to affairs of ordinary administration, the Camerlengo may, in cases of grave urgency, having consulted the College of Cardinals and acting in its name, take decisions of great importance. He signs the administrative acts of the Church and represents the Vatican in its relations with the outside world. Cardinal Masella was assisted in his office by the heads of the three orders of cardinals: Eugene Cardinal Tisserant, representing the cardinal bishops; Santiago Luis Cardinal Copello, representing the cardinal priests; and Alfredo Cardinal Ottaviani representing the cardinal deacons.[2] Their chief business was to organize the Conclave and insure its secrecy.

[2] Cardinal bishops are the bishops of the sees near Rome. However, they are occupied with the affairs of the Curia, the central administrative arm of the Church, entrusting to others the ordinary jurisdiction and administration of these suburban sees.

Cardinal deacons also devote full time to Vatican administrative posts. This order was formerly made up of priests, not bishops, but Pope John XXIII ruled in 1962 that all cardinals would thenceforth be given episcopal consecration. Cardinal deacons hold titular bishoprics, mostly of sees that have disappeared but whose memory is preserved in name.

Most numerous are the Cardinal priests—cardinals who rule sees removed from Rome. They are assigned titular pastorates of Roman churches but do not operate as pastors there.

It was Cardinal Masella's decision, in accord with the wishes of Pope John, that his funeral be private; that the body of the Pope not lie in state in the Sistine Chapel but be borne from the apostolic palace through Saint Peter's square into the basilica, there to rest for two days before being buried in a provisory tomb in Saint Peter's while a permanent tomb, also according to his wish, was prepared near his cathedral of Saint John Lateran. On the day after his death the body of Pope John, dressed in white alb, golden mitre, crimson and gold gloves, chasuble, buskins and slippers, was carried on a litter through a silent crowd of 50,000 jammed into Saint Peter's square, to the mournful cadences of the *De Profundis*. Inside the basilica the body rested on a high catafalque before the main altar, crowned by the great Bernini *baldacchino*, while twenty-one candles burned around the bier on almost the exact spot from which Pope John had addressed the Council nine months previously.

For two days the people came to pay their last respects. More than one million passed through the doors of Saint Peter's for a last glimpse of the man who had been always, as Domenach had said, supremely a Pope of tradition. The grief of the world was genuine and profound. In the United States an unprecedented tribute welled up across the country. In Cuba, Fidel Castro proclaimed a three-day period of mourning; the United Nations lowered its flag to half-mast in his honor; and the archbishop of Canterbury, for the first time since the Reformation, did the same with his personal emblem. Nikita Khrushchev hailed the Pope as one who had "won the respect of peace-loving peoples"—and the Chinese Government sneered that all that remained now for the Russian premier to do was have his people baptized. But for the most part it was a loss which transcended all political and religious differences and found the world confessing its poorer state in the loss of one so good.

He had been, Cardinal Montini said, "an incomparable Pope." But now he was dead and the Church's nine days of mourning for him, the *novendiali,* began in Rome, while cardinals across the world prepared to go to Rome for the conclave which would elect his successor. The final three days of the *novendiali* are the most solemn, with the Masses celebrated each day by a different cardinal. The five absolutions are given by the celebrant and four assisting cardinals at the high-raised catafalque, ablaze with ninety-six candles, topped by a tri-regnum crown, twenty-five feet above the floor.

The final Mass of mourning was said on the morning of June 17th in the presence of seventy-five cardinals, members of European royal families, the diplomatic corps, and the representatives of eighty-four governments sent as special delegations. Present from the United States was the vice president, Lyndon B. Johnson, with a three-member party. Two Russian Orthodox churchmen, Bishop Vladimir Kotliarov and Archpriest Vitaly Borovoy, were the first of their Church to attend the funeral of a Pope since the great Schism of 1054. Following the mass and benedictions given by Cardinal Tisserant, clad in sumptuous embroidered vestments of gold and black velvet, and Cardinals Spellman, Wyszynski, Giobbe, and Lienart, the final word of eulogy was spoken by Monsignor Giuseppe Del Ton, Secretary of Latin Letters. In a Latin which was classically elegant, he spoke of the Pope's goodness and humility, and of the "almost incredible" number of great enterprises he had achieved during his brief reign. "He truly was the master of peace, the announcer of peace, the angel of peace."

For the first time in the two weeks since the Pope's death, Cardinal Montini was in Rome and present for this final mass of obsequy. Although the cardinals already in Rome, their number increasing daily, had been meeting each day in general congregation to decide the affairs of the Church, Cardinal Montini had remained in Milan, intent upon his work there. On Friday, June 7th, he had preached in his cathedral, and had spoken out strongly for a continuation of Pope John's program by his successor in the Papacy. He said, "John has shown us some paths which it will be wise to follow. Can we turn away from these paths so masterfully traced? It seems to me we cannot." He returned to a theme which he had stressed in his pre-Council discourses, and which he had defended vigorously in one of his public appearances before the Council: the role of bishops in the government of the Church. He called for spiritual and practical conditions to insure the harmonious collaboration of the episcopate in that sphere.

It was a theme which he had developed at length and publicly before without drawing invidious attention, but in the nervous days of the interregnum, with the world abuzz with rumor and speculation as to Pope John's successor, the words were seized upon by a press more imprudent than informed as a declaration of candidature by the cardinal. The *New York Herald Tribune* headlined the story: "Montini Felt to Offer Self as Next Pope." The article, by Sanche de Gramont, regular Vatican correspondent of the paper, said: "The Cardinal's words were interpreted in Vatican circles as a pledge that if he is elected Pope by the Sacred College at the conclave starting June 19, he will pursue the chief aims of Pope John." Also: "Vatican officials said that Cardinal Montini, a cautious man who spoke only twice during the Council, was apparently stating his position now with unexpected candor in preparation for the conclave."

Such imputations, suggesting a kind of electoral manifesto by the cardinal, were clearly unjustified and impudent in the light of his many earlier affirmations of the need of the Council to clarify a confusion regarding the role of the bishops in the Church resulting from the definition of the dogma of papal infallibility by the First Vatican Council in 1870. In his pastoral letter for 1962, he had said: "The treatise on the nature and function of the episcopacy in harmony with the Roman Papacy is one which could result in a new and harmonious affirmation of the unity, not only juridical but living, of the Church around the chair of Saint Peter, and give a start, without any vindicative intention, to a greater and more organic internationalization of the central government of the Church." There was no reversal here of positions previously held, no affirmations of new positions impetuously taken.

The cardinal's last days in Milan had been marked by the same calm ordering of his schedule which characterized his regular program. His personal appointment book was full of notations in his own hand: June 19: consecration of the church, Curé of Ars; June 22: general assembly of the committee for new churches; June 28: ordination of priests in the Cathedral. The evening before his departure for Rome, Monsignor Milani, vice-president of the committee for new churches, conferred with the cardinal who that day had signed a decree of erection of a new parish. "There are seven more decrees to be signed, Your Eminence. What should we do if you do not return?" "No, no," the cardinal replied, "when I return from the conclave we'll come back to this." To Don Virginio Rovera, advocate general of his curia, who pressed the cardinal for a document he wanted before his departure for Rome, Cardinal Montini replied: *Periculum non est in mora*"—there is no danger in delay. And two days previously at the seminary, in speaking to some priests, he said: "Perhaps the time is ripe for a non-Italian Pope."

Before leaving for Rome, he traveled one more time to Bovezzo to visit his brother Francesco, ailing with a heart condition, and to spend a few hours with him and with his family in a setting of warmth and of intimacy which only a brother or sister's family can give to a priest. His brother Ludovico was also present. His departure from Milan was, characteristically, by plane, and as he entered the craft with his secretary, Monsignor Macchi,[3] he turned, and with a wave and a blessing, bade good-by to the city which had first welcomed him eight years earlier.

He arrived at the Rome airport late in the day, and drove immediately to Castelgandolfo where he was the guest of Dr. Emilio Bonomelli, director of the papal villa. The next morning he moved to the novitiate of the Sisters of the Child Mary in Via della Camilluccia, Rome. He had slept poorly at Castelgandolfo, and on the morning of the last Mass of repose for Pope John, as he sat in Saint Peter's, splendid in his mourning robes of purple wool, his face looked strained and somewhat severe. The eyes of many among the few thousand present were drawn often to the thin, erect figure of the cardinal, for already Rome was alive with rumor and speculation. Pope John was dead, this was the day of final farewell, and the report was abroad that in his diary the Holy Father had revealed his hope that the College of Cardinals would choose the brilliant archbishop of Milan as his successor. During John's lifetime, his lips, like those of the cardinals, had been sealed against discussing or influencing the choice of his successor, but now the signs of his predilection were recalled. It remained to be seen how the senate of the Church would react.

The press of the world, in reflecting on the reign of Pope John and in speculating on the role of his successor, articulated the gratitude the world felt to John and the hopes it

[3] Monsignor Macchi, who would remain as private secretary to Pope Paul, became secretary to the then Archbishop Montini shortly after his appointment to the Lombard see, in 1954. Father Macchi was at the time professor in the seminary of Saint Peter, Martyr, having been ordained in 1946, and having received his doctorate at the Catholic University of Milan, with a thesis entitled *Bernanos and the Problem of Evil*. He joined the archbishop in Rome and accompanied him on his entrance into Milan.

nourished regarding the man who would follow him in the Papacy. There was agreement that the Church under John had come to realize that the Church and the world have the same frontiers. The question posed was: Would there be an expansion of this concept or would there be a gradual and imperceptible contraction? The Polish Communist Review *Argumenty* inquired, "Has the pontificate of John XXIII been a moment of caprice in history or is it something lasting in the policy of the Church?" The *New York Herald Tribune,* in its editorial for June 5, 1963, said: "It remains to be seen what the attitude of the new Pope will be—in what direction he will throw the great weight of his office. If that should be toward the goals for which John XXIII strove, even on his deathbed, the result might well be the unleashing of the most powerful spiritual forces which have moved this world in many centuries. For when the accretions of centuries of polemics over the differing approaches to Christianity are stripped away, fundamental unities emerge; when the differences among Christian churches diminish, their great world mission becomes clearer, its influence stronger. The spirit [of the Council] itself cannot die. Its workings may be checked, or they may be accelerated by the choice made by the College of Cardinals. . . . That is why the Conclave will be watched, as seldom before in recent history. For the world will be waiting to know if the legacy of John XXIII is to be perfected in the months to come."

"The Pope," said the *New York Times,* "seemed to have caught at the flood one of those 'tides in the affairs of men.' It will surely flow onward to make our tormented age a little less divided." Walter Lippman spoke of the "miracle of Pope John": "The modernizing movement [begun by Pope John] can perhaps be arrested but it cannot for long be turned back. For what Pope John began will have very big consequences, and the history of our world will be different because he lived."

Barbara Ward in the London *Observer* (June 9, 1963) asked pointedly: Can the influence of Pope John endure? The answer, she indicated, was not an easy one. "At least a part of his astonishing impact on his fellowmen sprang from something potentially evanescent—the irresistible attraction of his personality." "All who came to him," she said ". . . left him with a sense of having encountered a profound paternal affection which was theirs not for this or for that distinction or achievement but simply because in each of them he saw a child of God. . . . Paternal affection is the precise opposite of superficial sentiment. It is rooted, it is reliable and resistant, it lies beyond all play of circumstance. . . . But now the man who projected this image of fatherhood in the single human family is dead. Will the work which sprang from his moving dedication to unity survive his loss? His greatest effort of spiritual reconciliation lay . . . in the calling of the Ecumenical Council. . . . Yet the Council is now, by the fact of his death, automatically disbanded with its labours no more than begun. One cannot doubt that it will be recalled by his successor. But will the earlier *élan* survive?"

Miss Ward spoke of the question mark hanging over Pope John's work of secular reconciliation. His policy of *détente* with Communism was, she said, no mere tactical desire to work out a *modus vivendi:* "John XXIII avoided all oversimple distinctions between a wholly virtuous West and a monstrous conspiracy on the other side." And she added words which seemed almost as much a description of the cardinal archbishop of Milan as of Pope John: "He grew up in one of the first Italian dioceses to react seriously to the challenge of modern industrialism. His whole thinking was influenced by the liberal tendency in French social Catholicism. He could see that man can lose his way, not only by the false doctrines of Communism but equally by the West's besetting temptation—that of seeking a 'well-being based exclusively on the comforts of life.' "

"There is no denying that the Pope's approach aroused profound misgivings in some Catholic ecclesiastical and political circles," she continued. "Conservative Italians accused him of making Communism respectable and thereby adding a million votes to the Communists in Italy's recent general elections (April 18, 1963). Right-wing Germans stonily attacked him for 'selling out' German interest to the Poles and Russians. A few American leaders clearly preferred the old black and white simplicities of the cold war. Mr Khrushchev's condolences and flags at half-mast in Havana hardly reassured them."

Miss Ward ended by pointing out that there might possibly be in the conclave and the *politique* resulting from it, a counter-attack in favor of more cautious policies in the political area. "But," she concluded, "one can be far more confident over the work of religious conciliation. The Vatican Council may not have completed much work but it demonstrated clearly the extent and vitality of the Church's modernising tendencies. The Bishops, assembled from the ends of the earth, took a more liberal view of their opportunities than the Rome-bound *Curia*. They were not only encouraged by the Pope. They were encouraged by one another. Thus he helped to articulate and dramatise the growing readiness for more liberal policies. But he did not create it, and it will therefore survive him."

No pontificate wins the complete approval of all in a church as diverse and catholic in its thinking and emphasis as it is in its diffusion throughout the world. The lines of difference had been most clearly seen because most sharply drawn in the first session of Vatican Council II, with its world-wide representation of bishops from every continent and land. In subscription to one faith in its entirety and integrity the Church was one in Council. In its willingness to examine the statement of that faith, to open windows, to build bridges, to bring the Church "up to date," there was division along the conventionally expressed conservative/progressive lines. The progressive thinking of the Council, in line with the exhortation of Pope John to "open windows" had predominated in the first session, and a sharp distinction between the majority thinking of the Council and that of the Curia became apparent. It was to be highlighted again by an extraordinary oration delivered in Saint Peter's basilica a bare forty-eight hours after the final Mass celebrated for the soul of Pope John.

On the morning of the day of conclave, Wednesday, June 19, eighty cardinals, still in their robes of mourning, made their solemn entrance into Saint Peter's for the celebration of the Mass of the Holy Spirit, invoking divine guidance on the voting which they would begin the next day. Only two of their total number were missing: the 89-year-old and seriously ill cardinal archbishop of Quito, Ecuador, Carlos Maria de La Torre, and the cardinal primate of Hungary, the 71-year-old archbishop of Esztergom, Josef Mindszenty, living in sanctuary since the Hungarian uprising of 1956 in the American embassy in Budapest. The cardinals, through their Dean, Eugène Tisserant, had already sent Cardinal Mindszenty a telegram in Latin which read: "According to the norms of the Constitution, 'Vacantis apostolicae sedis,' I have the honor to inform you that the conclave of cardinals for the election of the Supreme Pontiff in succession to the deeply loved John XXIII of venerable memory, will take place in the Vatican Apostolic Palace on the 19th of June of this year at five P.M. The Sacred College of Cardinals in these days feels itself profoundly united to you in fraternal memory and in fervent prayer to the Holy Spirit."

The Mass of the Holy Spirit reminds the cardinals in the

words of its gospel that "the Paraclete, the Holy Spirit whom the Father will send in my Name, he will teach you all things and bring to your mind whatsoever I have said to you." And the petition of the Mass, contained in its Collect asks: "O God, Who on this day didst instruct the hearts of the faithful by the light of the Holy Spirit, grant us, by the same Spirit, to relish what is right and ever to rejoice in His consolation . . ."

When the Mass was finished, the cardinals sat on their banquettes and awaited a discourse which turned out to be one of singular outline. They composed the senate of the Church, they alone would enter the conclave, one of the number present would emerge as Supreme Pontiff—and now they awaited a prelate of the Roman Curia, the Secretary of Briefs to Princes, to deliver the traditional allocution, *"De eligendo Pontifice"*—On choosing a Pontiff. This privilege is one of the rare ones which outlives the death of the Pope, since with his death all major offices cease to be held, and Monsignor Amleto Tondini, Secretary of Briefs to Princes under John XXIII, was, in effect, no longer Secretary. For all the sonority of his title, the Secretary is an interpreter, a translator, an executor, and it is more for the elegance of his Latin than the high dignity of his office that he is chosen to address the cardinals on this significant day. Although there have been previous exceptions in history, the oration is usually a generic exhortation to the cardinals to remember the responsibility which is theirs before their conscience, the Church and the world, and a laudatory recollection of the deceased Pope.

Monsignor Tondini's praise of Pope John was cautious and generic: "the good Pope," "the Pontiff of charity and of peace." He spoke of the "heavy" inheritance left to his successor, and outlined, more than once, a pessimistic picture of the contemporary world which, it appeared to some of his listeners, seemed to counterpoise, as illuminated and prudent, the pessimism of the speaker against the incautious and childlike optimism of him who as Pontiff had embraced the world of his century. Pope John had given much importance to natural values in establishing dialogue with the world: the orator insisted on the importance of the supernatural order and said that the successor of Pope John "ought to endeavor, with total effort, to reestablish the supernatural virtues in the life of Christians." He should guide the bark of Peter to the advantage of all, but especially of Catholics. For the speaker, "the days in which we live are days when the relations [between peoples] are based not on a moral order but depend on a politique of suspicion and of fear" in which "the air of true peace is not breathed." Governments do what they can, but often with damage to the souls of men "because they consider him [man] a machine from which to draw temporal advantages for himself and principally for the State." Only the Pope can resolve international problems "placing himself above any suspicion of partiality."

As for the Council, surely it would be continued. "The Catholics of every continent pray that the great undertaking will be carried through to fulfillment. But it will be for the Pope, whom you, eminent Fathers, will choose from your midst, to establish the suitable time for its renewal. And to him especially will it belong to determine and judge if the questions, the studies and particularly the spiritual dispositions have yet attained that maturity which will bring about the results awaited by the soundest part of humanity: that is to say, the light of sure direction in the midst of the dominant confusion of ideas, and an auspice of sure peace in the midst of mutual distrust and the antagonisms of people."

It seemed to many present like a bristling speech; it had little of the pacific spirit of John. "It was a manifesto of the most reactionary current of the Curia and attempted to trace a new program for the Pope," said one commentator. The speaker seemed unaware of the irresistible thrust of humanity toward truth and salvation, to which end the Church exists that it might evangelize, bless and consecrate such a yearning. Pope John had not set it in motion—but he had recognized it, accepted it and blessed it with a special insight and patience, with a rare sense of the times and the men of the times. It seemed unlikely that the words of Monsignor Tondini would reverse this movement of the Church and the boldness of a charismatic insight which had given her new life under Pope John. The Rome correspondent of the London *Tablet* commented drily, "Whatever may be said of the sermons preached at them, Masses of the Holy Ghost are clearly good things to have." [4]

Now it was the College of Cardinals alone, the senate of the Church, which would decide the question of succession. With eighty present in Rome, gathered from thirty-one nations, their entrance into conclave at five o'clock on Wednesday afternoon would make the conclave the largest since the election of the Pope became the exclusive prerogative of the cardinals in the twelfth century. Through them the opinions and hopes, the particular problems and the contrasting perspectives of the Church diffused throughout the world would enter the Sistine Chapel and be resolved. The symbol of their reconciled differences and of their converging wills would rise from their midst, and as Pope sit enthroned under the Last Judgment of Michelangelo to receive the prostration of their persons and the acceptance of their fealty. The Church would have a Pope and her life, constrained and suspended without a head, would resume again.

Pope John XXIII was elected in 1958 by a diminished college of 53 cardinals, dwindled under Pius XII from its traditional 70, established by Sixtus V. The new Pope shortly announced that he was raising the limit from 70 to 75, but that he would not, however, be bound by this figure, and would

[4] June 29, 1963, p. 703.

shortly issue norms regarding the number in the College. These were never presented, but in successive consistories Pope John raised the number to 79, 85, 86 and 87. In all he created 52 cardinals. The largest number, 23, was created on December 15, 1958. In 1959, 8 were created, followed in 1960 by 7, in 1961 by 4 and in 1962 by 10.[5]

The electors of his successor for the first time in history would all be bishops. In the long history of the College many had been elevated to the cardinalate as laymen and had thus remained through their lifetime, eligible for the Papacy, as is indeed any baptized male Catholic, but since 1378, when Urban VI was elected, not chosen.[6] But until the time of John XXIII those constituting the order of "cardinal deacons" were still priests.[7] On April 15, 1962, Pope John had issued a *motu proprio* ("Cum gravissima") which ordained that in the future every new cardinal not already a bishop would immediately receive episcopal consecration. And four days later, on Holy Thursday, he personally consecrated the twelve cardinals

[5] Pope John loved to give allegorical significance to their number. The first 23 corresponded to the 23 Popes, himself included, who had chosen the name John. The next 8 symbolized the number of the beatitudes, the following 7 the number of infused virtues, three theological and four cardinal, and the four symbolized the four-sided wheel of Ezechiel. The last 10 created by John received no symbolical meaning.

[6] The last layman to be named a cardinal was Giacomo Antonelli, secretary of state to Pius IX until he died in 1876. He considered it "outrageous" that the American John McCloskey, archbishop of New York, be raised to the cardinalate in 1875, his opposition being not to McCloskey but to the idea that the Church universal had anything to learn from the presence in the College of Cardinals of a representative of the Church in North America. Cf. E. E. Y. Hales, *The Catholic Church in the Modern World* (New York: Doubleday & Co., Image Books, 1961), p. 150.

[7] Cardinal Alfredo Ottaviani, prefect of the Holy Office, was a priest and remained so until his consecration as bishop by John XXIII.

of the college who were still priests in his cathedral of Saint John Lateran.

Pope John had also contributed to the internationalization of the College. Until the conclave which elected Pius XII, the Italian cardinals had for centuries been in absolute majority. In the early nineteenth century, Napoleon had sought by threats, and in vain, to insure the presence in the College of at least 30 French cardinals, and in 1846 there were only 8 non-Italians, but their number had increased to 25 by 1878. At the death of Benedict XV there were still only 29, and by the time Pope Pius XI died in 1939 their number had dropped to 26, as opposed to 39 Italians. It was Pius XII who decisively increased the number of non-Italians in the Sacred College, and when he died there were 17 Italian cardinals and 36 non-Italians (the Italian Cardinal Constantini and the American Cardinal Mooney of Detroit had died before entering conclave). The non-Italians counted 19 Europeans, 13 Americans (North and South), 3 Asiatics and 1 Australian.

In the College preparing to elect a successor to John, the Italian representation had become little more than a third of the total, 29 as against 52 non-Italians. 46 had been created by Pope John, 26 had been named by Pope Pius XII, and 8 by Pius XI. But the number of 52 non-Italians did not tell the complete story of the broad representation which John had given to the College. The numerical representation of the various continents had been further modified. Europe had seen its number increased from 19 to 27; North America from 4 to 7; South America from 9 to 12; and Asia had received its first Japanese and first Philippine cardinals. Africa, too, had its first African Negro representative in the tall, striking Cardinal Rugambwa of Tanganyika.

There seemed little possibility, however, that a non-Italian would be elected. The consensus in the Church was that the time had not yet arrived, yet the emergence in Vatican Council II of distinguished non-Italian Europeans indicated that the time might not be too distant when a four-hundred-and-forty-year tradition would be reversed.[8]

Observers were quick to point out that in bestowing red hats Pope John had been generous rather than politic, as far as insuring the success of the program of his pontificate was concerned. He had named to the cardinalate many whom he had known through his years of service to the Church, seemingly without regard to whether the recipients shared his outlook or his desire to make the Church more open to the world. He had staffed the Curia with men in their seventies and even eighties, contemporaries of himself, many with broad experience of the world through long years of diplomatic service abroad, but marked too by what many considered excessive prudence, caution and an undifferentiated desire to maintain things as they had always been, startled and resentful of change. During the Council it had been noted that of the 36 cardinals who had shown themselves by their interventions to belong to the "conservative" wing of the church, 21 had been named by Pope John.

[8] 215 Popes (including John XXIII) were Italian. France had given 17, Germany 6, Spain 3, England, Portugal, the Netherlands and Switzerland 1 each. The last non-Italian was the Dutch Adrian VI (1522-1523).

Cardinal König, interviewed after the conclave which elected Paul VI, said with regard to the possibility that a non-Italian might have been elected to succeed John XXIII: "Yes, some Italian cardinals told me before the conclave that they were in favor of a non-Italian being elected Pope this time. I think the time was not yet ripe. But it may come about that in the foreseeable future a non-Italian will be elected to the Chair of Peter. The cardinal-electors were concerned above all to find a suitable man: nationality probably played hardly any part in this. It was a question of trying to find the best man. I think they succeeded in doing this."

But there was a counterbalancing factor. Pope John's "conservative" appointments were for the most part less dominant men than his "progressive" ones. The leaders of the conservatives—Cardinals Ottaviani, Siri and Ruffini—were creations of Pius XII. Those more generally conceded to be of a progressive tendency—Cardinals Montini, Bea, König, Suenens, Alfrink, Cushing, Landazuri, Ricketts and Ritter—had been elevated by Pope John.

Two further influences, traceable to Pope John's reign, were considerable factors in giving a particular personality to the College. The first was that Pope John's pontificate had made it much more difficult for the cardinals to elect an "inward-looking" successor. "If in 1958 an unadventurous Italian cardinal had been chosen, had taken the name of Pius XIII and had pursued a policy of keeping the Church to itself, of guarding the citadel but attempting few forays into the outside world, no one would have thought very much about it. It would have seemed a continuation of the natural order of things. But for such a choice to have been taken in 1963 would have been as an overt repudiation of everything that Pope John stood for." [9] It was almost certain that the majority would not be thinking about a change of direction, even though many would opt for a change of emphasis and pace.

Secondly, Vatican Council II had given the cardinals an opportunity to know one another, not merely personally, but in their thinking and perspective on the Church. Fifty of them had risen to speak during the first session, and the two months of almost daily contact made of the Council a kind of ante-chamber to the conclave they were about to enter. They would not enter it strangers to one another, and in this lay one of the greatest hopes of the Church which awaited a new Pontiff—that the voice and spirit not only of John but of the

[9] Roy Jenkins, "Inside the Conclave," *The Observer,* London, July 21, 1963, p. 17.

Church as revealed through its bishops at the Council would find expression within the Sistine Chapel through the eighty men who by their votes would shape the Church for years to come.

Thus it appeared that the central issue at the conclave would be *aperturismo*—an openness toward new trends in Catholic thinking, toward ecumenical relations with other Christians, toward new political approaches to Communism —a continuation, in short, of Pope John's programs. Those alarmed at the nature and scope of those programs and desirous of muting what they considered their excessive theological and political stridency, were considered, in pre-conclave speculation, to number about 36, and were called the conservative wing. The progressives, enthusiastic supporters of Pope John in his confrontation with the world and with other religious bodies, but individually possessing particular reservation especially in the political sphere, were considered to have some 32 cardinals in their ranks. The remaining 14, mainly members of the Curia whose thinking was little known, constituted the moderate group.

The College possessed some towering figures. It was headed by the Dean, the stern, bearded Orientalist and former cavalry officer, the 75-year-old member of the French Academy, Cardinal Tisserant. There was the Armenian-born prefect of Propaganda, also bearded, Cardinal Agagianian, 67, who reportedly had received several votes in the 1958 conclave. The stocky and loquacious Cardinal Urbani, 63, interested in social questions and something of a scholar, former bishop of Verona, had been appointed by John XXIII to succeed him as patriarch of Venice. Prominent was the 80-year-old archbishop of Paris, Cardinal Feltin, who on his arrival in Rome for the conclave had asked prayers for himself and his fellow cardinals that from their number would come "a new pastor under whose guidance the work of renewal, of peace and of unity, already initiated" would be realized.

There was the former apostolic delegate to the United States and Secretary of State to Pope John, the 80-year-old Cardinal Cicognani. Cardinal Roberti, 73, was little known but a brilliant canonist and lifelong curialist. Cardinal König of Vienna, 57, was a suave diplomat and expert in Eastern religions and emissary of Pope John behind the Iron Curtain. Cardinal Cushing of Boston, 67, noted for his prodigality in charity, was a missionary *manqué* for whom Pope John had felt an intuitive affection.[10] The tall, graceful archbishop of Bombay, Cardinal Gracias, 62, kept in his chancery the saddest file in the world: the number who die of hunger each week in the area in his charge.

There was Cardinal Bea, German and Jesuit, 82, bent and smiling, a biblical scholar, confessor to Pope Pius XII and the right arm of Pope John in his work of union of Christians. The handsome 75-year-old Cardinal Ruffini of Palermo was also a biblical scholar, strongly traditionalist, alarmed at new trends. The archbishop of Warsaw, Cardinal Wyszynski, 61, archfoe of the Communists in his country had spent five years in prison. A major figure was the almost blind, personally charming, dogmatically intransigent prefect of the Holy Office, Cardinal Ottaviani, 72. The dark and brilliant archbishop of Genoa, Cardinal Siri, 57, in his funeral oration for Pope John had said: "The moment is not yet at hand to speak of his work, also because this work has need of the perspective of history to properly judge it"; his diocesan newspaper, *Il Nuovo Cittadino,* had said: "No pontificate can repeat itself," and also, that if every pontificate was not new "it would betray its fe-

[10] The *New York Herald Tribune* did not exclude the possibility of an American succeeding to the papal throne in the person of the archbishop of Boston.

cundity and the expectation of incarnation and the demands for redemption of a world always in the process of becoming."

The 71-year-old Cardinal Lercaro was the short, gentle archbishop of Bologna, interested in social reform, with orphans living in his residence, a liturgist and dramatic foe of the Communists; he, too, while praising the goodness and holiness of the deceased Pope had carefully refrained from saying anything about his pontificate. Cardinal Frings of Cologne, vigorous at 76, on his arrival in Rome had given voice to the generally known intention of the German cardinals to elect a successor to Pope John who would follow in his footsteps. In this the Germans joined with the position which the French cardinals and those of The Netherlands and of Belgium were openly maintaining.

Outstanding, too, was the patriarch of Antioch in Syria, Cardinal Tappouni, 83, who had one time been imprisoned by fanatic guerillas in the Middle East; the scholarly and progressive Cardinal Suenens of Malines-Brussels, who had distinguished himself at the Council and had been invited by the United States Committee for the United Nations to explain the content of the encyclical *Pacem in terris* before the General Assembly—his name had been on the list of hostages prepared by the SS in Belgium during the war: Cardinal Alfrink, 62, the archbishop of Utrecht in The Netherlands, whose pastoral letter on the Council, translated into Italian, was withdrawn from the Italian bookstores for unexplained reasons. The dynamic archbishop of New York, Cardinal Spellman, 74, would be called one of the "grand electors" of the conclave. And the intense and dedicated archbishop of Montreal, Cardinal Léger, 59, was one of its leading and progressive figures.[11]

[11] Cardinal Léger had complained during the pre-Council days that where he had suggested reforms "no one listened to me. I spoke in a desert. I advanced many bold proposals, but I don't know if they will ever be approved." He had gone to the Pope and had been con-

It remained for Cardinal Ciriaci, a Roman, now 77, an astute diplomat, nuncio for years in Portugal, to advance, according to reports, the most startling suggestion during the pre-conclave days. He proposed that the cardinals elect a committee from their number to act as a permanent board which would advise the Pope in areas not strictly spiritual. It pointed up the disaffection felt by many in the overtures which Pope John had made to international Communism, and had overtones of vast complexity and interest.

There was distinction marking each of these men and of the others who together with them composed the College. Many were unwell, two almost blind, one (Cardinal Morono) 91-years-old; divergent in background and age and thinking, some presiding over the richest cities of the world, others with personal vows of poverty; some living in palaces, others in religious houses, some ambitious, some proud—all bishops with a purpose, which they would swear to fulfill according to their lights and with the assistance of the Holy Spirit, to give to the Church the man whom God would have to choose.

The pre-conclave assaying of papal possibilities swirled around the names of at least six cardinals. Most often mentioned was the cardinal archbishop of Milan. Favored by John, progressive, but a proud traditionalist as well, brilliant, a pastor and diplomat, a master of organization, only 66, eight years at the head of the most complex archdiocese in Italy, a linguist, knowledgeable about Rome and the Curia, widely traveled, uniquely a man of his time—all of his attributes were exposed, dissected, and reassembled as the mania of speculation on the eve of conclave reached its climax.

Counterpoised to Cardinal Montini's candidacy as the pro-

---

soled. The Pope told the cardinal: "The march of the Church today is irreversible. The Council will not end." The cardinal had also said: "The Church has become conciliar; the bishops will meet in Rome more often."

gressive he was considered to be was that of Cardinal Lercaro, presented as a moderate-progressive. The kindest of men, his social thinking in the reign of Pius XII had seemed extreme to many, but with the advent of John it had appeared in contrast to be somewhat to the right. His conception of social work had been criticized as unsophisticated, his personal reactions to problems as emotional. Yet he had made an immediate impression on the Council when he had pleaded for a church "poor in the image of its Master." He had won wide applause from some for his statement that he would never shake hands with Premier Khrushchev, and it was maintained that the conservatives in conclave would swing their votes to him should their own first and conservative candidate seem to have no chance of success. That candidate, it was said, was the handsome young archbishop of Genoa, Cardinal Siri, but it was felt that his age and his negative attitude toward much of Pope John's policy would militate against his election. The early votes which would be cast for Cardinals Suenens and König would represent, it was said, a transalpine warning that the election of Italians to the Papacy would not continue forever.

The "compromise" candidates were several: there was the spry and young-looking secretary of the Consistorial Congregation, the 73-year-old Cardinal Confalonieri. For years he had served as private secretary to Pius XI, and his grasp of curial life was profound. Others were Cardinal Roberti, the canonist; Cardinal Marella; the cardinal archbishop of Naples, Alfonso Castaldo. All were names proposed, extolled, defended and speculated about as the hour of conclave approached. The cardinals themselves were mute, their thinking revealed only by statements or speeches made days or months earlier, by their attitudes in council, by the administration of the offices they held. Frustration and expectation held Rome in iron grip on the Wednesday afternoon when the conclave would begin. A saying was making the rounds that Thursday (June 20th) means Montini; Friday belongs to Lercaro; the fourth day either to Confalonieri, Roberti, Antoniutti or Marella. The fifth day means either Traglia, Ciriaci, Cicognani or Siri. On Wednesday, a day of frantic rumor, the report spread that an agreement on the name of Cardinal Montini had been reached by Micara, Confalonieri, Urbani, Frings, Lienart, and Spellman.

There were "prophecies" and sayings, too, to consult when the matching and the weighing seemed to reach an impasse. The monk Malachy of Armagh in Ireland was papal legate for Ireland and died at Clairvaux in Burgundy in 1148. He visited Rome twice and from these visits was formed his list of "prophecies in the form of mottoes" for succeeding Popes. They cannot be traced in book or manuscript further back than 1595, and the noted Jesuit Herbert Thurston maintained that they had been compiled then to help the candidature of an ambitious cardinal. This leaves intact, however, the mystery of the striking aptness of many of them.[12] The motto selected by Malachy for the Pope now to be elected was *Flos Florum* —Flower of the Flowers. It was quickly pointed out that both Cardinals Montini and Wyszynski had three lilies in their armorial bearings, and as quickly that Cardinals Siri and Roberti also had flowers in their coats-of-arms. The manner of interpretation of the prophecies is everything. For example, *Flos Florum* could also refer to the Armenian Cardinal Agagianian as "the flower of the garden of the East"—thus did Rome amuse itself and protect its divinings against possibility of error.[13] Every man was a seer. It was pointed out

---

[12] Benedict XV, Pope during the First World War was characterized as *Religio Depopulata* and John XXIII, pastoral and the patriarch of Venice, as *Pastor et Nauta*—Pastor and Sailor.

[13] According to Malachy's prophecies the Pope to follow the *Flos Florum* will be *De medietate lunae*—from the middle of the moon—

also that a tradition at least a hundred years old demanded that a corpulent Pope be followed by a slim one, a Pope with an r in his surname by one without. This tradition had been maintained by every Pope elected since the time of Pius IX.

The man whose name was most mentioned spent the few free hours of that Wednesday afternoon in typical fashion—he visited a seminary. Cardinal Montini arrived at the Lombard Pontifical Seminary, his alma mater, at one-thirty on Wednesday afternoon and spent more time with the students. One brave lad, Luigi Serentha, said to him at one point, "Good-by to Milan, Your Eminence." The cardinal raised his arms and smiled, as one who was present said, "enigmatically." He spoke of the conclave. "It is a mystery," he said, "there are so many influences which shape the decision, but more powerful than all is that of the Holy Spirit." He posed for the inevitable photographs saying, "If you want them as a sign of your affection, then it is a great consolation to me." And the last informal poses of the man who will go into history as Paul VI were captured by the cameras of young Lombard seminarians.

---

or it could mean a half-moon (heraldic). Two more Popes will follow: *De labore solis* and *Gloriae olivae,* and finally Peter II; now is the time of anti-Christ, the final apocalypse, the end of the world.

9.   Successor to Peter—
Successor to John

*"For every high priest taken
from among men, is or-
dained for men in the
things that appertain to
God. . . ."*

—Saint Paul

The procedure of locking cardinals and their attendants in a
building until a Pope has been chosen is, for all of its antiquity
and the solemn procedures which envelop it, something of a
grotesquerie. It had its beginning almost seven hundred years
ago when, on the death of Pope Clement IV in 1268, eighteen
cardinals met in the papal palace at Viterbo, about fifty miles
north of Rome to elect a successor. For two years, nine months
and five days they wrangled while the Church remained without a Pope, and the Papal States which he ruled underwent
great suffering.

Finally, the mayor of Viterbo conceived the idea of locking the cardinals in the palace, seeking to isolate them from

worldly contacts and distractions which were delaying their decisions. Even this failed of its effect. It was then that the roof of the palace was removed, exposing the cardinals to the elements, and when the first rain fell the cardinals quickly agreed on the name of Teobaldo Viconti di Piacenza, who, on September 1, 1271, became Gregory X. It was he, with the memory of those two and a half years in mind, who published the norms establishing the procedure of conclave, thereby insuring secrecy and the absence of outside pressure on the electoral college.

This curiosity of history reveals that conclave has not always been the method of election employed in the Church. A tradition maintains that Saint Peter, before undergoing martyrdom in the year 67, suggested the names of his three assistants or coadjutors, Linus, Cletus and Clement, as those who should follow him in his position of Bishop of Rome and thereby as the one preeminent in the Church. For a long time such a procedure was followed, the Pope suggesting his successor, the name being confirmed by the assembly of bishops, the opinion and approval of the people being not a small part of the decision. In the eighth century it was decided that the election would rest with the clergy of Rome alone and the Pope be chosen from among the cardinals, although this was often ignored. Further precise directions were issued by Alexander III (1159-1181), imposing as necessary a two-thirds majority in order that the election be valid.

Secrecy and isolation continue to be key words in conclaves to this day, and the conclave to choose a successor to Pope John was scrupulously prepared. The cardinals, with few exceptions, were allowed one assistant only, and within the sealed-off area there were another twenty Vatican officials and some seventy-five attendants and servants. Twelve nuns were assigned to staff the kitchen. A doctor, a surgeon, two architects, two barbers and a confessor were included in the number of conclavists. Cardinals Confalonieri, Browne, and Traglia were commissioned by the College to determine and assess the probity, morals and commitment to secrecy of all conclavists.

Pius XII had sought, following his election, to set aside a section of the rambling Vatican Palace as an area in which suitable accommodations for the cardinals could be provided, and over fifteen apartments were installed, but the increased number of cardinals with their attendants made these inadequate, and called for ingenious improvisation. The cells,[1] as they are called, some of them large rooms used ordinarily for other purposes, now had simple furniture moved in, their usual furnishings, for the most part, undisturbed. The ceremonial halberds of the Swiss Guard kept watch over the bed of one cardinal. Temporary walls were erected to subdivide large throne rooms, and even the kitchen of the Pope's apartment contained a bed for a prince of the Church, with a bed in an adjoining pantry for his secretary.

The feeling of improvisation and of temporary provision was everywhere, Franciscan simplicity of furnishing contrasting with the overwhelming painting and frescoes of some of the temporary cells. Cardinals Ciriaci, Di Jorio and Testa supervised their preparation. They were assigned, contrary to custom, by drawing lots, although those ill or advanced in age were assigned the more comfortable cells and those closest to the Sistine Chapel. Cardinal Spellman was fortunate in draw-

---

[1] Gregory X, in 1274, had indicated that the sleeping quarters of the cardinals should be a communal dormitory. Clement VI, in 1345, permitted the bed of each cardinal to be separated by a curtain or a wall. When the conclaves began to be held in convents "cells" were constructed, at least 30 centimeters apart. It was Leo XIII in the late nineteenth century who allowed the cardinals each to have his proper room, although the word cell attaches to them to this day.

ing the sumptuous official apartment of the Cardinal Secretary of State. Cardinal Cushing was lodged in the reconverted office of an accountant. Cardinal Meyer of Chicago received the apartment of the chief of the Vatican Library. Cardinal McIntyre of Los Angeles drew a Spartan bedroom in the quarters of the pontifical Noble Guard, and Cardinal Ritter of St. Louis was assigned a small furnished storeroom.

Within the conclave area, doors were sealed, windows covered, radio and television banned; the only telephones were for use within the area itself. The whole maze was under the care of the governor of the conclave, Monsignor Callori di Vignale, with the marshal of the conclave, Prince Sigismondo Chigi Albani della Rovere, entrusted with guarding its secrecy. Contact with the outside world was not entirely severed; it simply became rigidly controlled. Only two "roundabouts" allowed this contact once the conclave was sealed. No conversation with an outsider was allowed except in the presence of the custodians of the conclave and in a language understood by them. No uninspected letter was permitted to leave the conclave except by the Grand Penitentiary. The introduction of newspapers carried an *ipso facto* excommunication. The courtyard of San Damaso was sealed within the conclave area and provided ample space for exercise outdoors, while the spacious frescoed corridors gave the same opportunity indoors. There was no feeling of constriction nor of crampedness— the area was too expansive for that.

The kitchen where the cardinals' food would be prepared was a high vaulted room, its fourteenth-century walls recently uncovered and restored. It contained gleaming stainless-steel worktables and sinks, and modern gray-enameled refrigerators. The dining room, the largest room of the Borgia apartments, was once the armor room of the Borgia family. Thirty-five feet above the U-shaped table was a fifteenth-century fresco by Il Pinturicchio. The china and silver appointments of the table were simple. To feed the cardinals and their entourage tons of food were stored: 1,600 pounds of pasta, 4,000 pounds of potatoes, 1,500 litres of white and red wine, 6,000 bottles of mineral water, 3,000 bottles of beer, 200 pounds of coffee, and three large slabs of Parmesan cheese were among the provisions. If it was to be a long conclave, logistically it would be invulnerable.

Shortly before five o'clock on Wednesday afternoon, the procession of the cardinals and of their attendants to the conclave began. They approached the Pauline Chapel through the Ducal Hall, watched in silence by special visitors crowded behind barricades. The cardinals, still in mourning purple, moved slowly, their entrances widely spaced, grave in their remembrance of the charge given them that morning at the Mass of the Holy Spirit: ". . . to give the Holy Roman and Catholic Church a pastor both capable and worthy in the shortest time possible and with the greatest zeal, leaving aside all worldly considerations and having God alone before their eyes."

Some walked, bent and aged, leaning heavily on the arms of their attendants, others strode purposively in the direction of the chapel. When the cardinal archbishop of Milan appeared, solemn, his hands clasped, head lowered, applause broke out among some of the spectators, and audible whispers of "the Pope, the Pope!" were heard. The cardinal heard them too, and raised his head and hands in a gesture of annoyance and silence. Minutes before he had knelt at the tomb of Pope John, and it was from there that he had begun his entrance into conclave.

The cardinals prayed briefly together in the Pauline Chapel, its walls lined with Michelangelo's awesome "Conversion of Saint Paul" and "Martyrdom of Peter." Then, led by a master of ceremonies bearing a glittering cross, they filed into the

Sistine Chapel, a hundred feet away. They made their way to their places in the chapel while choristers sang the *Veni Creator Spiritus*. The chapel glowed softly, alive with light and movement, displaying the treasures of art which make it unequaled in the Western world. For some centuries it has been the private chapel of the Popes, but it is only in the last hundred years that it has been used as the setting for the papal elections.

The chapel is divided into two unequal portions by an elegant Florentine Renaissance screen, providing a kind of antechapel, and it was here, just inside the door to the left, at table 39, that Cardinal Montini took his place, flanked on one side by Cardinal Gracias of India, and on the other by the patriarch of Venice, Cardinal Urbani. The chapel floor and the hangings other than the eighty-two purple thrones, with their collapsible canopies, were covered in green. A purple-covered desk stood before the altar, the scrutineers' tables and benches nearby. Behind the altar with its silver candle-sticks hung a tapestry depicting the scene of the first Pentecost. And behind this, soaring to the ceiling, the "Last Judgment" of Michelangelo brooded over the assembly.

The hymn and prayer concluded, all those not of the conclave were ordered to depart, and the constitution governing the procedure to be followed was read to the cardinals. Each took an oath to observe the constitution in all its parts, to defend the rights of the Church if elected Pope, to keep secret everything happening in conclave, and neither to receive nor countenance any veto. The Cardinal Dean addressed them on the gravity of their task, the principal officers of the conclave were sworn in, and then the cardinals retired to their cells, some in the nearby Borgia apartments, others traveling by staircase and elevator and along corridors leading to wings of the palace a city block away.

Now the solemn ceremony of sealing the conclave began.

The bell in the courtyard of San Damaso was rung three times, the cry, *"Extra omnes"*—all outside—rang out, the lights were switched on throughout the area, a search made of every corner by the Camerlengo and his assistants, the conclavists inspected to insure that no unauthorized person remained inside. The doors leading to the outside world were finally locked from the inside by the Cardinal Camerlengo and from the outside by the marshal of the conclave, Prince Chigi, dressed in his ceremonial Spanish uniform of black velvet and white lace. Over the Bronze Door, leading into the Vatican palace the flag of his family, bearing the coat-of-arms in red and blue, proclaimed that in his person was vested the keeping of the palace during the conclave, a role his family had received from Pope Clement XI in 1712.

To insure the secrecy of the conclave, the marshal could call on the papal forces, the Swiss and Palatine Guards, who are under his command during this time, and in the highly unlikely possibility of necessity, raise a militia of Roman citizens. A notary witnessed to the sealing of the conclave from outside, and another did the same within the conclave. Cardinal Tisserant, in the name of the cardinal bishops, Cardinal Liénart of the cardinal priests, and Cardinal Ottaviani of the cardinal deacons, alone remained outside their cells while the sealing was accomplished. Then they too withdrew and the silence of the conclave was joined to its secrecy as Wednesday night closed in.

Thursday morning began with a low Mass celebrated by the Cardinal Dean and a hymn to the Holy Spirit. The voting began at nine o'clock, with two sessions scheduled for the morning and two for the afternoon. The Pope can be elected in any of three ways. The first is by "inspiration"—this is the unanimous acceptance by the College of a declaration by one or more cardinals that one of their number is freely and spontaneously chosen. The second method is by compromise, which means that the College can delegate its choice to a committee of three, five or seven.[2] The committee is instructed by the College as to how many votes will be necessary to elect the Pope—four out of seven, three out of four, etc. The third method, by election, is the traditional method and the one used on this occasion by the cardinals in their voting sessions.

Ballots were distributed and all who were not cardinals were ordered out of the chapel. On each ballot was printed: "I elect as Sovereign Pontiff, the Lord Cardinal _____." (The formula ignores the fact that outsiders, even laymen, may be nominated.) The procedure is for the cardinal elector to write the name, in as disguised writing as possible, fold it, take it between the thumb and first finger of his right hand and in his turn, according to seniority, carry it to the altar. He kneels in prayer, and then rising says: "I call the Lord Christ, who will be my Judge, to witness that I am electing the one whom in the sight of God I think the most proper to be elected." He then places his ballot on a paten and tips it into the silver chalice resting in the center of the altar.

There are four votes taken each day, in two pairs. The cardinal scrutineers read the ballots aloud, allowing each cardinal to keep his own score. The cardinal revisors count the ballots again, and the last of the cardinal scrutineers passes a needle through the center of each ballot and binds them with a thread. The burning of the ballots takes place twice a day, once in the morning, once in the afternoon, for four scrutinies in all. The cardinal scrutineers bring the ballots from the altar to the stove, dilapidated rather than ancient, standing just inside the door of the chapel. With the aid of old copies of the *Osservatore Romano* and, if the balloting is in-

[2] This procedure would be used most probably in a case of hopeless deadlock when no candidate could receive two-thirds of the votes (or two-thirds plus one if the number present is not divisible by three).

conclusive (two-thirds plus one is required), with dampened straw added, the fire is ignited which destroys the cardinals' ballots and gives out the black smoke of "no election" to the crowds waiting in Saint Peter's square.[3] The tally sheets for each scrutiny are not burned, nor are the notes made by the cardinals. They are preserved in the Vatican archives to be opened only on orders of the reigning Pope. Following the election, it is the Cardinal Camerlengo's charge to draw up a report on how the voting went at each session, and after the approval of the senior cardinal bishop, cardinal priest and cardinal deacon, it too is sealed away in the archives.

In the intervals between the rounds of balloting the cardinals were free to leave the chapel and to mingle in the less cramped area of the conclave as a whole. They were free, too, to discuss the election, to voice their opinions, express their choice and if possible, and if they chose, to seek to persuade those who remained doubtful or as yet unconvinced. They were summoned back to the election precinct by a bell, and the procedure of the first balloting was repeated.

The first ballot of the day is traditionally cast in "favorite son" fashion and is often called "demonstrative voting." It provides the cardinals with an opportunity to express their respect for the office or person of certain of the cardinals without regard to their being serious candidates. An opportunity is also afforded to estimate the relative strength of the principal candidates.[4] The number of possible ballots is limit-

[3] To avoid confusion concerning the color of the smoke, electronic signals were installed, marked white and black, to inform Vatican Radio. During the conclave which elected Pope John XXIII the Vatican radio mistakenly informed the world one day early that a Pope had been elected.

[4] The Vatican correspondent of the Roman morning newspaper, *Il Messagero*, reported later that Cardinal Cushing of Boston had sought in this first balloting to gain the Papacy for an unidentified cardinal by the method of inspiration. He had, said the newspaper,

less and there is no process of elimination. Candidates may be put in and taken out at will. If a cardinal is ill and obliged to remain in his cell, three cardinals are delegated to obtain his vote. It is received in a box with a small opening at the top, which has first been shown to all the cardinals to be empty, then locked, and the key laid on the altar. Should a cardinal be unable to leave his throne, he pronounces the ritual formula in his place and consigns his ballot to the cardinal scrutineers.

Two rounds of balloting took place on Thursday morning. Outside in St. Peter's square some 20,000 people waited. At 11:45 A.M. the first puff of smoke appeared. It was whitish, and pulses quickened, but then it darkened and thickened and floated away in the clear Roman air. At four o'clock that afternoon the balloting began again, and at 5:47 the smoke rose, this time unmistakably black, and the conclave was sent into its second day.

Friday, the first day of summer, dawned hot and humid in Rome. The first days of June had been fresh and cool, and people grumbled about the heat and speculated lazily over coffee whether the Pope would be elected today. A newspaper vendor was certain: "They'll elect him today. If there's a cold war going on inside, this heat will put an end to it." It was the feast of the Sacred Heart, and in the Roman churches the Mass of the feast was being offered, and with the added Collect from the Mass for the Election of a Pope: "We most humbly entreat Thee, O Lord, that Thy boundless goodness

---

announced his intention previously, and rose in his place to proclaim: "My Lords, considering the virtues and qualities of the Lord Cardinal _____, I judge him worthy to be elected Supreme Pontiff, and from this moment I myself choose him as Pope." It was later reported that the cardinal in question was Cardinal Montini.

may grant as bishop to the most holy Roman Church one who shall ever be both pleasing to Thee, by his loving zeal in our regard, and, by his beneficent rule, deeply revered by Thy people to the glory of Thy name."

In the Vatican palace, shuttered and enclosed in its second day of conclave, the cardinals attended Mass, again celebrated by the Dean. Breakfast was a quick affair, and by nine o'clock the cardinals were in the Sistine Chapel and the balloting began again.[5] It appears that the first vote of the day, the fifth of the conclave, was the final one. At 11:19 a grayish trickle of tentatively white smoke emerged from the tube on the roof of the Sistine Chapel. Suddenly it billowed upward in a huge and unmistakably white cloud. The Pope had been elected! A cheer went up from the thousands already in the piazza, and

[5] Nothing certain is known of the balloting; the secret of the conclave prevents such information from being revealed. The accepted speculation maintains that Cardinal Montini showed unexpected strength on the first ballot, supported strongly by the Americans. Cardinals Siri and Antoniutti received support as did the cardinal archbishop of Bologna, Lercaro, but Montini's strength was sufficient to have carried him, on the fourth ballot of Wednesday's voting, to within a few votes of election. The first ballot of Friday, concludes this version, gave him 79 votes.

La Stampa, a respected daily of Turin, in its issue of June 23, referred to the importance some had attached to the visit Cardinal Spellman of New York had made to Cardinal Montini on the Tuesday night before the conclave. It was considered significant, said the newspaper, because the archbishop of New York was considered a leading exponent of the conservative position in the Church. The newspaper continued: ". . . yesterday, in the rejoicing following the election, Cardinal Spellman let fall a revealing phrase in one of the halls of the apostolic palace, in the presence of many witnesses. He was walking with his colleague Cardinal Micara, and at one point, in a somewhat playful and happy mood, he exclaimed: 'You saw, Your Eminence, you saw! We did as you ordered us to do.'" The paper adds that it was no secret that in pre-conclave days Cardinal Micara was Cardinal Montini's most avid supporter.

from all over Rome, informed by radio and television, people started converging on Saint Peter's square.

Inside the Sistine Chapel the scrutiny of the ballots had ended. The tally was announced to the cardinals; one among them had a majority. The junior of the cardinal deacons, Cardinal Albareda, moved slowly to the door of the chapel and called the principal officers of the conclave to enter as witnesses. They waited as the Cardinal Dean of the Sacred College, Cardinal Tisserant, together with Cardinals Goncalves Cerejeira and Ottaviani, moved majestically down the chapel, through the screen, turned to the right and stopped before the green-covered table with the neat N. 39 on it. Behind it sat the cardinal archbishop of Milan, immobile, his lips barely moving in prayer. In Latin the Cardinal Dean asked: "Do you accept your election as Supreme Pontiff which has been canonically carried out?" Cardinal Montini looked at him for a brief moment, then said: "I accept—in the name of the Lord." "By what name will you be known?" asked the Dean. "I will be called Paul," came the firm reply. The Dean bowed to the new Pope, the canopies were lowered over the thrones of the cardinals and one alone remained enthroned—the successor to John, the successor to Peter.

Accompanied by the cardinal deacons, the Pope went immediately to the sacristy adjoining the chapel to put on one of three white cassocks, together with a white sash, a rochet, mozzetta, a red stole embroidered in gold, white stockings, shoes of red velvet with small crosses of gold, and a white skullcap. He returned to the Sistine Chapel, blessing the cardinals as he walked to the *sedia gestatoria,* resting on the footpace of the altar, and sat to receive the first reverence of the cardinals. It was at this point that the ballots were burned and news of the Pope's election reached the outside.[6] The

[6] The conclave had lasted 42 hours: one of the shortest in history. Pius XII was chosen in less than 24 hours, Pope John XXIII in 3 days.

Fisherman's Ring was placed on the Pope's finger by the Cardinal Dean, and he rose to go to the balcony of Saint Peter's for his first appearance before the world.

As high noon approached, the sun beat down on the piazza in front of the basilica, which was filling rapidly. Under their blue umbrellas the photographers waited, and high on the colonnades in flimsy wooden booths the television cameras had been set up to record the scene. Italian soldiers marched smartly into the piazza and took up positions before the stairs of the basilica. The Palatine Guard appeared. A band played. The people chatted, voicing their choices, shielding themselves against the sun, cameras to the fore. A few minutes after twelve, the glass doors opening onto the central balcony of Saint Peter's swung wide, and a great roar went up. A red-bordered white papal tapestry, still bearing the coat-of-arms of Pope John, was draped over the balustrade, and Cardinal Ottaviani appeared in the midst of jostling ecclesiastics.

The crowd of 100,000 was still. The voice of the almost blind cardinal was strong and clear: *"Annuntio vobis gaudium magnum: habemus Papam,"* he began. There was a burst of applause and the crowd tensed, waiting. *"Eminentissimum ac Reverendissimum Dominum Cardinalem Joannem Baptistam*—the Most Eminent and Reverend Lord Cardinal John Baptist——" The crowd exploded; no need to hear the final name, but it came strongly: "Montini, who has taken the name Paul VI."

The announcement of the name brought a renewed roar. "It is a program in itself," shouted a priest, beside himself with excitement. The cheering continued, and suddenly present on the balcony was the slight, slim figure of the new Pope, diminished against the perspective of the church. He stood directly under the name of the Borghese Paul V, emblazoned across the façade. He lifted his arms and hands in a gesture of greeting and acknowledgment, a slight smile on his lips.

Then in a strong voice, and without tremor, he imparted his first blessing to the city and to the world. "Blessed be the name of the Lord," he chanted. "Now and forever," answered the crowd. "Our help is in the name of the Lord," called the Pope. "Who has made heaven and earth," came the response. Then with a majestic sweep and elevation of his arms, he traced his blessing in the Roman air: "May the blessing of Almighty God, Father, Son and Holy Spirit, descend upon you and remain forever."

Across Rome the bells rang out jubilantly, and across the world the news spread that Cardinal Montini, long the servitor of Popes, had himself become the Servant of the servants of God. He joined the cardinals for one last meal together, refusing to preside in the place of honor, choosing to sit in the position assigned to him when he first entered the conclave. That afternoon the Pope formally lifted the conclave enclosure and received once again the "adoration," or more properly, the expression of respect and fealty, of the cardinals. Afterward he insisted on having his photograph taken with all of the cardinals clustered around him, the first such to be taken following a conclave.

The press of the world greeted the election of Paul VI with praise. The emphasis throughout was of gratification that one who had identified himself so intimately with the spirit and program of Pope John should be his successor. Said the *London Times:* "The most significant point in the election of Paul VI is indeed the fact that the cardinals or the majority of them chose a Pope who would pursue the innovating work of John XXIII." The French press unanimously expressed its delight. "There is no doubt," said *Le Monde,* "that Paul VI is, of all those who might have succeeded Pope John XXIII, the one who is closest to his thinking." The press in the Iron Curtain countries expressed cautious optimism regarding the program that the new Pope would foster in promoting world peace. Said the *New York Times:* ". . . the cardinals could not have chosen anyone more clearly calculated to carry on where Pope John had to leave off. . . ."

President Kennedy sent a message to the new Pope which wished him "long years of leadership in the cause of peace and goodwill so nobly advanced by your great predecessor." The Queen of England, General de Gaulle, Premier Khrushchev, all sent their felicitations. The Russian premier expressed his best wishes "for success in your activities favorable to peace and to the peaceful coexistence of peoples."

Many saw in the name he had chosen a presage of his program. It was a name unused for centuries, as had been the name chosen by John XXIII. The Pauls who had preceded the new Pope were recalled. Pope Paul I, a brother of Pope Stephen II, came to the throne in 757, and consolidated the temporal holdings of the Holy See. Pope Paul II sought to bring the Russian Orthodox Church back into union with Rome. Alessandro Farnese, Paul III, was elected in 1534. He summoned the Council of Trent, founded the congregation of the Holy Office, issued a condemnation of slavery, and defended the rights of the Indians in the newly-discovered America. Gian Pietro Cardinal Carafa, who succeeded him in 1555 as Paul IV, had no faith in the reforming success of the Council of Trent and suspended it, preferring to deal directly with the problem of heretics. Pope Paul V, elected in 1605, was an intransigent man, more rigid than diplomatic, more a challenger than a reconciler of men. He nevertheless sought, as had Paul II, to effect union with the Russian Orthodox Church.

Many of the problems which confronted his predecessors bearing the name of Paul—efforts at Christian unity, the problems attendant on holding an ecumenical council—faced the new Paul. There is little doubt he chose his name because of his devotion to Saint Paul the Apostle. The zeal and Chris-

tian breadth of Paul had always challenged the new Holy
Father. Said the *Osservatore Romano* of the choice: "The
Apostle to the Gentiles . . . is a symbol of ecumenical unity,
venerated by Catholics, Protestants and Orthodox Christians."
It was pointed out that it was Saint Paul who had internation-
alized the early Church, the great missionary apostle who
sought to become all things to all men that he might win them
to Christ.

At the beginning of June Pope John XXIII still lived. On
the last day of June, his successor was crowned. For nine days
already he had been Pope, from the moment he had replied,
"I accept" to the question posed him by the Cardinal Dean in
the Sistine Chapel. They had been days of intense activity,
sustained and pastoral, and now for a few hours the Pope and
the Church paused, while in centuries-old symbol and pag-
eantry the choice of the cardinals was declared with public
pomp.

To some, the glittering ceremony of coronation of the Pope
is an incongruity and anachronism, unworthy of the successor
of the simple fisherman and the vicar of the simple Christ. He
is a pastor—and pastors do not wear crowns. He is a servant
—and the trappings of monarchy are not for servants. But the
ceremony of coronation of the Pope is unique, a declaration of
supreme spiritual significance, historically rooted and grown.
Conceived and developed, as is much of the ceremonial of the
papal court, in imitation of the Christian Roman emperors, it
sought in times past to affirm, not mere equality with them,
but an exaltation of the office of the Pope in order to proclaim
the ascendancy of the spiritual over the merely temporal. As
the Church, her position established, moves further into the
modern world, there is sure to be modification, curtailment,
but it will be gradual, almost imperceptible. It took three hun-

dred years to evolve papal coronations, the work of a hundred Popes.

Because the great nave of St. Peter's basilica, traditional setting for the coronation ceremony, was still filled with the tiers of seats prepared for the bishops in Council, the Pope decided that the ceremony should take place in front of Saint Peter's, with the great gradines of the church serving as the sanctuary, and the immense curving piazza, enclosed by Bernini's columns, as the sweeping nave of the outdoor church. The altar was set forward on the rim of the steps, with the great throne placed against the central door of the basilica. Wisely, too, it was decided to hold the ceremony at 6 P.M., when the shimmering heat of the Roman June day would have somewhat abated.

Already much of the piazza was in shadow when the tribunes, to the left and right of the altar, began to fill with the diplomatic corps, the Roman nobility, and the special representatives of ninety-two nations, international organizations, and churches. The King and Queen of the Belgians were among the heads of state present, also the Presidents of Italy and of Ireland. President Kennedy, although already in Italy, had appointed a distinguished representation. It was headed by the Chief Justice of the Supreme Court, Earl Warren, and included Senator Mike Mansfield of Montana, Mr. Charles W. Englehard, Jr., and Rabbi Louis Finkelstein, chancellor of the Jewish Theological Seminary, New York. The naming of the outstanding Jewish scholar was remarked in the United States as the first time a rabbi had ever served in such capacity, and was hailed as "a high watermark in Vatican-Jewish relations."

The procession formed in one of the great palace rooms of the Vatican, and moved slowly down the magnificent Scala Regia, through the Bronze Door and into the square where two hundred thousand people waited to hail the Pope. The crowd was quiet as the procession moved into view, led by the Swiss Guard in their orange, red and blue; the chamberlains in their purple; the lay dignitaries in their black; the *bussolanti* in their violet cassocks and red capes; followed by the chaplain carrying the tiara. The penitentiaries appeared, dressed in black, followed by chaplains in violet and red, and then row upon row of white-mitred and caped patriarchs, archbishops and bishops, followed by the similarly attired cardinals. Then, borne aloft on his *sedia,* the great ostrich feather fans waving beside him and the canopy above him, came the Pope. A vast roar greeted him. Shouts of "Long live the Pope!" were drowned in the cascading applause, as he turned from left to right, blessing the crowd. Three times in the procession to the altar and throne the *sedia* carrying the Pope halted, while a friar burned a piece of flax, and in a voice which reverberated through the piazza called out: "Holy Father, thus passes the glory of the world."

Once seated on the throne within the temporary sanctuary, the obedience of the cardinals began, each approaching singly to kiss his ring and to be embraced. Some he steadied as they tottered, some lingered for a word, anxiously watched by the prefect of ceremonies, Archbishop Dante, hovering nearby.

The long, solemn pontifical Mass followed, celebrated at the altar facing the crowd. The Epistle and Gospel were sung in Latin and in Greek, to mark the universality of the Church, and the Gospel reminded the Pope: "Thou art Peter. . . ." At the end of the Mass one of the most charming of customs during the long ceremony was fulfilled. The dean of the Vatican chapter, accompanied by two canons, approached the Holy Father and gave him a small bag of white silk, decorated in gold thread, containing twenty-five coins *"Pro Missa bene cantata"*—for a Mass well sung.

Darkness had settled over the square and floodlights illuminated the sanctuary as the Pope took his place on the throne.

The moment of coronation was at hand, and a bearer approached with the tiara, the triple-tiered, beehive shaped crown, a gift to the Pope from the people of Milan. It glinted softly in the light as Cardinal Ottaviani, senior deacon of the College of Cardinals, raised it high above the Pope's head and slowly lowered it, saying as he did: "Receive this tiara, adorned with three crowns, and know that you are the father of princes and kings, guide of the world, and vicar of Jesus Christ, our Saviour."

The coronation speech of the Holy Father was given in nine languages. He spoke first in Latin, then in Italian, French, English, German, Spanish, Portuguese, Polish and Russian. In Latin he spoke of the solemnity of the spectacle of the coronation, his obligation to speak, the weight of his office, the role of the Church and the frailty of his human nature on whose slender powers God had seen fit to impose such a task. "We flee finally to Paul, from whom we have taken our name, so that we may place ourselves under his auspices and gain his protection. . . . May he choose to be our heavenly model and patron through all of the days of our life."

Because French was more widely understood he chose it, the Pope said, to announce to the world his attitudes toward the Catholic communities, the separated Churches and the modern world. "The Church . . . regards as incomparable wealth," he said, "the variety of languages and rites in which it carries out its dialogue with heaven. The Eastern communities which continue in their noble and ancient traditions are, in our eyes, worthy of honor, esteem and confidence . . . To those who, without belonging to the Catholic Church, are united to Us by the powerful bond of faith and love of Jesus Christ and marked with the unique seal of baptism—one Lord, one faith, one baptism—we address ourselves, doubly encouraged by an immense desire, the same which has moved so many among them: to hasten the blessed day which will see, after so many centuries of deadly separation, the realization of Christ's prayer on the eve of His death—*ut sint unum,* that they may be one. . . . No more than he [Pope John XXIII] do We nourish illusions about the exigencies of the problems to be solved and the gravity of the obstacles to be surmounted. But, faithful to the great Apostle whose name We have taken, rather are We to practice the truth in love (Ephesians 4,15). We intend leaning only on Our weapons of truth and charity, to pursue the dialogue that has been begun and, as far as We are able, to help the work already undertaken."

As he had so often done in Milan, the Pope referred to the dialogue of the Church with the modern world. "But beyond the frontiers of Christianity, the Church is engaged in another dialogue today, the dialogue with the modern world. On superficial examination, the man of today can appear to be more and more a stranger to all that is religious and spiritual. Conscious of the progress of science and technology, inebriated by spectacular successes in domains hitherto unexplored, he seems to see his own power as divine and to want to do without God.

"But behind this grandiose façade it is easy to discover the profound voices of this modern world, which is also worked upon by the Holy Spirit and by grace. It aspires to justice, to a progress that is not only technical but also human, to a peace that is not merely the precarious suspension of hostilities among nations or among social classes, but that would permit at last an openness and a collaboration among men and peoples in an atmosphere of reciprocal confidence."

In the English part of his sermon Pope Paul said: "To our venerable brothers and beloved children who use the English language a word of greeting and of blessing in their mother tongue . . . your language makes a notable contribution toward increased understanding and unity among nations and races. . . . We exhort you, Our children and all English-speaking men of good will, to strive and pray that this priceless blessing [of peace] may be given and preserved upon earth, as announced by the Angels when Christ, Our Saviour, was born."

The Pope spoke in Spanish and Portuguese before turning to German, in which he paid tribute to the faith of the people of Germany, Switzerland and Austria. Then in Polish he said: "In a special way We salute and bless Our beloved Poland which has always been faithful, where We stayed for a time, and which remains always very dear to our heart." And closing in Russian, he said, "Our thoughts are directed to all the Russian people to whom We send a fatherly blessing with all Our heart."

Night had fallen when the ceremony of coronation finally ended. In the glare of the lights, under a sky which lay low over Rome, the Pope was borne back to his palace. He had been crowned, and now it was the quiet words and actions of his pontificate to which the world would look and which would receive the judgment of history.

10.   The Pauline Pontificate

Gregory the Great, according to legend, after his election to the Papacy, escaped from Rome in a grain basket. For three days and nights he wandered in forests and caves outside the city to avoid mounting the throne. In the end he submitted humbly. Pius XII, more credibly, is said to have cried out asking God's mercy when his election was announced. The initial reaction of Cardinal Montini has not been recorded, other than his acceptance, but if one may deduce it from a knowledge of his temperament, one may suppose that he sustained the voice of the divine imperative in almost complete quiet.

Like Pius XII, he brought to the papal throne something of the "sense" of the Papacy. His Vatican years had been served under Pius XI and Pius XII, and his dialogue with John XXIII had been exchanged in a close bond of mind and heart. In his forty years as a priest, he had had an opportunity to see a gradual change develop in the role of the Vicar of Christ in the world. Within the term of his own service in diplomacy, the gradation could be traced from the idea of public monitorship in Pius XI, a role partly inherited, partly thrust upon him by historical events, and partly the product of his own temperament. It grew more dominant with the advance of world

Communism in the 30's and its promotion of the materialism which posed such strong threats to the Church and to society. Pius XII, too, had matured as Pope in a context of tangibly crucial opposition and world convulsion, his challenge not only the visible enemies of Fascism and Nazism, but the intellectual uncertainties and disillusions that followed on the Second World War. Thus he had conceived his role, in large part, as that of the teacher of the Catholic world, the clarifier of its spiritual and social doctrine, the defender of a threatened Christendom. It was a pontificate in the tradition of the Constantinian era which was to end with his reign.

Since the middle 50's, there had evolved a still more extensive and responsive regard for what the Pope thinks and represents in all aspects of human concern. In its confusion and imbalance the world had, to some degree, recognized in the Papacy a center of stability and proportion. To this was to be added under John an affection for the man and an appreciation and comprehension of the Church he led, which was unique in this century.

The Papacy entered the 60's vital and renewed, aware of its own spiritual preeminence, the volume of its voice, and the gravitational pull of its sanctifying burdens. Under Pope John it became more recognizably the bond of unity among all Christians, and to some degree, among all men.[1] The secular press had been emphatic in insisting that it was John who gave the Papacy "an urgent and abiding interest in the minds of millions of non-Catholics." It is difficult to believe that had John lived longer his words on any issue of moral significance would have fallen unheeded. Attack and strong opposition he might have known, but hardly dismissal. And Paul is the suc-

---

[1] "The Petrine office is understood . . . as Christ's own provision of a final court of arbitration and mediation in the service of unity."— H. Kung, *The Council, Reform and Reunion* (New York: Sheed & Ward, 1962), p. 133.

cessor not only of Peter but of John. John's expressed approval
of him, and his own avowal of the duty to follow the path of
John, made the world alert from the beginning of his pontificate to even the least obtrusive manifestations of his official
response to human situations.

Throughout his life there has been every indication that
Pope Paul knows, not only in concept but in wisdom and in
spiritual touch, the nature of the world he has come to mediate.
It is a world of the common man—and the common man in a
diversity of races, beliefs, national and cultural backgrounds.
It is a world in which, as Yves Congar has described it, "one
man out of every three lives under Communism, and one
Christian out of every two is not a Catholic." It is a world in
which there still persists a stubborn reluctance to believe in the
individual and corporate power of the common man, a power
which Pope John knew intuitively. Pope Paul by his wide
reading among writers concerned with the plight of modern
man—Camus, Mann, Malraux—deepened intellectually an
already profoundly human and spiritual insight to which his
pastoral years in Milan gave added dimension.

In the first months of his reign Pope Paul, even though already evincing an emphasis and language more his own than
John's, seemed to capture the mood and spirit of John's pontificate. It should not be forgotten, however, that between
these two Popes, men with a patent affinity for each other,
there exists a polarity which has both separated and united
men as leaders and thinkers from earliest times—separated
men as they approach human problems frontally or laterally,
as they accept or refuse to accept the fact of tension; united
men as the world expresses a need for them together, and con-
fronts one with the other.

It might not be too extreme to compare Pope Paul's interpretation and shaping of the ideas and aspirations of John to
the process of the refraction of light, whereby the many faceted

prism breaks down the ray into its original components, each thereby gaining a new depth and beauty. John's rare gift of holy simplicity could be misleading to those who hastily judged it to be merely an absence of complication. John's long pastoral life could not have been as fruitful as it was, had his simplicity been anything but a profound fusion of many diversified elements and capacities, made one by an integrating bent of mind and by what Paul himself called John's "goodness," his purity of heart. Upon Paul, however, the practiced "translator" of the mind and will of the Popes he served, devolves the duty of analysis, of workmanship, the careful second stage in *aggiornamento,* the creative unfolding, exposing, distinguishing and consolidating of the aspirations of his predecessor and of the hopes of the Church.

When the history of his pontificate is completely chronicled, a glance over the initial months will show a comprehensive sensitivity to the diverse forces currently at work in the world. From the highly charged equilibrium of amity and power of the Test Ban Treaty[2] following within a month of his coronation to the "great game of friendship" of the World Jamboree of Boy Scouts at Marathon, Greece, Paul VI almost immediately caused himself to be heard, speaking with a knowledge and calm immensely reassuring to the Church and to the world.

---

[2] On July 22 he wired President Kennedy, Premier Khrushchev, Prime Minister MacMillan and Secretary-General U Thant: "The signing of the treaty banning nuclear experiments has very intimately touched Our heart because we see in it a testimony of good will, a pledge of harmony, and a promise of a more serene future. Welcoming in Our soul, always solicitous for the welfare of humanity, the echo of satisfaction and hope which rises from every corner of the world, We express our felicitations on completion of an act so comforting and so significant and We pray God that He prepare the way for a new and true peace in the world."

In fulfilment of his pledge of fidelity "to the great canons of his [John's] pontificate," Pope Paul in the first hours of his reign took a significant step. He confirmed as his Secretary of State Amleto Cardinal Cicognani, who had served Pope John in the crucial final months of preparation for the Council and during its first session, and who was at the center of the various delicate diplomatic experiments which John had initiated. He was therefore in a position to provide the continuity and background necessary for the new Pope in the period of his orientation. The Sostituto of the Secretariat, Archbishop Angelo Dell'Acqua, was also confirmed in his office, and thus the Holy Father assured himself of a knowledgeable and expert team to bring him quietly to the center of the problems and challenges facing him.

Other gestures were more homely. To his former diocese of Milan, already jubilantly celebrating three days of holiday in honor of its former archbishop, he sent one of his first telegrams. There were words of gratitude and a special expression of "affection for so many of the poor, the suffering, the aged, the children, waiting for a word of comfort and encouragement." He remembered his brothers, too: "To you, my dearest Ludovico and Francesco, and to your families, in the holy memory of our dear dead parents, who taught us faith in Christ and love of the Church, the first of the apostolic blessings from your always most affectionate brother, today by divine disposition, Paul VI."

At ten o'clock in the evening of the day of his election, the Pope phoned his former vicar general in Milan, Archbishop Schiavini. He disposed of some matters with him and then asked that one of his secretaries in Milan, Don Luigi Sala, be called to the phone. "Today is the feast of San Luigi Gonzaga," he said to the overwhelmed young priest, "and I wanted to give you my fondest wishes for your feastday." Then it was the turn of the superior of the sisters who maintain the residence in Milan. "I have so many things in my head (*per la testa*) that I cannot speak," he said to her. "But I bless you all."

The light in his office burned late into the night as with his secretary he dealt with the big and small changes in his life. Appointments were made for the fitting of cassocks and shoes and hats, the full regalia of a Pope. They would come after his appearance in the Sistine Chapel the next morning. The baggage left at Castelgandolfo must be fetched, the Pope wanted his desk from his library in Milan, his books must be forwarded immediately. The message which he was to address to the world the next day was drafted and corrected, and shortly after one-thirty in the morning the lights went out in the Pope's office, and he slept the few hours which remained until five o'clock, when he arose for his first full day as Supreme Pontiff.

Within twenty-four hours of his election, Pope Paul again entered the Sistine Chapel, there, in the presence of the College of Cardinals, through television and by radio, to deliver his first message to the world. The scene was visually overwhelming, and there was a festive, almost jubilant air about the cardinals as they arrived for the ceremony. The Pope sat enthroned before the tapestry of the Pentecostal scene, looking almost fragile in the high gold mitre and sumptuous cope which enveloped him. The third and final obedience of the cardinals preceded the Pope's speech, and each approached in order of seniority, his scarlet *cappa magna* fully extended, to kneel and be embraced by the smiling, courteous Holy Father.

Monday would be the feast of Saint John the Baptist, after whom he had been named, and Cardinal Tisserant, in his charming and fluent Italian, presented the *"auguri"* of the cardinals, closing with the words: "We are ready, we cardinals who reside in Rome and those of us spread throughout the world, to obey and to collaborate in the plans of Your Holiness with a dedication which knows no limits." The Pope was

visibly touched. He seemed for a moment to lose his compo-
sure, and when he spoke it was slowly, spontaneously, in Italian. "I feel," he began, "to the point of suffering, my own
limitations." He paused. Then he continued: "I have experience, my Lord Cardinals, of the immense and dramatic problems which confront the Church and the world, and I feel the
need of that trust and support which you can offer."

The Pope's first message to the world was delivered in
Latin. He spoke firmly, strongly. He first paid tribute to his
predecessors, "who left Us a spiritual, sacred and glorious
heritage." He remembered Pope Pius XI under whom he had
begun his Vatican service forty years earlier, ". . . with his
indominitable spiritual strength"; Pius XII, whom he had
served through the years of war and in the postwar period, and
who ". . . illuminated the Church with the light of a teaching
full of knowledge."

But it was to Pope John XXIII that he referred in his most
affectionate and moving words: "But in a very particular way
we love to remember, with mindful and moving piety, the
figure of the late John XXIII, who in the brief but very intense
period of his ministry, was able to bring near to him the hearts
of men, even those distant, with his unceasing solicitude, with
his sincere and concrete goodness for the humble, with the
clearly pastoral character of his actions, qualities to which the
particularly enchanting and human gift of his great heart was
added. The enlightenment exercised on souls was a steady
progress, clearer and clearer, and an ardent flame, up to the
final personal sacrifice, suffered with that spiritual strength
that moved the world by uniting mankind around his bed of
pain and by making them a single heart and a single spirit in
a united outpouring of great respect, veneration and prayer."

And then he spoke the words which many waited to hear:
"The preeminent part of our pontificate will be occupied by
the continuation of the Ecumenical Council Vatican II, on

which the eyes of all men of goodwill are focused. This will be the principal labor on which We intend to expend all the energies that the Lord has given us so that the Catholic Church, shining over the world like a sign to all nations afar off (Isaiah v.26), can attract all men to itself with the majesty of its organization, with the youthfulness of its spirit, with the renewal of its structure, with the multiplicity of its strength."

Pope John XXIII had set as the third intention of his pontificate, following the holding of the Roman synod and the convening of the Ecumenical Council, the long-awaited reform of the Code of Canon Law which regulates the intracommunity life of the Church. It had been proposed first by Pius XII, and now Pope Paul spoke of it: "In this light will take place work for the revision of the Code of Canon Law, the furthering of efforts, following the lines set by the great social encyclicals of Our predecessors, for the consolidation of justice in civil, social and international life, in truth and freedom and in respect of reciprocal duties and rights."

Those who were watching for the Pope's "liberal" utterances were not disappointed, as he spoke more specifically on social problems: "The certain order of love for others, a test of love for God, demands of all men a more equal solution of social problems, demands aid and care for underdeveloped countries in which the living standard is often not worthy of human dignity—all require a voluntary study on a universal scale for the improvement of the conditions of life.

"The new epoch that the conquests of space have opened to mankind will be singularly blessed by the Lord if men know truly how to recognize each other as brothers rather than competitors, and build a world order in holy fear of God, in respect for His laws, in the sweet light of charity and mutual collaboration.

"Our work, with the aid of God, will also be to undertake every effort for the conservation of the great good of peace among peoples—a peace that is not only an absence of warlike rivalries and armed factions, but a reflection of the order wished by the Lord, Creator and Redeemer, a constructive and strong will for understanding and brotherhood, a clear-cut expression of good will, a never-ceasing desire for active concord, inspired by the true well-being of mankind, in unaffected love."

There was a word for "the brothers and children in those regions where the Church is impeded from using its rights." He sent his blessing to them, that they might "feel themselves near to us. They have been called to share more closely in the cross of Christ which, we are sure, will be followed by the radiant dawn of resurrection."

With a universality of concept and vision, and in the heightened tone to be expected of the Supreme Pontiff, the Pope in this first address had succeeded in striking a note of immediacy, and had spoken to the world of the world's most urgent concerns. All of the issues over which men are at present divided and fiercely united were not only touched upon; they were placed in their proper relevance in a Christian scheme and seen in the light of eternal values. And this enlightenment was achieved with a combination of warmth and conciseness which men intent on more restricted ends might envy.

His official charges with the world and with assemblies of men momentarily complete on this first day, Pope Paul characteristically turned to concern for individual men. In Milan, on the day after he had taken possession of his cathedral, he had gone to visit the sick, and the day after his election to the Papacy was to be no different. Shortly after three in the afternoon, the Pope descended into the grottoes under Saint Peter's, to pray at the tomb of Pope John. He knelt for a long time, his head bowed, his hands clasped. He prayed, too, at the tombs of Pius XI and Pius XII, and then, leaving the basilica, went to the Hospice of Santa Marta nearby, to greet the aged and ailing Archbishop Angelo Rotta, former nuncio in Hungary and close friend of Pope John. There was a visit also to Archbishop Josyf Slipyi, primate of the Ukraine who, following his release from eighteen years of detention in Siberia, had been living in the Vatican. He lay ill, and the Pope spent a few moments with the frail little man who had suffered so much for his faith.

The Pope's next visit was to take him outside of Vatican City, to the Spanish College, where the cardinal archbishop of Toledo, the heavy-set, progressive Enrique Pla y Deniel, was sick with influenza.[3] The black papal Mercedes, carrying the Pope and Monsignor Macchi, moved through streets filled with startled and cheering people, obviously pleased to see the Pope so soon among them. At the College, the Pope spent a short time with the cardinal, and then greeted the students and the other cardinals resident in the College during their sojourn in Rome. His first visit outside the Vatican was hailed as a mark of the Pope's esteem for Spain,[4] and the proud nation received the visit as a compliment, but it was also the simple gesture of a man who throughout his life had had a special affection for

[3] Later in the summer (August 11) the *New York Times* printed a short article on Cardinal Deniel's "pastoral exhortation" to the Catholics of Toledo, underlining Pope Paul's concern with labor problems, and his pastoral mission in Milan, carried out "in such a way as the modern world demands." The account mentioned the likelihood of Cardinal Deniel's presiding over a meeting of the Spanish hierarchy possibly to discuss, among other things, a draft bill "emancipating" Spain's 30,000 Protestants.

[4] In honor of the coronation of Pope Paul, the Spanish government issued a decree of amnesty on July 1, which applied to all sentences involving loss of liberty and to all crimes and offences which come under the penal code, the special penal laws, and military legislation. In addition, all persons who on the day the decree was issued, had served twenty years of effective imprisonment were set free.

the sick, and whose first visit into the city of which he was bishop, as it had been in Milan, was to one who was ill.

The whirlwind activity of the Pope in his first week seemed to substantiate the remark made by his chauffeur in Milan, Antonio Mapelli. "He would say to me, 'Hurry, hurry, Antonio! Speed it up if you can, because I am in a hurry.' He never wanted to arrive late for anything, never!" In that first week he began the routine of audiences with his closest associates and assistants which are held every day except Sunday. He received his Secretary of State, Cardinal Cicognani, every day, and began also the so-called *di tabella* or regular audiences on fixed days of the week, with the prefects and secretaries of the Roman congregations.[5] There were audiences also on fixed days for the heads of the offices and tribunals of the Roman Curia, or central administration of the Church. He also instituted a practice he had begun in Milan of meeting his closest collaborators at lunch each Friday so that the problems confronting them could be discussed freely during the meal.

In this same week, the Cardinal Secretary of State, acting in the Pope's name, signed a papal rescript or formal ruling setting the opening date of the second session of the Ecumenical Council as September 29, 1963. The Council coordinating committee met to put the finishing touches to the 17 schemata to be presented to the Fathers of the Council, and the Council press office issued a statement recalling the words of Pope Paul the day after his election, that "All men of good will have their eyes fixed on the Council."

His concern with the Church universal as expressed through the Council and with world problems did not distract Pope Paul from what he, in receiving the 2,500 parish priests of Rome called "the first title of Our Mission and of Our authority"—his office as Bishop of Rome. "We feel, having spent thirty-four years of our priesthood here, that we know the reli-

[5] These can be likened to the ministries of a civil government.

gious life of Rome, but we know, too, how many are the new religious needs of the city, and the practical difficulties of satisfying them. We know the formidable challenges posed to pastoral activity by the cosmopolitan character of the city, by its urban growth, and the influence of all the currents of modern culture and habit. It is to these that we must dedicate our primary solicitude." "It is," the Pope added, "Our years in Milan which have prepared Us for this pastoral confrontation of the sacred ministry with the most characteristic expressions of modern life."

The juxtaposition on the same day of the audience for his priests with the audience for the members of the diplomatic corps accredited to the Holy See from forty-nine countries, highlighted the multifaceted ministry of the Pope. To his priests he spoke in Italian; to the diplomats in French. To his priests he underscored the challenge of modern life to the pastoral ministry in a great and growing city. To the diplomats he spoke of the challenge to peace in a world at once grown small in its dimensions and large in its conflicts. In his first meeting with the corps, the Pope said: "This is almost a family reunion: a meeting where one finds, after some years' absence, friendly faces which bring to life cherished memories. After the teachings of our predecessors—and we refer particularly to the *Pacem in Terris* encyclical—it is hardly necessary for us to repeat to you the respect of the Church for the dignity and mission of every country in the world, both those distinguished by a long historic and cultural past and those which in our time have acceded to independence. . . ." He spoke of "true peace . . . this incomparable treasure which is unceasingly menaced. . . ."

In his first message to the world, Pope Paul, out of his own conviction, and in the spirit of *Pacem in Terris,* had spoken of the needs of newly emergent countries and of the obligation of more prosperous and economically developed nations to help any country where "the level of life often is not worthy of human beings." The phrase "the third world" has been used to describe not only Africa but that part of Asia not ruled by the Communists, and also, with somewhat different emphasis, Latin America. It signifies those parts of the world where human misery walks largely unchecked, but where hope is beginning to stir and where independence has in part been achieved—nations which have not yet entered the industrial and economically viable society of the twentieth century. Two messages which Pope Paul delivered in the first weeks of his pontificate revealed that the Papacy under him would have a more insistent preoccupation with the conditions of misery and need which still afflict large portions of the world.

The first was addressed to a group of one hundred Nigerian Catholics in Rome for his coronation. The Pope had visited Nigeria during his African tour, and it was with evident pleasure that he received these first representatives of the continent which in its Catholic life had impressed him so profoundly. "It is with admiration and joy," he said, "that We greet the reawakening of Africa to civil maturity, and in consequence to liberty, to independence and to progress. While We recognize the merits of all those who have helped the African people to walk the road of civilization, We nourish the hope that these people may be able to enjoy the rights proper to modern civil society and, fraternally assisted by countries economically and culturally more developed, may attain in liberty and peace that prosperity which corresponds to their common human dignity."

A part of the third world which lay neglected and exploited for centuries and which today smoulders in misery is the vast continent of South America, where Catholicism had been the religion, in name at least, of all the people for hundreds of years. Pope Paul chose his meeting with the Pontifical Commission for Latin America,[6] dedicated to fostering the socio-religious apostolate in one of the most troublous and destitute areas in the world, to speak about the Church in that continent.

He assured the members of the commission that the plight of the Church in Latin America had been one of the deathbed concerns of Pope John XXIII; that, after receiving the last rites of the Church, he had spoken of the great work to be done there. Again a mark of affinity for John, modulated by his own finely sharpened and realistic response to the contemplation of the widespread distress in Latin American countries, led him to pronounce a word of praise, which could never be mistaken for triumphalism, for the work the commission had done during the past five years. Thanking Canada particularly, because she had immediately sent a number of priests and religious into Latin America in answer to the appeal of the commission during the reign of John, he praised also the United States which had given personnel and economic aid "with its usual generosity."

He reminded the commission that, although the mission of the Church is not specifically social or political, "having 'compassion on the crowd' in the manner of the Divine Saviour is part of the working program of the priest, who will not remain indifferent, insensitive or inactive before his brothers and sisters who suffer. . . . Thus, social action, properly understood, finds its place among the duties of the priest. It will be an extension of the priestly ministry, understood in the true sense. We are happy to know that Our venerable brothers the bishops and Our beloved sons of Latin America have this pastoral sensitivity which urges them to care for bodies as well as the good of souls, while bearing in mind always the supreme end of man."

[6] Founded by Pius XII in the last year of his pontificate, it had done most of its work under John XXIII.

Thus while praising whatever the Church had accomplished in the past three hundred years, the Pope injected a note of realism which pervades the account of this meeting. Archbishop Miranda, in his address to the Pope on this occasion, had quoted Pius XII's title for Latin America, calling it "the continent of hope," yet even a cursory glance at this hungry, angry continent impresses on the mind that Paul's words concerning the care of bodies as well as the good of souls are key words, and that Pius' continent of hope is still dark. It is a mark of Christian hope, no doubt, that priests are living with and helping the poor in Latin America. It is a confirmation of it that Pope Paul emphatically blesses this form of the Church's activity.[7]

The audience in which the Pope received the Secretary General of the United Nations, U Thant, was noteworthy for the tribute which he paid to the United Nations for answering the dreams of his predecessors and mirroring the same universality as the Catholic Church. "The Church," Pope Paul said, "considers the United Nations to be the fruit of a civilization to which the Catholic religion . . . gave the vital prin-

[7] On the day following, a report from Washington cited Cardinal Raul Silva Henriquez of Santiago, Chile, as saying that Pope Paul would further develop the "determination of Pope John to use the power of the Roman Catholic Church to promote social and economic reforms in Latin America. . . . The center of our campaign is to hasten the improvement of the living standards of the Latin American peoples, while retaining their political and religious freedom. If we can prove that ours is an effective solution to poverty and ignorance, I am convinced that Communism shall be decisively defeated in all our hemisphere." He stressed that the gap separating the wealthy from the destitute masses of urban workers and peasants "must be urgently closed, for there is no time left." He added that if he lived under the conditions that prevailed in most of rural Latin America, he "would be a Communist."

ciples. It considers it an instrument of brotherhood between nations which the Holy See had always desired and promoted. . . .

"The ideologies of those who belong to the United Nations are certainly multiple and diverse, and the Catholic Church regards them with due attention. But the convergence of so many peoples, so many races, so many States in a single organization intended to avert the evils of war and to favor the good things of peace, is a fact which the Holy See considers as corresponding to its concept of humanity, and included within the area of its spiritual mission in the world." Reverting to history, he made reference to the desire of Benedict XV for such an organization; its "fundamental criteria traced with happy foresight by Pius XII" at Christmas 1939 and in September 1944, and the underlining of its importance and the encouragement given it by John XXIII.

In retrospect it seems that the mind of Paul was able to see in this meeting and in the very existence of the United Nations, more penetratingly and more reasonably than many Catholic commentators saw fit to remark, the possibility of a fruitful cooperation between the Church and the United Nations. An astute observation in the London *Tablet,* however, pointed out an urgent relevance in the meeting: "The words addressed to U Thant can be very useful to the Organization, for it is in the older and richer countries, most of them with large Catholic populations, that there is most impatience, disillusion, and dislike for a body which seems to be chiefly a stamping ground for Afro-Asians with one dominant and unfriendly idea. . . . Thus the Pope's words may need to be remembered when the Vatican Council in its next session reaches the schema, specially dear to the heart of Cardinal Suenens, which covers mundane activities like the work for peace, aid for poor countries, the corporal works of mercy on the large scale of contemporary international life. There may be temptation to think that the Church herself should try to create her own agencies, collect her own lay experts, and ask them to formulate detailed programmes. . . . But there is no need for an expert on disarmament or nutrition to be a Catholic. The place of the lay expert is with other lay experts, to pursue tasks which, as they are for the benefit of all humanity, are properly to be undertaken by men of all faiths."

A few days prior to his discussion with U Thant, involved as it was with the emergence of new nations and their socio-political problems, Pope Paul had made one of his first statements of political philosophy in a letter to the 50th convention of the *Semaines Sociales de France,* meeting in Caen. From the Christian point of view, he said, democracy does not necessarily result from any particular political institution or organization, but rather it is a state which exists wherever there is effective dialogue between government and governed, between authority and the people. The "tyranny of social groupings," and the "abandoning of the individual to mechanisms in which his liberty disappears" were enemies of democratic progress. "Democracy as supported by the Church is not so much linked to a specific political regime as to the structures on which depend the relations between the people and the authorities in their request for the prosperity of all."

"Democracy can be found in any regime that is not totalitarian," the Pope said. "It requires a society of free men, equal in dignity and fundamental rights, a society that takes note of personalities, of responsibilities and rights." [8] In the

---

[8] In August of 1963, during the crisis in Vietnam involving Buddhist protests against harshness and intolerance of the government led by Roman Catholic President Ngo Dinh Diem, the Pope received 41 Vietnamese students studying in European universities. He urged them to discover that unity is the secret of the Church, and that this vocation to unity applies to their nation as to others, "with this essential priority: that it does not ignore the rights, the merits, the character-

same letter he had also spoken of the function of the press in a democracy, urging that the people be properly informed, adding even more cogently, however, that "the people must strive to judge and weigh the information they receive." "And," he added, "the instruments of diffusing (the news) must not be at the exclusive disposition of any single political viewpoint."

Americans have, from the beginning, found Pope Paul an appealing figure. His two visits to this country, accounts of his activities as archbishop of Milan in major news weeklies, and his sympathy with John, predisposed Americans to look with favor on Cardinal Montini before his election as Pope. When he received Cardinal Spellman after his election, he spoke of the impression made on him during his 1960 visit by the devotion and participation of the faithful in Saint Patrick's cathedral, an impression that had inspired him to encourage the same devotion and participation in his cathedral in Milan. He praised the works of charity in the United States and the Catholic school system, and recalled his visit to the New York Foundling Hospital, and the Archbishop Stepinac High School in White Plains.

Early in his pontificate he received four hundred members, priests and laymen, of the archdiocese of Philadelphia, who had come to Rome for the beatification of John Nepomucene Neumann, a bishop of that see in the nineteenth century. The ceremony had been cancelled because of the illness of John XXIII. Pope Paul promised them that he would proceed with it as soon as possible, and spoke to them in English about their country, its hospitality and generosity. It was the new Pope's first audience to a large group of Americans.

At about the same time the Holy Father granted a half-hour audience to the Richard Nixons and their two daughters.

---

istic aspects of the country named; that it does not suffocate the genius of the people to which it addresses itself."

The former Vice-President had sought and received the audience a few days before President Kennedy's arrival.

On July 2 the President of the United States and his party were welcomed at the Vatican with what many American newspapers referred to as "centuries-old ceremony." The President spent forty minutes in private conversation with Pope Paul, after which the Pope greeted the official party, including Secretary of State Dean Rusk, and delivered a formal speech of welcome.

Paul's sense of the rightness of time and his sensitivity to the gravity of human distress, wherever found, were clearly expressed in this address: "In the discourses of Your Excellency . . . we find a spontaneous harmony with that which our venerable predecessor, Pope John XXIII, said in his last encyclical letter, *Pacem in Terris,* when he presented anew to the world the dignity of the individual human person, a dignity which the Almighty bestowed in creating man to his own image and likeness. We are ever mindful in our prayers of the efforts to insure to all your citizens the equal benefits of citizenship, which have as their foundation the equality of all men because of their dignity as persons and children of God."

The recognizable reference here to integration and the civil rights program caused mixed reaction in the United States. The *New York Times* included a gratified comment in an editorial: "The message will doubtless have its effect in our country. History was made when the two men met. If the visit to Italy proved valuable, President Kennedy will have Pope Paul to thank."

The audience concluded with the Pope's extending greetings and blessings to all the members of the President's family, and to the citizens of the United States. There was the traditional exchange of gifts between the two rulers, autographed photographs, desk sets, medallions, and, from the Pope to Mr.

Kennedy, a marble reproduction of Michelangelo's *Pietà*, the original of which is to be sent to the New York World's Fair in 1964.[9]

On July 17, 1963, the Swiss Bishop François Charrière of Lausanne-Fribourg-Geneva rose to speak before the leaders of the Orthodox Church gathered in Holy Trinity Monastery in Zagorsk, about forty miles north of Moscow. Sent by Pope Paul VI as his personal representative to the golden jubilee celebration of the Patriarch Aleksei, he was the first Roman Catholic prelate ever to speak in this holiest shrine of Russian Orthodoxy.

The bearded patriarchs of the Orthodox Churches with their graceful, draped headdresses, gave deep, meditative attention to the full-faced, spectacled Westerner as he spoke. Aleksei, patriarch of the Russian Orthodox Church, seemed to incline his darkly-crowned gray head forward at a more eager angle than the others. The moment was historic and the words of the bishop, full of grace and conciliation, leaped across almost a thousand years of separation.

". . . In the age when brave pioneers strive to reach the heavens in a thrilling adventure of space exploration, we cannot view our old quarrels from the standpoint of narrow provincialism . . . we must apply the dimensions of the planet. We must view these old quarrels from the standpoint of the exploration of space, and this perspective will reduce them in our own eyes to their proper importance and size."

Accompanying Bishop Charrière was the Very Reverend Christophe Dumont, O.P., of Paris. The two men had been carefully chosen for their ecumenical experience and a natural

---

[9] Pope Paul sent a medallion on a small gold chain of the Madonna and Child for Mrs. Kennedy's unborn child. A little more than a month later, when the child died, Paul sent a personal message of condolence to the Kennedys.

affinity for the movement by Cardinal Augustin Bea, chairman of the Vatican Secretariat to Promote the Unity of Christians. In Bishop Charrière's diocese the World Council of Churches and other international Protestant organizations have their headquarters, and Father Dumont is director of Istina in Paris, a center which specializes in studies of Eastern Orthodoxy. Not since the eleventh century had there been a formal and ceremonial relationship between the two Churches. Even in the autumn of 1962, when the Russian Church had accepted John's unprecedented invitation to send observers to Vatican II, the exchange was less direct, less specifically religious. But John's invitation had been the forthright and disarming overture that was necessary for this more precise, dimensional step, this overture to dialogue. "To go out to them" had always been the animating principles of the priest who is Pope Paul, and now, in the first days of his pontificate, he had sent wise men to the East, that the Eastern and Western Churches might develop through such encounters a relish for brotherhood. But a rapprochement, Bishop Charrière felt obliged to point out, could not be reached except on these terms: "The foundation can only be truth and justice; the climate, freedom; the motive and the inspiration, charity and love. This rapprochement cannot be directed against anybody."

The addresses of Bishop Charrière and of Father Dumont were reciprocated in speeches of amity expressed by their Russian hosts, and the participation by the Vatican in the jubilee was acclaimed also by members of the Russian Orthodox Church meeting in Montreal, in July 1963, at the fourth World Conference on Faith and Order. Such responses to evidence of openness and Christian charity had given the Church under John, and now under Paul, a sense of nearness to men and institutions, mentally and spiritually distant for centuries. The Pope, in this gesture of response to the invitation of the Russian Orthodox Church, had opened another window. In the matter of *aperturismo,* the words, the world noted, were the words of John, but the voice was the voice of Paul.

The Russian Church had sent observers to Vatican Council II, but the Greek Orthodox Church had maintained its reserve. A little more than a month after the address of Bishop Charrière at Holy Trinity Monastery, Pope Paul visited the eleventh-century monastery at Grottoferrata, not far from Castelgandolfo, where the Eastern rite is followed in the liturgical observances. Here he celebrated Mass for the monks and then delivered an unprepared address in which he pleaded for unity with all Eastern Churches.

"Does my vision stop here?" he asked, after paying tribute to the spiritual ties which bind Western and Eastern Christianity. "You, yourselves, in your rites invite me to look toward all the Eastern Churches that have the same baptism, the same fundamental faith, a valid hierarchy, and sacraments full of grace." Referring to the delegation to the jubilee of Patriarch Aleksei, he continued: "It was done with the intention of rendering homage, of showing that there is no reason for rivalry for prestige, neither for pride nor ambition nor for any desire to perpetuate dissonances and dissidence existing in the past, but which are now, it seems to me, totally anachronistic. Let us seek to render common and solid our creed, seek to render articulate and fitting our hierarchical union." In praying that Christian unity be achieved, he added, "if not in our age, at least in succeeding ages."

And again the Christian world which seeks to understand Paul discovers here a combination of John and Paul: the voice of John in the implicit plea that the Greek Church be among the observers of Vatican Council II;[10] and Paul in the

[10] The Greek newspaper *Ethnos* reported in July that the Patriarch Athanagoras of Constantinople and the leaders of the Church in

patient attitude of being willing to wait, to work out the divine design by progressive steps.

In the constellation of qualities which Pope Paul brought to the Papacy was his desire to continue the heritage of Pope John's willingness to open his heart to men of all faiths and of no faith, to men of all political credos, if they came prepared to enter into honest, active dialogue.[11] This was one point of the heritage of John left unmentioned in some analyses appearing after the election. After his death, John was praised for this willingness in *Nedelya,* the Sunday supplement of *Izvestia,* and Paul, after the conclusion of the conclave received commendation from the same journal.

Like John, Paul believes that the West must deal with Communism—but the position to him is not doctrinaire. Describing himself in Milan as "a priest of the workers, yes—a priest of the Left, no," he went into factories employing hundreds of Communist workers, not asking that they cease to be Communists before he spoke to them. He was called "a strong proponent of coexistence," yet many observers maintained that since the Italian elections in April 1963, when Communist gains amounted to over one million votes, his attitude as archbishop of Milan had stiffened. Paul had been known to condemn "selfish" wealth, but in doing so, had not been accused of compromising with Marxism. In Italy, shortly after the conclave, some leftist groups, made anxious by what they called his "Christian Democratic background," urged him to

---

Greece had agreed not to send observers to the second session of the Vatican Council.

[11] Pope John was quoted by Archbishop Roberti, nuncio to the Congo, as having said that there had been overtures made by the Soviets to the Holy See in regard to diplomatic relations. "But he (Khrushchev)," the Pope had added, "must first assure us freedom for the Church. We are hopeful that this will be done."—Archbishop Roberti at a memorial convocation at Louvanium University, Leopoldville, June 17, in honor of John XXIII.

avoid "ideological crusades." American newspapers, on the other hand, on the eve of President Kennedy's visit, expressed the hope that Communism would be an area of discussion. And in July, when speaking to an association of Roman Catholic workers in Italy, with a directness characteristic of his Milan days, Pope Paul recommended to Church assistants in the association that they study the psychology of the worker, thus indicating his awareness that response to workers' unrest must make use of more than merely religious means. There is often, he said, a contrast between the psychology of the worker and the language of the priest which leads to difficulty in their understanding one another.

During the reign of Pope John XXIII, quiet negotiations had been begun in order to effect more favorable conditions for Catholics in Iron Curtain countries. Shortly after Pope Paul's election, the Most Reverend Endre Hamvas, bishop of Csanád, acting head of the bench of Hungarian bishops,[12] in an audience with the Pope reported the Hungarian government's desire for the continuation of talks on the relations between the Church and State in Hungary. Interviews leading to the release of Cardinal Josef Mindszenty were repeatedly referred to after Pope Paul's election by "unusually reliable sources." Although the negotiations were apparently dropped after the illness and death of Pope John, his unbounded fraternity seems to have kept them alive until now, and in the first period of Paul's pontificate they passed into the more delicate and hazardous final stage.

[12] Cardinal Mindszenty, primate of Hungary, whose fate is the most sensitive of questions to be discussed between the Vatican and the Hungarian government is reported to have asked, in conversation with Monsignor Casaroli of the Secretariat of State who visited Budapest in May, that he should not be succeeded by Bishop Hamvas, who is thought to be close to the "peace priests." (London *Tablet,* July 20, 1963, p. 803.)

In an apostolic letter sent to the Czechoslovak hierarchy in connection with the eleven-hundreth anniversary of the arrival of SS. Cyril and Methodius in their country, Pope Paul expressed the wish that "as soon as possible good news about the position of the Church in the Czechoslovak Republic might reach the Vatican." [13] Cardinal Wyszynski, primate of Poland, assured members of the Polish colony in Vienna that Paul intended to continue John's policy of improving relations with Iron Curtain countries. Further assurance was discerned in the proposed plan of Cardinal König of Vienna to visit Czechoslovakia "to explore chances for a relaxation of the Czechoslovak government's attitude toward the Church,[14] and to revisit Hungary and Cardinal Mindszenty. In midsummer, Deputy Premier Kallai of Hungary spoke encouragingly about the possibility of filling the vacant episcopal sees in Hungary, while later, Italian sources quoted Plojhar, minister of public health in Czechoslovakia, as saying that the situation of Archbishop Beran might admit of solution, "if the Vatican continues to proceed according to the way outlined by Pope John XXIII." Marshal Tito of Yugoslavia was quoted as saying: "I think we can improve relations with the Vatican."

Thus it appears that for the Communists the resolution of many problems lies essentially in following the program of Pope John. The difficulty of doing this over a period of years cannot be overestimated. Pope Paul's qualities of ingenuity and acumen will be called upon to their deepest fathom by

[13] In Prague, the weekly *Katholicky Novim* described Pope Paul as one who would continue the "peace-loving line" of Pope John XXIII. It was certain, the paper said, that he had taken the name Paul because he was striving for a lasting and just peace throughout the world.

[14] Archbishop Beran had been under house arrest in Prague since 1948.

what he knows of the Church in these Eastern European countries. This position may be, as one Italian writer sees it, subject always to the humor of the government, but the politico-religious question "is now at grips with the actuality of a Church which enjoys enormous prestige and is considered a mediator of world peace."

The state of relations between the Church and the Communist world in the summer of 1963 seemed to justify the hope of Pope John. Denunciation had not been the answer, but rather the renewal and strengthening of the Church through an infusion of charity and a willingness to speak to man of the things of man, if not of the things of God. And because life is a sequential existence, the occasions which seek and challenge this charity, this openness to encounter, will constantly arise and seek recognition. To discern these, to meet them, to use them justly—this is the towering task of Pope Paul VI.

It is a truism to say that a man's life centers around his conflicts. Yet the conflicts of the successor to Peter tend to become submerged, not only before the public, the press, and the faithful—they become submerged within the man himself. Without ceasing to be, as all men are, both the arena and the protagonist of psychic struggles, the man who is the Vicar of Christ, especially in modern times, begins to take on dimensions commensurate with the Body of Christ. He may suffer cosmic agony. He risks universal obloquy. The corners of his cross knock at the poles; he is stretched taut, with the protective contraction which all men learn, both willingly forgone and denied him by the reaches of his commitment. His new selfhood becomes such that it absorbs his former self, so that he may, in an odd moment of leisure, regard it quizzically and with affection, touched by its former isolation, but feeling its deep consanguinity with all men. Small men have been Popes, and have remained small. Were Paul VI's dimensions less than they are, however, it would be impossible for him in today's world not to grow beyond accustomed limits in a way which he himself might at one time have thought impossible.

Even on the level of his assessable dealings with men and his thoughts about them, the present Pope has been called a global thinker. In his diplomatic relations, in his writing, in his pastoral activity, he has never been "European" in the sense of Charles de Gaulle. The native turn of his mind has always been one in which the words of *Pacem in Terris* would find quick understanding: "One cannot overlook the fact that even though human beings differ from one another by virtue of their ethnic peculiarities, they all possess certain essential common elements, and are inclined by nature to meet each other in the world of spiritual values, whose progressive assimilation opens to them the possibility of perfection without limits. They have the right and duty therefore to live in communion with one another." Paul's interest in coming to the United States and Canada, in visiting South America and Africa, does not mean that he has something in him to which the peculiar quality of Americans (or Latin American, or Africans) appeals almost by reflex (as has been hinted by Americans writing about the new Pope). It means that rather he sees these continents as the places of man.

Paul's great challenge will be the study of unity, and teaching of unity, the apostolate of unity and ecumenism. His early announcement of the date of the reconvening of Vatican Council II and his declared dedication to the Council indicate this.[15] As archbishop of Milan he was once quoted as saying:

[15] One week before the Council's second session began, Pope Paul announced plans for reorganizing the structure of the Roman Curia, in-

"The truth is that the world's inability to achieve a unity of thought and to end spiritual divisions is the real reason why society is so deeply unhappy, so poor in ideas and enthusiasm, and so lacking the shared spiritual concepts which are its own inner joy, nobility and strength."

There are personal marks about this man which are noted with surprise and delight, even in reading of them, by those who are in the habit of seeing the Pope as rather a symbol than a man. Much that he did during the first days of his pontificate reveals the person. Certain semiofficial acts also show how his personality shapes his public gestures. He wrote a letter in his own hand to two Protestant ministers who wished him well in his pontificate. He celebrated Mass in the Ambrosian rite on the Feast of SS. Peter and Paul for pilgrims from Milan who brought him the tiara to be used in his coronation—the first Pope ever to celebrate Mass in this rite. On September 8 he twice offered Mass for the people and in their midst—at Genzano and Pavona—becoming the first Pope in modern history, at least, to celebrate two Masses on a Sunday.

He said Mass for the townspeople in Castelgandolfo in the local church of Saint Nicolas on August 15—and urged them in a homily on the feast not to forget in their prayers those whom suffering prevented from enjoying the beautiful summer holiday weather. His acceptance of a miner's lamp from Belgian miners who felt a special fraternity with this priest of the workers; his special appeal for the prayers of pilgrims, beyond his personal messages of sympathy and gifts of money for the victims of the earthquake in Skopje, Yugoslavia; his instruction to *L'Osservatore Romano* and *Acta Apostolicae Sedis* to drop grandiloquent titles and refer to him

---

cluding its internationalization. (Confer appendix for excerpts of his address.)

simply as "Holy Father"—all these are more than the indiscriminate minutiae that go to fill the many moments in a Pontiff's life. They constitute a medium by which a many-faceted man becomes known to his people. He may, as some writers have put it, have a subtle mind, and a strong hand. The hand, however, is fine and sensitive, and the mind is on good terms with the heart.

These things will reveal him personally more effectively at the beginning of his pontificate than any effort to make a thorough study of his official acts. It is because we are in a life of Christian hope, especially in the present age of the world, that an account of him can be only an essay. The charity which this Father to his people deserves is the effort to look on the prospect of his pontificate with his own eyes. It is likely that Paul will estimate his own acts in the light of the priesthood which has shaped his life and his opinions. If there is a priestly type, even his physical appearance places him in this category. Tall, thin, with an unusually high forehead, he has penetrating gray-blue eyes under bushy brows, a large straight nose, and two vertical lines in his brow which add another note of individuality and reserve to a face which is strongly handsome. It is a mobile face, capable of multiple shades of human expression and arresting expressiveness. And the man who looks from it on the world is also flexible, reserved, resilient and firm.

The direction of his power he himself has expressed in speaking of Christianity: "The Christian message is not a prophecy of condemnation. It calls to penance in order to call to salvation. It is not bitter; it is not ill-tempered; it is not discourteous; it is not ironic; it is not pessimistic. It is generous. It is strong and joyful. It is full of beauty and poetry. It is full of vigor and majesty. Indeed, it raises the Cross: suffering, sacrifice, death, but only to bring comfort, redemption, and life."

Appendix

The following are excerpts from Pope Paul VI's address to the Roman Curia on September 21, 1963.

. . . the Roman Curia is the instrument of which the Pope has need, which the Pope uses to undertake his divine mandate. Its function calls for high capabilities and virtues, because its office is high.

As everyone knows, this old and complex body in its most recent reordering dates back to Pope Sixtus V's famous constitution *Immensa Aeterni Dei* of 1588. St. Pius X gave it new life with his constitution *Sapienti Consilio* in 1908, and the Code of Canon Law in 1917 substantially made its architecture. Many years have passed: It is understandable that such ordering has been aggravated by its venerable old age, as is shown again by the disparity of its organs and practices to the needs of new times and usages of new times, and as it shows at the same time the need to be simplified, decentralized, to enlarge itself and adapt itself to new functions.

Various reforms are therefore necessary. They will certainly be pondered, set in motion according to venerated and reasonable traditions, on one hand, and according to the needs of the times, on the other. And they will certainly be functional and beneficial, because they will have no other aim than that of allowing to fall that which is already perishing and superfluous, in the forms and norms which regulate the Roman Curia, and to put in being that which is vital and provident for its more efficacious and appropriate functioning. They will be formulated and promulgated by the Curia itself!

The Roman Curia will not be frightened, for example, to be recruited with larger supranatural vision, nor to be educated by a more careful ecumenical preparation.

The Roman Curia will not be jealous of temporal prerogatives belonging to other times nor of external forms no longer fitted to express and impress true and high religious meaning. It will not be miserly of functions that bishops can today exercise better themselves locally without injuring universal ecclesiastical order. Neither will economic aims or advantages ever have any weight in suggesting some reserve or some centralization on the part of the Holy See's organs, if this is demanded by the good of ecclesiastical administration and the welfare of souls.

It is the sacred norm of the departments of the Roman Curia to question the bishops and weigh their judgments in dealing with affairs.

Among the consultors of the sacred congregations, there figure not a few bishops, coming from various regions.

And we will say more: If the Ecumenical Council wishes to see some representatives of the episcopacy, particularly bishops heading dioceses, associated in some way and for some questions in conformity with the doctrine of the Church and canon law, with the supreme head of the Church, in the study and responsibility of ecclesiastical government, it will certainly not be the Roman Curia that will oppose the suggestion. On the contrary, it will feel a growing in the honor and burden of its sublime and indispensable service which is, as we know well, specifically administrative, consultative and executive, apart from the due procedure of the ecclesiastical tribunals both in the Roman Curia and in the dioceses. The Roman Curia, yet again, will thus feel even more strongly its vocation to give an example to the whole Church and to the secular world.

The Roman Curia is not an anonymous body, insensible to the great spiritual problems, that automatically dictates laws, but a live body faithful and docile to the head of the Church, a body made of grave responsibilities and functions, and imbued with reverence and solicitude to those prelates who *"spiritus sanctus posuit episcopos regere ecclesiam Dei."*

Therefore let the Roman Curia not be a bureaucracy, as some have wrongly judged it, pretentious and apathetic, legalistic and ritualistic, a fighting ground of hidden ambitions and deaf antagonisms, as others accuse it of being. But let it be a true community of faith and charity, of prayer and action, of brothers and sons of the Pope, who do all to serve him, with a sense of collaboration, in his duty to the brothers and sons of the universal Church and all the world.

We know that our wish expresses yours, sincere and good, and that it is this wish that in us and in you makes prayer, so that our Lord Christ, with the intercession of the most Holy Mary and the holy apostles Peter and Paul, will cause this old and ever new Roman Curia to shine like a lantern *"ut luceat omnibus qui in domo sunt in domo,"* that is, in the Church of God!

Index

Africa, 135-37; Cardinal Montini's impressions of, 136-37; Pope Paul on, 216
Agagianian, Cardinal, 176, 181
Ambrosian Social Institute, 106
Art: Cardinal Montini on, 133
Association of Catholic Italian Workers, 107
Association of Catholic University Graduates, 44
Association of Christian Workers (ACLI), 72
Atheism: Archbishop Montini on, 115-16

Bea, Cardinal, 175, 177
Benedict XV, Pope, 3, 4, 25-27, 48
Berlin, 56
Bishops, role of: Cardinal Montini on, 162-63. *See also* Collegiality
Boston, 135
Brazil, 135
Brescia, city of, 1 ff
Budapest, 50-51
Bulgaria, 128

Canada: visit by Msgr. Montini, 74-75
Canon law, reform of: Pope Paul on, 211
Canterbury, archbishop of, 160
Carroll, Msgr. Walter S., 75
Castro, Fidel, 160

Catholic Action, 3, 5, 33
Catholic Centre Party, 47
Catholic Electoral Union of Italy, 3, 5
Catholic University of Milan, 108
Cesare Arici Institute, 11-14, 16, 18
Chicago, 75, 135
Christian Democratic Party, 5, 43, 73, 139
Christian unity: Cardinal Montini on, 148; Pope Paul on, 225
Cicognani, Amleto Cardinal, 75, 128, 177, 181, 208, 214
College of Cardinals, 127, 171 ff
Collegiality of bishops: Cardinal Montini on, 144-45
Communism, 205, 226-29
Communist Party: in Italy, 73, 96; in Milan, 88, 96-98, 100-101, 107, 116
Concesio, village of, 1, 9, 10, 17, 106
Conclave after death of Pope John XXIII, 159 ff
Congar, Yves, 132, 206
Coronation of Pope Paul VI, 198-203; coronation speech, 201-203
Cuba, 160
Cushing, Richard Cardinal, 128, 135, 175, 177, 186

Delp, Alfred, 59-60, 94
Democracy: Pope Paul on, 220-221

235

Der Stellvertreter, 57-59; Cardinal Montini on, 61-64
Diplomacy, papal: Msgr. Montini on, 29-32
Diplomatic corps, 81; addressed by Msgr. Montini, 81-82

Eastern Europe, Church in, 71-72
Ecumenical Council. *See* Vatican Council II
Education, Catholic: Archbishop Montini on, 124-26
Eisenhower, President, 133-34
Englehard, Charles W., Jr., 199
Eucharistic Congress, Budapest, 50

Fascism, 4-5, 25, 27, 34-35, 38-40, 73, 205
Fascist University Youth, 36, 40
Federation of Italian Catholic University Students, 34-40, 42-43; Cardinal Montini on, 43
Finkelstein, Rabbi Louis, 199
Flos Florum, 181
Franco, Generalissimo, 54; Cardinal Montini telegram to, 141
Free Federation of Labor, 108
Frings, Cardinal, 56, 178, 181
FUCI. *See* Federation of Italian Catholic University Students

Gaggia, Bishop Giacinto, 19-23
General Confederation of Workers, 107
Germany, 55-60
Ghana, 136
Greek Orthodox Church, 225-26
GUF. *See* Fascist University Youth

Hitler, 47, 56, 59
Hochhuth, Rolf, 57 ff
Hughes, Philip, 118

Il Cittadino, 5-6, 41
Introduction to the Study of Christ, 44
Ireland, 76
Italian Federation of Church Schools, 124

Jewish refugees, 54-55
John XXIII, Pope, vii, 19, 52, 137, 141, 150, 224; and Vatican Council, 141 ff; death of, 154 ff; evaluation of reign of, 164 ff; creation of cardinals by, 171-175; Cardinal Montini on, 148-149, 157-58, 161; Pope Paul on, 210
Johnson, Lyndon B., 161
Journalism: Pope Paul VI on, 7, 79-80
Journet, Charles, 132

Kennedy, President, 155, 197, 199, 222-23
Khrushchev, Nikita, 160, 180, 197
König, Franz Cardinal, 129, 174, 175, 177, 180, 228

Labor: Archbishop Montini on, 99-100. *See also* Workers
La Sapienza, 37-38
Lateran Treaty, 27, 39
Latin America: Pope Paul on, 217
Lercaro, Giacomo Cardinal, 116-117, 178, 180-81

Liceo Arnaldo da Brescia, 16, 18
Liturgical movement: Archbishop Montini, 106
Lombard College, 24-25

Macchi, Msgr., 130, 136, 164, 213
McIntyre, Cardinal, 186
Malachy of Armagh, papal prophecies of, 181-82
Management: Archbishop Montini on, 103-104
Mann, Thomas, 35, 132
Mansfield, Senator Mike, 199
Marian Year, 1953, 74
Maritain, Jacques, 35, 132
Marxism: Archbishop Montini on, 97
Milan, ix, 8, 80, 86 ff; Great Mission of, 113 ff
Mindszenty, Josef Cardinal, 71, 168, 227-28
Montini, Francesco, 8, 163, 208
Montini, Giorgio, father of Pope Paul, viii, 2-10, 15, 17, 19, 21, 23, 25, 51, 71, 130
Montini, Giuditta Alghisi, mother of Pope Paul, viii, 2, 8-10, 17, 19, 23, 71, 130
Montini, Ludovico, 8, 40, 85, 163, 208
Montini, Vittorio, 9
Mooney, Cardinal, 75
Mussolini, 4, 25, 40, 47, 67

National Catholic Welfare Conference, 75
Nazism, 27, 57, 205
Negro Catholics, 75
New York City, 133, 135
New York Herald Tribune, 162, 165

New York Times, 75, 97-98, 163, 197
Nigeria, 135
Nixon, Richard, 222
Notre Dame University, 133-35; citation of Cardinal Montini, 134-35
Nuclear test ban treaty: Pope Paul on, 207

O'Hara, John Cardinal, 75, 128
Osborne, Sir D'Arcy, 57, 64
Osservatore Romano, 67, 109, 117, 133, 143, 155, 190, 198, 231
Ottaviani, Alfredo Cardinal, 159, 175, 177, 189, 194-95, 201
Overseas College, Milan, 126

Pacelli, Cardinal Eugenio, 48-49, 50-51. *See also* Pius XII
Peace: Cardinal Montini on, 157; Pope Paul on, 211-12, 215
Persico, Father, 16-17
Pirelli factory, 103
Pius IX, Pope, 3
Pius X, Pope, 48
Pius XI, Pope, 27, 32-33, 36-41, 48, 51-52, 88, 95
Pius XII, Pope, viii-ix, 49 ff, 65-71, 76 ff, 85, 92, 120, 127, 132; Cardinal Montini on, 61-64
Pizzardo, Giuseppe Cardinal, 28, 32, 34, 39, 41, 49
Pontifical Academy of Noble Ecclesiastics, 28-32, 35
Pontifical Gregorian University, 4, 24, 28
Pope, divine rights of: Cardinal Montini on, 145
Priesthood: Archbishop Montini on, 122

Priest-worker movement, 73, 139; Cardinal Montini on, 73

Randall, Sir Alec, 48, 70
Reform of the Church: Cardinal Montini on, 145-47
Rhodesia, 135
Ricketts, Cardinal, 175
Ritter, Cardinal, 75, 175, 186
Roman Question, 26-28, 36, 48
Roncalli, Angelo, 127. *See* John XXIII
Roosevelt, Franklin D., 65-67
Rugambwa, Cardinal, 172
Russian Orthodox Church, 161, 223-25

Saint Laurent, 75
Secretariat of State, 32, 41, 47 ff
Sesto San Giovanni, 94, 97, 104
Social Progress: Archbishop Montini on, 105, 106
South Africa, 135
Spain, 213; Spanish Foreign Office, 141
Spellman, Francis Cardinal, 72, 76, 135, 161, 178, 181
Stritch, Cardinal, 75
Suenens, Cardinal, 150-51, 175, 178, 180

Tardini, Cardinal, 65, 68, 78, 128, 142
Taylor, Myron, 65
Tisserant, Eugene Cardinal, 83, 159, 161, 168, 176, 189, 194, 209 ff
Trent, Council of, 118; Cardinal Montini on, 145
Turkey, 128

United Nations, 160, 178; Pope Paul on, 218-19
United States, 221-22; visit by Msgr. Montini, 74; visits by Cardinal Montini, 133, 161
University, the: Cardinal Montini on, 134
University Conscience, A, 44
Urbani, Cardinal, 176, 181, 188
U Thant, visit to Pope Paul, 218-220

Vatican Council, First, 162
Vatican Council II, 139 ff; Cardinal Montini on, 142 ff; Pope Paul on, 210-11
Vatican Radio, 53, 117
Verolovecchia, 8, 10, 15, 17

Ward, Barbara, 166-67
Warren, Earl, 199
Warsaw, 32 ff
Way of Christ, The, 44
Washington, D. C., 75, 135
Women's Italian Center (CIF), 73
Workers: Archbishop Montini on, 94, 95, 96, 97, 98, 102-103, 106; Pope Paul on, 227. *See also* Labor
World Conference on Faith and Order, 224
Writing: Cardinal Montini on, 132-33
Wyszynski, Cardinal, 161, 177, 181, 228

Youth: Archbishop Montini to, 117, 126